Treacherous Translation

THE SEOUL-CALIFORNIA SERIES IN KOREAN STUDIES

The Seoul-California Series in Korean Studies is a collaboration between the University of California, Berkeley, and the Kyujanggak Institute for Korean Studies, Seoul National University. The series promotes the global dissemination of scholarship on Korea by publishing distinguished research on Korean history, society, art, and culture by scholars from across the world.

Treacherous Translation

Culture, Nationalism, and Colonialism in Korea and Japan from the 1910s to the 1960s

SERK-BAE SUH

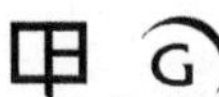

Global, Area, and International Archive
University of California Press
BERKELEY LOS ANGELES LONDON

The Global, Area, and International Archive (GAIA) is an initiative of the Institute of International Studies, University of California, Berkeley, in partnership with the University of California Press, the California Digital Library, and international research programs across the University of California system.

University of California Press, one of the most distinguished university presses in the United States, enriches lives around the world by advancing scholarship in the humanities, social sciences, and natural sciences. Its activities are supported by the UC Press Foundation and by philanthropic contributions from individuals and institutions. For more information, visit www.ucpress.edu.

University of California Press
Berkeley and Los Angeles, California

University of California Press, Ltd.
London, England

Library of Congress Cataloging-in-Publication Data

A catalog record for this book is available from the Library of Congress.

ISBN: 978-0-520-28985-7

22 21 20 19 18 17 16 15 14 13
10 9 8 7 6 5 4 3 2 1

For my parents and family.

Contents

Acknowledgments

A shorter and earlier version of Chapter Two was published under the title "Treacherous Translation: The 1938 Japanese-Language Theatrical Version of the Korean Tale *Ch'unhyangjŏn*" in *positions: east asia cultures critique* (18:1, spring 2010). Part of the preface is derived from the same article. An article based on Chapter Three appeared in the *Journal of Asian Studies* (70:1, spring 2011) under the title "The Location of 'Korean' Culture: Ch'oe Chaesŏ and Korean Literature in a Time of Transition."

Archival research for Chapter Two was funded by generous support from the Japan–Korea Cultural Foundation. I extend my thanks to Mizuno Naoki of Kyoto University for his help and support in Japan.

I also thank the UCI Humanities Center, which provided financial support for preparing the final draft of the manuscript.

Last but not least, it should be noted that this book was supported by the Academy of Korean Studies Grant (AKS-2012-S-01).

A number of people have read parts of the book at various stages of its development and offered invaluable comments. I especially thank Tani Barlow, Michael Bourdaghs, Leo Ching, Henry Em, Edward Fowler, Takashi Fujitani, Theodore Hughes, Hajime Imamasa, Walter Lew, Liao Chaoyang, Seiji Lippit, Seo Youngchae, and Gregory Vanderbilt. Their comments, offered in various forms ranging from formal discussions at conferences to casual conversations over drinks, inspired me to formulate my arguments in the ways in which they are presented in the book. Many thanks also go to the two anonymous reviewers. I tried to integrate their incisive and insightful comments and suggestions into the final draft of the book. I only hope this book measures up to their support and expectations.

I have been blessed to work with amazingly talented and intelligent graduate students. Numerous conversations I had with them gave me the invaluable opportunity to sensibly spell out some of the theoretical problems I tackle in the book. My special thanks go to Hyonhui Choe, Jessica Conte, Kazuko Osada, and Ken Yoshida. If they have learned from me as much as I have from them, I will deserve to be very proud of myself as a teacher.

I am equally lucky to have a number of colleagues at the University of California, Irvine, and beyond who took an interest in the book and encouraged me to keep going, especially when I felt it would never come to fruition. I would like to express my gratitude to John Duncan, James Fujii, Bruce Fulton, Jonathan Hall, Martin Huang, Kelly Jeong, Kyung Hyun Kim, Jinkyung Lee, Namhee Lee, Margherita Long, D. Cuong O'Neill, Robert Oppenheim, Bert Scruggs, Annmaria Shimabuku, Alan Tansman, Jeffrey Wasserstrom, Linda Vo, Lisa Yoneyama, and Jun Yoo for their words of encouragement. Some of them might not be aware how greatly their few words of kindness touched me and eased my doubt about whether I could get this book published. Indeed, its publication seemed an extremely remote possibility at times. Thus, I would like to extend my sincerest thanks to Yung Sik Kim and John Lie, then editors of The Seoul–California Series in Korean Studies, and Nathan MacBrien, the publications director of the Global, Area, and International Archive, for deciding to publish the book. I only wish I could thank them enough.

My thanks are also due to my editors Debbie Hardin and David Peattie, whose professionalism and efficiency turned the potentially stressful experience of editing into a pleasant one. Working with them led me to realize once again that writing a book is truly collaborative work on many levels. Needless to say, however, all errors remain mine.

Finally, I mention Miriam Silverberg. Yes, I pronounce a proper name, the name of my graduate adviser, a sign of her singularity, instead of thanking her. First of all, she gave me so much support at the initial stage of this book project that I cannot thank her enough in any sensible way. More relevantly however, I cannot even attempt to thank her for her support if thanking her is an attempt on my part to reciprocate the generous gift from her.

I thank many people here but Miriam belongs in another category. When you thank somebody, you declare not only your gratitude but also your willingness to reciprocate what you have received. The promise of reciprocity is implicit in the simple expression of gratitude, "thank you." Here, at this moment, I thank my students, colleagues, and friends not only because I feel grateful to them for what they have generously provided for me but also because I know I will endeavor to reciprocate their help and support, a generous gift, even though I am well aware that my endeavors will miserably fail in the end. I will fail to reciprocate their gift no matter how much I will try not because my feeling of gratitude is insincere but because a genuine gift cannot be reciprocated. We cannot but fail to reciprocate a genuine gift because, if it can be reciprocated, it is not a gift anymore in the most fundamental sense of the word. Once a gift is matched up with another gift of equal value in return, it has already entered the cycle of favors in exchange between the giver and the receiver. Although the symmetrical relationship bound by the exchange of favors falls in the arena of economy, the asymmetrical relationship established by an unreciprocated gift belongs in the realm of ethics.

I know my attempt to reciprocate my students', friends', and colleagues' help and support will end in ultimate failure. Their support and help is a genuine gift I cannot pay back in exact proportion to how much I have benefited from it. Nevertheless, I should and will endeavor to reciprocate the generous gift from those who have extended their helping hands. The spirit of "nevertheless" is intrinsic to human decency.

I cannot even attempt to thank Miriam for her generous gift, however, in the same way I thank my students, colleagues, and friends. I cannot even make an ultimately failed attempt at reciprocity toward her because she is not here with us anymore. If I thank her, there is a danger it will be a mere pose lacking sincerity. Thus, here, at this very moment when I am acknowledging all the help and support I have been blessed with, I only mention her name: Miriam Silverberg.

Preface

This book grew out of my endeavor to examine the ways in which the issues of translation and language were embedded in Korean and Japanese discourses on nation, culture, and literature in the context of Japanese colonial rule and its aftermath in Korea. More specifically, the book examines the role of translation in shaping attitudes toward nationalism and colonialism in Korean and Japanese intellectual discourse from the 1910s through the 1960s. Critiquing the conventional view of translation as a representation of an original text, a view that was prevalent among both Korean and Japanese intellectuals, I argue that, when theorized as an ethical and political practice, translation challenges the ethnocentric view of culture and language embedded in both colonialism and cultural nationalism.

Translation in the colonial context means not just the translation of texts between the language of the colonizer and that of the colonized. It also entails the representation of the colonized's culture and of the colonized themselves. When framed as the faithful rendering of a text from one language to another, translation is supposed to represent the original text. In addition, there is another level of representation involved in translation. In the commonly held view of translation, it is expected to facilitate understanding of the culture to which the original text belongs.[1] The assumption underlying such a view is that the translated text represents the source culture from which the original derives.

As further examined in Chapters 2 and 4, the issue of representation comes up even more conspicuously in the case of translating a text from the language of the colonized to that of the colonizer. Furthermore, not only is the colonized's culture represented but the colonizer's cultural identity is also imagined in terms of its difference from that of the colonized through translation. As Edward Said pointed out in *Orientalism*, the Western orientalists' translation of Middle Eastern and Indian classics in the 18th and 19th centuries enabled the West to imagine its civilization with respect to what it considered the Orient in the time of modern colonialism.[2] Focusing on cases of translation from the colonized's language to that of the colonizer, Tejaswini Niranjana has astutely criticized the conventional view of translation as the faithful representation of the original, a view that, she argues, is collusive with regimes of colonial domination.[3] However, the problem of representation is not limited to the case of translation from the language of the colonized to that of the colonizer. When translating from the colonizer's language to that of the colonized, the translator, whether colonizer or colonized, cannot help but continuously compare the culture of colonizer with that of the colonized so long as translation is defined not just as a linguistic transfer of meanings but as the rendering of an original text rooted in one culture to a different language whose signifying system is specific only to its culture. In the course of translation, the original text that is understood to represent the colonizer's culture is thus made to help essentialize the colonized's culture in terms of the latter's difference from the former. Furthermore, not only are the cultures of the colonizer and of the colonized reified through representation, but the former also is made to register as the norm against which the supposed deficiencies of the latter emerge in the course of translation. Thus, for example, instances in which there are no words in the colonized's language that correspond to ideas highly valued by the colonizer are often ascribed to failings in the colonized's culture.

As in the case of translations by writers from Western colonizer nations, Japanese translations of Korean history and literature represented the colonized and their culture and shaped Japanese colonial discourse on Korea. Korean cultural nationalism arose primarily in response to such colonial representations of culture and nation, as is the case of the Korean intellectual An Hwak, whose treatise on Korean literary history will be examined in Chapter 1.[4] However, because of its ethnocentric view of culture and language, Korean cultural nationalism failed to effectively challenge colonialist claims about the legitimacy of colonial rule.

Despite political and economical disparities in power between the colonizer and the colonized, the cultural nationalism of the colonized enables them to imagine their own language and culture to be equal to those of the colonizer. It does so by positing an autonomous and homogeneous national community of language and culture. Linguistic and cultural nationalism can also empower a politics of resistance by the colonized against colonial domination. However, it can also spur something akin to the multiculturalism found in the United States, which carves out an autonomous space for the cultures of the minority while fully accepting the legitimacy of the dominant ruling groups. In other words, the linguistic and cultural nationalism of the colonized stops short of questioning the legitimacy of colonial rule. Cultural nationalism consequently fails to provide a radical critique of colonial domination. Furthermore, the linguistic and cultural nationalism of the colonized rests on the fixed identities of the colonizer and the colonized that rest on such essentialist foundations as ethnicity, tradition, culture, and language. Even while occasionally causing friction with colonial rule, linguistic and cultural nationalism as ideology thus works concentrically with colonialism, which also depends on the same essentialist foundations.

If a nation is "an imagined community," as Benedict Anderson has argued, the act of imagining a nation is never complete but must be repeated constantly not only to police borders with other nations but also to reformulate boundaries to adapt to political, economic, and cultural changes in society.[5] Culture is the arena in which imagination draws and redraws the boundaries of the nation. Although race as a pseudo biological concept has been denounced as an illegitimate marker, culture remains accepted as an authentic delimiter of a nation, because a specific culture is, with very few exceptions, associated with a national community. Colonialism and its legacies have erected the frame in which the nation is imagined in the realm of culture. As Nicholas Dirks reminds us, not only has modern culture been shaped by colonialism, colonial domination itself is enacted through culture.[6]

Literature is one main cultural institution in which nationalism and colonialism converge in the imagining of national boundaries. The modern literary conventions of genre and narrative technique originated in the European tradition and spread to non–Western societies through colonial expansion. Through adaptation and appropriation, the modern literature of non–Western societies has been written in vernacular languages, which, with few exceptions, are thought of only in connection with national communities. Thus, literature is viewed as the linguistic expression of a specific culture that is linked to a national community.

One of the common definitions of a national literature is a body of literature created for the community of a nation. The concept may seem natural, but the word *nation* resists clear definition, and even if its blurry boundaries are determined, the community depends on transparent communicability among its members. One of the prerequisites for transparent communicability is a common language. Dependence on translation to communicate marks one's foreignness and condemns one to exclusion from the community. In short, one who does not speak the language is not really a member of the community.

It is often said that a major part of Koreans' indignation at the Japanese arose from the colonial policy of assimilation. This so-called *dōka seisaku* (assimilation policy) consisted of a set of institutional measures devised by the colonial government to make Koreans and other ethnic groups within the empire into good subjects of the Japanese state.[7] However, in contrast to its stated goals, the assimilation policy never aimed to entirely assimilate the Koreans into the Japanese nation. Although the Japanese colonial government occasionally denounced discrimination against Koreans by the Japanese, the need for such admonitions only underscored the enduring discrimination that reflected the deeply rooted prejudice among ordinary Japanese against Koreans. Furthermore, although the stated aim was to eliminate institutionalized discrimination at some future point when Koreans were thoroughly assimilated into Japan, the goal remained always out of reach. Discrimination could disappear only when all the differences between the colonized and the colonizers would vanish. The present differences between the colonized and the colonizers served to justify discriminatory practices. Difference cannot be dissociated from discrimination under colonialism. It should not be surprising that some Koreans called for the renunciation of Korean culture, language, and whatever differentiated them from the Japanese.[8] However, the total abolition of discrimination was always deferred to the future. Here was a case demonstrating how colonialism pivots on difference between the colonizers and the colonized to preserve the colonial hierarchy on which colonialism exists. Colonialism does not eradicate difference. It reconfigures it.

Just as colonialism maintains differences between the colonized and colonizers while claiming to erase them, translation simultaneously points to the gulf between two languages while trying to bridge the gap. As examined further in Chapter 2, translation can hypostatize borders between two languages and thus accentuate the difference between two autonomous and homogeneous communities.[9] It is linguistic and cultural nationalism that posits an autonomous and homogeneous community of nation. The imagined autonomous and homogeneous community masks the fact that no community is completely sterilized of foreignness and free from the contamination of otherness.

If translation aims at transcending the difference between linguistic and cultural communities, which are externally independent and internally unified, the ideal of translation is to transfer a text from one linguistic and cultural community to another without losing any semantic or syntactic meaning. In other words, the ideal of translation in this context is an equal exchange between two languages and cultures. The view of translation as an equal exchange rests on the assumption that it is possible to establish a reciprocal relationship between two languages, overcoming the differences between them. In this sense, translatability refers to the possibility of equivalents that bridge the gap between two languages. Previous studies on colonial translation by Niranjana and Lydia Liu, to name a few, have pointed out that the idea of translation as an equal exchange is incongruent with colonial domination and political asymmetry between the colonizer and the colonized. Whereas the previous studies have primarily problematized the colonial intervention in the process of translation, however, I want to focus my critique on the homology between the logic of translation as equal exchange and colonial discourse, which depends on narrative strategies that serve in the end to justify and defend colonial domination and exploitation.[10]

One might argue that translation has more to do with the commensurability between languages than with the exchange value between them. Karl Marx's analogy between the circulation of commodities and translation helps us see the relevance of the idea of exchange value in relation to the way in which translation is conventionally understood. To explain how money mediates the exchange of products and thus turn them into commodities in circulation, Marx likened the exchangeability of products to translatability. He wrote,

> To compare money with language is not less erroneous. Language does not transform ideas, so that the peculiarity of ideas is dissolved and their social character runs alongside them as a separate entity, like prices alongside commodities. Ideas do not exist separately from language. Ideas which have first to be translated out of their mother tongue into a foreign language in order to circulate, in order to become exchangeable, offer a somewhat better analogy; but the analogy then lies not in language, but in the foreignness of language.[11]

In other words, the foreignness of language requires translation in the same way as the difference between products in exchange necessitates the concept of exchange value, that is, the value of one product expressed as the use value of another product. Commensurability itself is not inherent in languages but is rather made possible by the equivalencies translation can provide for languages.

Since Marx, quite a few scholars in translation studies have employed the trope of exchange to explain translation. George Steiner is one notable example. Steiner suggests that the ideal for translation is "exchange without loss" between languages.[12] Liu also uses Marxian concepts of use and exchange value in her study of translations from Western languages to Chinese in the late 19th and early 20th centuries. As Liu points out, the creation of equivalents between languages is far from innocent of political intervention, and all the more so in colonial translation. In other words, in Liu's view, translation is not symmetrically reciprocal between two languages. Production of equivalents is conditioned by the power relations between two language communities. While acknowledging the relevance of a new approach in colonial and postcolonial studies that emphasizes translation as the site of resistance, Liu, however, warns us that the trend could reduce the history of colonial translation into a single narrative about the struggles of the colonized resisting the Western colonial domination. She insists rather on looking at translation as a more nuanced site of "resistance, domination, and appropriation."[13]

In contrast with Liu's view of translation as a venue in which the dominant and the dominated conflict and negotiate with each other, I posit that colonial translation is premised on the idea of exchange between the colonizers and the colonized as equal parties. In other words, I focus my analysis on the collusion between colonial discourse and the idea of equal exchange implicated in the conventional view of translation that involves constituting equivalencies between languages. Insistence on equal and reciprocal exchanges in the conventional view of translation eerily parallels the emphasis on the reciprocal and equally beneficial relationship between the colonized and the colonizer in colonial discourse. For example, as discussed further in Chapter 2, Japanese colonial discourse was replete with rhetoric, as well as statistics, seeking to establish the belief that Japanese colonial rule was equally beneficial to Koreans as it was to Japanese, if not more so. Colonial discourse assumes a reciprocal relationship between the colonizer and the colonized even as power disparities enable colonial injustice and exploitation to prevail. It is not difficult to argue the absurdity of a colonial discourse that assumes the colonial relationship to be an equal exchange. But the complicity and homology between colonial discourse and the view of translation as equal exchange has not been closely scrutinized. Although colonial translation can be a site of struggle and negotiation between the colonized and the colonizers, as Liu argues, that definition does not offer a fundamental critique of colonial domination. In other words, the collusion between colonial translation and colonial domination cannot be exposed to make a radical critique unless the idea of equal exchange itself is carefully examined and critiqued. I am not proposing that translation is inherently collusive with colonial domination. Rather, I suggest a different view of translation as an ethical as well as political practice. Translation thus radicalized resists the lure of cultural and linguistic nationalism on the part of the colonized as well as the colonial enterprise of domination.

Drawing on the work of such thinkers as Marx, Emmanuel Levinas, and Jacques Derrida, I conceptualize translation as an ethical and political practice that interrupts the tyrannical dictation of the self over the other and thus enables the former to encounter the latter in language. Translation thus theorized highlights the ethical aspect of language as a venue in which self and other can engage in dialogue without silencing unbridgeable differences. It also emphasizes translation's potential to create an anticolonial politics by exposing heterogeneity within the languages and cultures of both colonizer and colonized, thereby disrupting the homogeneous linguistic and cultural communities promulgated by the colonial hierarchy.

There are three main reasons why I base my criticism of colonialism on Levinas's thought. First, Levinas's ethics is premised on the radical alterity of the other.[14] According to Levinas, the absolute alterity of the other subjects the self to questioning its own legitimacy and orders the self to act ethically toward the other.[15] The self should not and cannot speak, think, or behave on behalf of the other. Colonial domination is an exemplary mode of rule that prevents the self from encountering the alterity of the other. By the logic of colonialism, it is the colonizers who decide what the colonized should do. To legitimize their domination, the colonizers make it their moral obligation to bring in modern economic, political, and cultural institutions to enlighten the colonized, who they believe cannot civilize themselves on their own. Put simply, the colonizers believe they know better than the colonized what is good for them. Thus, after the Sino-Japanese War (1894–1895), the Japanese statesman Itō Hirobumi lamented that Korea was "quite incapable of reform from within" and that "those [reforms] which Japan had endeavored to introduce seemed a long way off from being realized."[16] Itō's words demonstrate the tyranny of colonialist subjectivity. The colonizers think, speak, and act on behalf of the colonized. There is no room for the absolute otherness in such a mode of thinking. In criticizing the logic of colonial domination that disrespects the alterity of the colonized, I rely on Levinas's ethics.

Second, recent trends in colonial and postcolonial studies have emphasized the importance of ambivalence in colonial discourse, as explicated in Homi Bhabha's seminal book *The Location of Culture.* I agree with Bhabha that colonial discourse is replete with ambivalence resulting from its simultaneous recognition and denial of the difference between the colonized and the colonizer. However, I am also concerned that emphasis on colonial ambivalence tends to dismiss the clear differences between the colonized and the colonizer. As Bhabha points out, the nationalist critique of colonialism bogs down in the binary opposition between the colonized and the colonizer. It is true that the nationalism of the colonized is as fixated on such essentialist foundations as ethnicity, culture, and language as the colonizer's justification of the colonial hierarchy.[17] Certainly, the cultural and linguistic nationalism of the colonized often fails to offer radical resistance to colonial domination exactly because it does not aim to eradicate the mode of the essentialist identification and instead merely reverses the order of the hierarchy. Such nationalism also does not capture "the third space" of colonial reality that Bhabha regards as the site of resistance to colonialism and the criticism of both colonialism and nationalism that are based on binary oppositions. More important, colonial nationalism seldom tackles colonial injustice done to people who are outside of the supposed national community of the colonized.

Nevertheless, it is still necessary to retain a clear separation between the colonizer and the colonized to force the colonizer to face his or her all-encompassing ethical responsibility for colonial violence. Levinasian ethics offers a way to criticize the essentialist identity on which both the colonized's nationalism and the colonizer's domination hinge, while at the same time retaining the irreducible difference between the colonizer and the colonized. The ethical argument Levinas inspires me to make does not blur the separation between the colonized and the colonizer even though it attempts to criticize both colonialism and the cultural and linguistic nationalism of the colonized. The ethical relationship that I advocate entails a clear demarcation between the colonized and the colonizer. However, the separation between the colonized and the colonizer does not rest on such essentialist foundations as ethnicity, language, tradition, or culture. The difference between the colonized and the colonizers rather is situated in the history of colonial violence. It is the history of Japanese colonial domination, not any essentialist foundations of identity that posit the differences between Koreans and Japanese.

Third, the Levinasian notion of eschatology leads us to reflect on the inherent violence in the representation of the past and offers a way into an "ethical history." It might be seen as implausible to invoke Levinasian ethics in defense of history because Levinas is critical of history for totalizing the differences between individuals' experiences into "a coherent discourse."[18] This violent aspect of history is inevitable when recounting the experiences of those in the past who are no longer present and thus deprived of their own voices. Thus, in history, the individual is presented only "in the third person." However, Levinas does not completely rule out the possibility of an ethical way of recounting the past, proposing that eschatology can disrupt the tyranny of history. In his view, eschatology upholds the singularity of the individual because, unlike history, it grants individuals the right to speak for themselves. But at the same time, eschatology does not allow individuals to say whatever they want because it prioritizes the alterity of the other over individual freedom. When an individual's fear that death will deprive her of her own voice turns into concern over the murder of the alterity of the other, the possibility of eschatology emerges.

Before proceeding further, however, I need to explicate in more detail the possibility of the political actualization of Levinasian ethics to justify this book's theoretical orientation.

Although Levinas is critical of politics as the realm of power relations, the problem of politics is at the heart of his thinking on ethics. As Levinas explains it, the self's ethical responsibilities to the other can come into conflict because the world is inhabited by multiple others. Often the self has to prioritize one "other" over another to uphold justice. This can only be accomplished through politics. Nevertheless, Levinas has been criticized for his political position. For example, many who admired him as a philosopher of ethics were befuddled by his hesitation in denouncing the state of Israel for the massacre in the Palestinian refugee camps at Sabra and Shatila in 1982. Thus, Slavoj Žižek criticizes Levinas for the unbridgeable distance between his "high theory" and his "vulgar commonsensical reflections" on real politics.[19]

As a matter of fact, Levinas's uncompromising insistence on the absolute alterity of the other poses an almost insurmountable problem to any attempt to ground criticism of such political injustice as colonialism in his ethics.[20] If the other is beyond the self's grasp, relentlessly resisting the self's assimilation of the other into the self's own consciousness and thus questioning the certainty of the self's legitimacy, is it still possible to thematize the other as the colonized? Once we tie the other to the colonized, will we not efface the absolute alterity of the other? In a word, the question is whether the other in Levinasian ethics can be concretized as others who suffer from injustices and thus calls for our intervention in politics to bring justice. This difficulty of making sense of the other as those who are oppressed in the real world is often interpreted as the ineffectiveness and impracticality of Levinas's ethics and has even been viewed as the result of his political conservatism. Thus when Levinas was hesitant to designate Palestinian refugees as the other, his failure to address the violence of the Israeli state against Palestinians seemed to have come not only from his never neutral attitude toward Israel but also from political ineffectiveness or even perniciousness inherent in his ethics.[21]

It is possible to push the issue even further to the point of questioning the very possibility of Levinasian ethics by raising the following question: How can Levinas speak of the other if it exceeds the self's cognitive power and evades the self's understanding? If talking about the other inevitably involves thematizing it in discourse and consequently regarding the other as an object knowable to the self, ultimately turning the difference of the other into something assimilable to the same, then did Levinas not end up betraying the very premise of his own ethical principle as soon as he spoke and wrote about the other? Is ethical language possible when incorporating the other into discourse unavoidably violates the alterity of the other?[22]

Levinas's *Otherwise Than Being* can be seen as his response to such questions. In the book, Levinas distinguishes the two aspects of language, the saying and the said. The said is the thematizing aspect of language, what is said, whereas the saying is the aspect of language that far exceeds thematization and thus remains beyond and outside what is said.[23] Risking oversimplification, it can be argued that the saying refers to an event of speech whereas the said constitutes the message or content of speech. The saying points to the essence of language that is ethical because it instances the primordial moment in which language begins with the other.

Being faithful to Levinas's words, it can be said that the other is never synchronous with the self. If the other were contemporaneous with the self, the other could be brought into the consciousness of the self.[24] The other never coincides with the self, however. Rather, the other comes up only as a trace, what Levinas calls the face. The face discloses itself as the saying. The face of the other demands that the self respond and orders the self to enact a saying of its own. Speech thus emerges with the other with whom the self desires to engage. The self's desire arises neither from free will nor from egoistic need but from the shame that the other evokes.[25] The self's shame in turn coincides with the demand to be responsive and responsible and constitutes the following questions: Have I not harmed the other to be here at this moment? Have I not usurped the other's place?

Without the saying, the said is oblivious of the essence of language that is ethical.[26] Such obliviousness misleads us into seeing language only as a tool for the transmission of ideas. If the essence of language is to transmit ideas (the said) between interlocutors, then such a view will ultimately confirm the self's cognitive power because that means the self can understand others in dialogue well enough to safely assume that what the self takes its interlocutor to mean corresponds sufficiently to what is actually meant. However, can the self hold up the absolute alterity of the other if it is complacent about its understanding of the other? Does complacency not lead to the confirmation of the self's legitimacy with respect to the other? Levinas's differentiation of the saying from the said makes it possible to see the ethicality of language, which the saying points to. Although the view of language as a tool for transmitting ideas is premised on the belief that interlocutors can understand each other well enough, Levinas's emphasis on the saying is a reminder that "enough" is never enough and language is never reduced to the said.[27] By illuminating the ethical aspect of language and questioning the primacy of the said in the conventional understanding of language, the saying disrupts the certainty of the self's legitimacy that the said prioritizes.

For Levinas, language is the privileged venue in which the self comes closer to the other. However, there is no guarantee that the self can ever reach the other. On the contrary, the self is always exposed to the risk of being ignored and misunderstood by the other in dialogue. Rather than being able to confirm the legitimacy of the self, the self is deprived of the certainty of its legitimacy in conversation with the other. The self is not only vulnerably exposed to misunderstanding and indifference but also held solely responsible for respecting the saying without reducing it to the said. If "I" is misunderstood and ignored, it is only "me" who should be responsible. If "I" is accused of misunderstanding and indifference, it is also "me" who should be found guilty.

The difficulty of actualizing politics based on Levinasian ethics persists, however, because politics, even if it is emancipatory, never allows for such rigorous insistence on the alterity of the other as demanded by Levinasian ethics. Then, despite the above justification for basing my criticism of colonialism on Levinas's ethics, should I not admit that Levinasian ethics inevitably falls into the fetishization of the other that is ultimately impractical and even completely useless, politically speaking? Is there any way to salvage Levinas's ethics from the aforementioned accusation? I believe one way to argue for the relevance of Levinas's ethics to politics involves answering the following question: How does the ethicality of language translate into anything relevant to politics? As discussed above, the seeming impossibility of transition from ethics to politics in Levinas's thought derives from the fact that his rigorous insistence on the absolute alterity of the other prevents the other from being readily concretized as others. The entangled and complicated relationship between the saying and the said is helpful in understanding the equally entangled and complicated relationship between ethics and politics in Levinas's thought.

As mentioned above, despite the obvious privilege he assigns to the saying over the said, Levinas does not fail to emphasize that the saying cannot manifest itself without the said.[28] Although the saying precedes the said, it cannot materialize without being coupled with the said. Put simply, the saying as an event cannot occur without being said. Thus, the manifestation of saying requires the said. Likewise, the other cannot manifest itself other than in the appearance of an other. Even though it is imperative to be alert to the fact that any understanding of the other as a concrete other, a person who suffers political persecution, inevitably risks assimilating the other to consciousness and thus violating his or her alterity, it is also necessary to recognize that no encounter with the other can materialize except as an encounter with a concrete human being with whom the self desires to engage not because it egotistically desires companionship but because the appearance of the other evokes shame in the self and demands that it be responsible for the other's sufferings.

It might be helpful to discuss Levinas's essay titled "Dialogue" to further examine how his ethics are indeed relevant to politics. Levinas begins the essay with an observation that, since World War I, not only politicians but also philosophers have valued dialogue as a venue in which people are meeting each other to talk out disagreements and differences and reach consensus peacefully. He however asserts that the idea of dialogue premised on the tradition of Western thought does not live up to the meaning of genuine dialogue, because, in the tradition of Western thought, dialogue is conventionally regarded as taking place between two interlocutors who share a common foundation for knowledge, be it God (as in Judeo–Christian theology), reason (as in rationalism), or custom (as in Humean empiricism). In the idea of dialogue premised on the common ground of knowledge, there is no room for encountering the other who is outside and beyond such a common ground. To Levinas, such a dialogue based on the common ground is not a genuine dialogue but rather a monologue. A more serious problem found in such an idea of dialogue is that the powerful often impose their ways of thinking on the powerless as the common ground for dialogue.[29] The lack of violence in this case is not real peace because it is contingent on the suppression of the voice of others. Levinas highlights in the work of Martin Buber and Gabriel Marcel on dialogue the possibility of ethics that enables "the I" to encounter the absolute other.

What captures my attention in Levinas's essay is the fact that his concern about real politics inspired him to engage with Buber and Marcel philosophically and to radicalize their thoughts by reading the ethics of alterity into them. For him, the conventional understanding of dialogue, which is based on a common ground of knowledge, cannot ensure genuine peace. Levinas calls for ethics to question the legitimacy of politics, which often masks the suppression of the powerless and mistakes the lack of physical violence for peace. In other words, in his view, ethics is called for to disrupt politics as the latter goes about its usual business. What we should call attention to is the fact that incongruity between ethics and politics enables the former to interrupt the latter. Ethics can disrupt politics because it is beyond politics. If the realm of ethics coincides with that of politics, there is no way ethics can interrupt politics from outside. When politics is put in line with ethical demands, it is interrupted by ethics, which demands that the self ask and answer the following questions: Am I good to others, the humanity who are other to me? How can I be in good conscience when fellow human beings are suffering? What should I do to bring justice to the powerless? The point is that, in order to be ethical, one must never be in good conscience. Thus, Levinasian ethics, which concerns the alterity of the other, passes toward a mode of politics, which infinitely demands that the self care about others, especially those who are oppressed.

It might be said that concern about the other without considering others is politically empty, and care about others without upholding the other is ethically blind. In that sense, radical politics inspired by Levinasian ethics is not so far away from the spirit of Marx, whose political program anticipates the advent of a new society founded on the ethical imperative, in other words, "from each according to his ability, to each according to his need."[30] In Chapter 2, I read Marx through the lens of Levinas to highlight ethics in Marx's political economy, and I read Levinas through the lens of Marx to rescue radical politics from the limits of Levinas's ethics.

Finally, Derrida is also relevant to my criticism of both colonialism and cultural and linguistic nationalism. His criticism of foundationalism calls into question cultural essentialist presumptions embedded in such phrases as *Korean nation, Japanese literature,* and *Western civilization.* For example, as demonstrated in Chapter 3, Derrida's theory of supplement is helpful for looking at how colonial ideology subsumes the colonized's culture within the colonizer's culture, while at the same time essentionalizing the latter as distinct from and superior to the former. Furthermore, Derrida, who was born and raised in colonized Algeria, deliberates on the linguistic situation of the colonial society in his book *Monolingualism of the Other or the Prosthesis of Origin.*[31] He provocatively argues that "all culture is originarily colonial" and that language plays the essential role in enabling culture to legitimize domination.[32] Derrida's insights are also helpful for examining the violent nature of the monolingual language policy that standardized the Korean language and stamped out the use of the Japanese language in liberated Korea after 1945. As discussed in Chapter 5, the majority of Korean intellectuals deemed it necessary to implement a monolingual language policy in liberated Korea. Derrida's insights offer a critique of the nationalist argument that the suppression of the Japanese language was necessary to unify Korean society and to purge Japanese colonial legacies.

ORGANIZATION OF THIS BOOK

Treacherous Translation: Culture, Nationalism, and Colonialism in Korea and Japan from the 1910s to the 1960s comprises an introductory essay and five chapters. By analyzing short stories written during the colonial period by the Korean writer Kim Saryang (1914–1950) and the Japanese writers Nakajima Atsushi (1909–1942) and Nakanishi Inosuke (1887–1958), in the introductory essay I aim to lay out the concerns and issues addressed throughout the book. More specifically, by focusing on the translators featured in the stories, I examine the ways in which those literary texts reveal the colonizer's unease over translation as the necessary but imperfect mediation that frustrates transparent communication with the colonized. I argue that the colonizer's anxiety over translation, as manifested in the literary texts, is related to the desire to reconfirm his or her authorial and authoritarian voice. Finally, by examining the preface the Japanese poet Kitahara Hakushū (1885–1942) wrote for the 1929 Japanese translation of Korean folk songs published by Kim Soun (1908–1981), I further argue that translation can open up the possibility of a critical reflection on the idea of the unified national subjectivity on which colonial discourse pivots.

In Chapter 1, "Translation and the Community of Love: Hosoi Hajime and Translating Korea," I examine the treatises the Japanese journalist Hosoi Hajime (1886–1934) wrote in the 1910s and 1920s on translation, culture, and Korea. A prolific translator of the Korean classical canon, Hosoi regarded his translation projects as an effort to facilitate Japanese understanding of the Korean nation and culture. He implored his Japanese readers to love and embrace Koreans as their own family. By analyzing Hosoi's texts on national character and literature in relation to Korean nationalist intellectual An Hwak's treatise on the same topics, I show how the concept of national literature intervened in shaping the identities of colonizer and colonized. I also aim in this chapter to examine translation's role in schematizing national character, as demonstrated in Hosoi's texts. Hosoi revealed his disregard of translation by using "translation" as a trope to signify "unreflective imitation" and "copying" that is inferior to the original, while simultaneously stressing the importance of Japanese translations of Korean literature. I argue that despite the seeming contradiction, Hosoi's high regard for, and mistrust of, translation both resulted from conventional views of translation as a representation of an original. Finally, I read Hosoi's treatises on Japanese colonial rule over Korea through the lens of G. W. F. Hegel, because Hegel's ideas of law, love, family, and community foreshadow the contradiction inherent in Hosoi's justification of Japanese colonial rule over Korea. Hegel is helpful for understanding the ways in which Hosoi's concept of love cannot but fail to bind Japanese and Koreans together despite his hope that the power of love can enable colonized and colonizers to overcome their differences in language, culture, and ethnicity.

In Chapter 2, "Treacherous Translation: The 1938 Japanese-Language Theatrical Version of the Korean Tale *Ch'unhyangjŏn*," I discuss the Japanese theatrical company Shinkyō's controversial 1938 Japanese-language staging of the popular Korean romance *Ch'unhyangjŏn* (The Tale of Spring Fragrance). Although the performance garnered favorable reviews from Japanese critics, the Japanese-language version *Ch'unhyangjŏn* received uniformly unfavorable, skeptical, and even hostile responses from Korean critics, who regarded it as a poor translation of the original story. Despite the disagreements between Japanese and Korean intellectuals about the play, however, the idea of translation as equal exchange was embedded both in the colonizers'affirmation of the play as an exemplary step toward cultural assimilation and the colonized's protests against it as an "inaccurate" or "unfaithful" translation. As discussed earlier, such insistence on equal exchange in translation colluded with the idea of symmetrical reciprocity between the colonizer and the colonized in colonialist propaganda. Moreover, such emphasis on reciprocity persistently pervades the current discourse that justifies neo-imperialist aggression on a global scale. I draw on Marx and Levinas in examining Korean and Japanese responses to the Japanese theatrical group Shinkyō's staging of the Korean folk tale *Ch'unhyangjŏn* because Marx and Levinas offer a valuable theoretical framework for criticizing the ideas of equal exchange and reciprocity that underpinned both Korean cultural nationalism, which ended up retreating from political resistance to a more conciliatory insistence on cultural autonomy, and Japanese justification of cultural interactions between Japan and Korea, which colluded with Japanese colonial rule over Korea.

In Chapter 3, "The Location of 'Korean' Culture: Ch'oe Chaesŏ and Korean Literature in a Time of Transition," I focus on Ch'oe Chaesŏ (1908–1964), a leading Korean intellectual, active translator of English literary criticism, and chief editor of *Kokumin Bungaku* (National Literature), a prominent Japanese-language journal published in colonial Korea from 1941 to 1945. Ch'oe asserted that the unfolding of history in the 20th century demanded a paradigmatic transition from liberalism and individualism to state-centered nationalism in culture and literature. He also privileged everyday life as allowing people to live as members of communities that ultimately are integrated into the state. By positioning Koreans as subjects of the Japanese state who were equal to the Japanese people, his argument implied that the colonized should be treated on a par with the colonizers. Further, Ch'oe advocated Koreans' cultural autonomy as an ethnic group within the Japanese empire. Rather than hastily celebrating Ch'oe's logic of collaboration as a subversive disruption of the colonial hierarchy, I contextualize his thoughts on nation, culture, and literature with those of contemporary Korean, Japanese, and Western intellectuals and explore how his concepts of history and everyday life enabled him simultaneously to justify Japanese colonialism's political domination of Korea and to defend Koreans' cultural autonomy. By comparing Ch'oe's critical essays on literature, culture, and politics with his own Japanese translations of the same essays, I also analyze the way in which the originals and the translations addressed a slightly different readership. I argue that such a miniscule difference in the assumed readership between the Korean originals and the Japanese translations, however, interrupts the univocal signification of such concepts as tradition, culture, Japan, and Korea on which Ch'oe's essays pivoted. The difference reveals that the meanings of such concepts are undecidable in

Derrida's sense. The undecidability inherent in the significations of the concepts ultimately undermines Ch'oe's discursive strategy that aimed to expand the conceptual boundaries of the Japanese nation (*kokumin*) to include Koreans and at the same time advocated the autonomy of Korean culture within the empire of Japan.

In Chapter 4, "Translation and Its Postcolonial Discontents: The Postwar Controversy over Tōma Seita's Reading of Kim Soun's Japanese Translations of Korean Poetry," I examine the postcolonial controversy over Japanese leftist historian Tōma Seita's interpretations of a collection of Korean poetry, which Kim Soun, on whose folk song translations Kitahara Hakushū commented, translated into Japanese during the colonial period. In a series of essays from 1954, Tōma read into the poems an allegory of the Korean nation's suffering under Japanese rule. However, Kim denounced Tōma's politicization of what he considered lyrical poems because, in his view, Tōma, who could not read Korean, misrepresented the poems and Korean culture by relying on Kim's own Japanese translations. What Kim did not mention in his denunciation, however, was the fact that some of what he considered Tōma's misinterpretations resulted from Kim's own problematically loose translations. The controversy poses questions concerning the relationship between history and literature, the ethics of translation, and the epistemological violence inherent in representation. In this chapter I attempt to respond to such questions by examining Tōma's essays on Korean poetry and Kim's criticism of them. To bring out the theoretical implications of the issues involved in the controversy, I discuss them through Fredric Jameson's controversial essay "Third-World Literature in the Era of Multinational Capitalism" in which he looked at non–Western literature as national allegory. In the 1950s, many Japanese leftist intellectuals saw the Japanese as a nation oppressed under U.S. hegemony and aligned postwar Japanese nationalism with the nationalisms of other Asian peoples, especially the Chinese and Koreans, whom they regarded as beneficiaries of national liberation. By contextualizing the controversy in the torrent of early 1950s debates among Japanese leftist intellectuals about what constitutes progressive national literature intent on challenging both rightwing nationalism and American dominance in Japan, I also treat the controversy's potential for encouraging a just relationship between the former colonized and colonizer by drawing on Levinas's notion of eschatology as an alternative to history in recounting the past.

In Chapter 5, "Toward a Monolingual Society: South Korean Linguistic Nationalism and Kim Suyŏng's Resistance to Monolingualism," I tackle national language in South Korea after its liberation from Japanese colonial rule. During the colonial period, Japanese was privileged and promoted as the official language of the Japanese empire in Korea. In the wake of the country's liberation from Japan, the whole spectrum of Korean intellectuals agreed, despite vast political differences, that it was necessary to rigidly standardize Korean as the national language while suppressing the use of Japanese to build a homogeneous national culture. The prominent poet and prolific translator Kim Suyŏng (1921–1968) belonged to the generation of Koreans who were forced to learn Japanese during the colonial period, only to be coerced again into using exclusively Korean after the liberation. Kim left a series of notes on his poetry that attest to the lingering presence of colonial bilingualism in postliberation South Korea despite the state's systematic efforts at suppression. In his notes, Kim confessed that his writing continually negotiated between Korean and Japanese. Kim's case raises questions about the ideology of a national language that works to obliterate the foreignness of language and reinforces monolingualism as a cultural community's normative linguistic condition. Kim's notes on his poetry highlight his role as a rare "critical intellectual" who warned against monolingualism's repressive nature in postliberation South Korea.

Introduction

Translation and the Colonial Desire for Transparency

Several years ago, while searching digital archives for Korean intellectuals' critical essays on literary translations published during the colonial period, I came across a newspaper article from 1930 reporting that six detectives from the Chongno Police Station in colonial Seoul had finished translating into Japanese within three days the mission statements and policies of a communist group under investigation for subversive activities.[1] The article conveys a sense of self-congratulation on the part of the police that they could successfully submit the translated evidence to the prosecutor's office so quickly. There was nothing new about the colonial authorities' persecution of Korean revolutionaries and the story would have escaped my notice except that it calls attention to the fact that Japanese colonial bureaucracy and colonial rule itself required a vast number of the colonial functionaries who performed the everyday task of translator.

As a matter of fact, the main task of most Korean officers in the Japanese colonial police was to translate between their Japanese colleagues and the colonized. After the March First movement in 1919, the colonial government used monetary incentives to encourage Japanese police officers to learn Korean. Although the number of Japanese police officers conversant in Korean gradually increased as a result, most Japanese police officers could not do their police work without the help of translators.[2]

Since my encounter with this article, which serves as a reminder that Japanese colonial rule depended on translation and its practitioners to sustain itself, various figures of translators have come to my attention from colonial-era literature written by both Korean and Japanese writers.

Nakajima Atsushi's 1929 *"Junsa no Iru Fūkei: 1923nen no Hitotsu no Sukecchi"* (Landscape with Policeman: A Sketch of 1923) tells the story of one such colonial functionary/translator, a Korean officer in the Japanese colonial police named Cho Kyoyŏng.[3] The majority of the translators working to make sure that colonial power pervaded every nook of colonized society came from the Japanese colonial police.[4] As a colonial functionary, Cho is disliked by the colonized. Unlike his Japanese colleagues, he is also mistrusted by the colonizers. In the eyes of the colonized, he is a traitor, a transgressor of the bonds of blood with his nation. On the other hand, he is viewed with suspicion by the colonizers as a potential saboteur who might manipulate communication between the colonized and the colonizers. In other words, he is a translator who performs the thankless task of translation. Witnessing daily discrimination by Japanese settlers against his fellow Koreans, Cho agonizes over his split loyalties to the Japanese state and the Korean nation.

In the end, Cho is fired because he clashes with his superior over how to treat the case of a brawl between Korean and Japanese teenagers. The story does not inform the reader what exactly is the cause of Cho's argument with his boss about but only implies that he demands fair treatment for the Korean students. After receiving the notice of termination and severance money, Cho wanders around and ends up squandering his severance money on a prostitute. The story ends with Cho running to a group of manual laborers sleeping in the street, and his final words are a lament: "you, you, this peninsula . . . this nation." Cho lost his stable source of income, but he has also broken free from the precarious position of translator between the colonizer and the colonized.

While Nakajima's story hints at the precarious position between the colonizers and the colonized to which the colonial translator/functionary is condemned, a scene in Kim Saryang's 1940 Japanese-language short story "*Kusa Fukashi*" (Deep Grass) describes the ways in which translation works to maintain the linguistic hierarchy in the colony.[5] The story concerns an unexpected reunion between Pak Insik, a Korean medical student at Tokyo Imperial University, and his high school teacher. While Insik is visiting his uncle, a magistrate in a remote mountainous region in Korea where he and other Korean students are to participate in a medical volunteer program for slash-and-burn farmers, he unexpectedly meets his high school Korean language teacher, whose students have nicknamed him "Noseblower." "Noseblower" was a laughing stock in Insik's high school, where nobody took the subject of Korean language and literature seriously. To make matters worse, the teacher's servility toward his Japanese colleagues embarrassed the Korean students. He was one of the teachers whose resignation Insik and his classmates had demanded when they organized a classroom walk-out. Now, six years later, Insik discovers that his former teacher is working as a clerk for his conceited and vainglorious uncle, the colonial bureaucrat.

In the scene in question, "Noseblower" is translating the magistrate's less-than-fluent Japanese-language speech for villagers. The magistrate's speech does not flow well in the ears of his nephew Insik, whose excellent Japanese has allowed him to enter the most prestigious university in the Japanese empire. The magistrate cannot tell voiced from unvoiced consonants (confusing *ga,* and *ka,* for example) and constantly mixes them up, a common mistake among Japanese speakers whose mother tongue is Korean. In other words, his Japanese is marked with traces of Koreanness. Overbearing and anxious at the same time, the magistrate is nevertheless speaking in Japanese about the colonial policy instituted in 1937 forbidding Koreans from wearing their traditional white clothes on the grounds that more time and water are required to launder them. Struggling to keep up, "Noseblower" is stumbling often over translation to Korean. The assembled villagers understand none of the foreign language coming out of the magistrate's mouth and are perhaps equally clueless about the rationale behind the colonial policy even when the speech is rendered into the language they understand. For all three parties in this farcical scene —speaker, translator, and listeners—the Korean language ought to have been a more effective medium of communication. Conveying a message, however, is not the primary concern of anyone present.

What is at issue is that through translation Japanese is reconfirmed as the language of authority. The magistrate reasons that the Korean language cannot evince the dignity he, an official of the Japanese empire, deserves. In other words, he thinks that if he were to speak in Korean, he could not command respect and obedience due him from his audience. Translation adds the final touch to the constant configuration of the colonial hierarchy of languages. The majority of the colonized, who are alienated from power, cannot access the authoritative voice directly but hear it only through the mediation of translation. The magistrate's Japanese, which is less than fluent, nevertheless registers in the minds of the villagers as the flawless language of authority, not least because it has been translated. The villagers cannot tell the awkwardness of the magistrate's Japanese, which to Insik's ears is less than standard Japanese, the imagined ideal speech without which the idea of the homogeneity of Japanese could not hold. The villagers know the speech is being delivered in a foreign tongue not only because they do not understand it but also because it requires translation to Korean. The language must be Japanese because it is coming out of the mouth of the magistrate, the representative of Japanese colonial power. In sum, the magistrate wants to speak in Japanese because it is the language of authority and the villagers know his speech is being given in Japanese because it is being translated into Korean and he is a colonial official representing the empire of Japan. Thus, the scene farcically marks language politics in colonial society and translation's collusion with it.

On the one hand, by showing in the case of Insik and his uncle that linguistic boundaries do not always coincide with racial or ethnic boundaries between colonizer and colonized because the colonized can learn the colonizer's language, the story subverts, in a way, the unreflectively immediate correlation between language and ethnicity embedded in colonial discourse on literature and culture. In Chapter 3, I will further discuss this issue of the often assumed correlation between language, ethnicity, and literature when I examine the writings of the Korean intellectual Ch'oe Chaesŏ. Kim Saryang's story, on the other hand, reveals that translation reifies linguistic boundaries between Japanese and Korean and demarcates those who can speak Japanese from the rest who cannot. Dependence on translation to communicate in the colonizers' language marks exclusion from power. Furthermore, in the story, language still functions as a relatively stable demarcation to set apart the Japanese from Koreans because the magistrate's awkward Japanese testifies to his less-than-complete mimicry of the colonizers.

Whereas translation's collusion with colonial domination does not go unnoticed in such literary works as "Deep Grass," the colonizer's uneasiness toward translation recurs throughout colonial literature. Nakanishi Inosuke's 1922 story "*Futei senjin*" (Recalcitrant Korean) memorably evokes from the perspective of a sympathetic Japanese intellectual the sense of unease and frustration the colonizers feel at their dependence on translation.[6] As a matter of fact, the story can be read as an allegory of colonial translation, or at least of one mode of colonial translation, and thus the failure of translation in its most fundamental sense. It begins with a Japanese man named Usui Eisaku traveling with his Korean translator to the far northwest region of Korea in the early 1920s. His destination is far from the urban areas that the Japanese keep under tight control. Anti–Japanese guerilla activities persist around the region. The purpose of the trip is to meet an old Korean man who is known to be one of the leaders of anti–Japanese resistance. Usui hopes to have honest conversations with him and other Koreans with strong anti–Japanese sentiments and to let them know that not all the Japanese support Japanese colonial rule and that quite a few sympathize with Koreans' demands for independence. His wish is sincere, but he cannot deliver his thoughts to the Koreans he meets without the help of a translator. His Korean translator, whose name is not given in the story, does not seem to care about Usui's sincere wishes, but instead worries more than Usui about the Korean insurgents, who do not hesitate to use violence for their cause.

The only protection available to Usui against the possible hostility of the insurgents is a letter of introduction from his friend from college, Hong Hŭigye, a socialist who had been the fiancé of the old man's daughter, now deceased. The letter, written in Korean—which Usui does not understand—is his sole protection. The old man has every reason to hate Japan. Not only has his country lost its independence to Japan but his daughter perished at the hands of Japanese forces during the March First movement.[7] Usui is understandably very nervous about meeting with the old man. His nervousness arises primarily from the assumption that these anti–Japanese Koreans will not discriminate between sympathetic Japanese like Usui himself and the rest of the colonizers at whose hands Koreans suffer. Usui can communicate with the colonized only through translation, and his limitations in communication with Koreans intensifies his nervousness. If he encounters hostility from the colonized, his fate will rest on his translator, whose reliability is in question not because of his Japanese abilities but because of his lack of commitment to Usui's cause. Usui is also distressed by the backwardness of the region so far from the civilized urban center he came from. Even though he is decorous enough not to say so in front of Koreans, he refers to them as "natives" (*dojin*), a pejorative revealing his sense of superiority over the supposed primitiveness of the indigenous people.

Getting off the train that brought him to this dismal place isolated from civilization, Usui looks around nervously. When he learns that the train station manager is Japanese, he asks him how long it would take to reach his destination on foot, speaking as clearly as he can to make sure the manager will know from his speech that he is Japanese, too. Usui does not need to ask the question because he knows the answer. He just wants to speak with a Japanese person, sentimentally thinking that it will be his last chance to talk to a fellow countryman until he returns. Concerned about Usui's safety, the manager recommends that he stay the night and set out the next morning. Although grateful for the manger's concern, Usui decides to continue his trip at once, following the suggestion of his translator, who urges him to depart as soon as possible so that they can arrive at their destination before night falls. The Japanese station manager stares ominously at the translator dressed in Korean clothes, which unmistakably marks him as a Korean, but the translator ignores him. As Usui leaves the train station, the lone post of modern civilization in the middle of an untamed land, his anxiety mounts.

Usui's encounter with a local is discouraging enough. The Korean boatman refuses to take Usui across a river because he is Japanese. The translator's attempt at persuasion fails as Usui's goodwill fails to translate. Usui's request to be ferried across is linguistically too simple to be untranslatable and thus the failure of translation does not derive from incommensurability between Korean and Japanese. Although the river seems to symbolize linguistic, cultural, and emotional barriers between the colonizer and the colonized, Usui's helplessness in the face of the boatman's refusal hints at the vulnerability of the speaker with respect to the addressee's rejection and the misunderstanding to which the self might be subject when engaging in conversation with the other with whom the self shares no common ground. Does not such an occasion of conversation between ultimately heterogeneous interlocutors call for translation in its true sense, the translation necessitated by failure of communication? Does not such genuine translation require the self's commitment to conversation with the other despite the risk of being ignored and misunderstood? Certainly, leaving his linguistic, cultural, and emotional comfort zone, Usui is willing even to risk being harmed by the colonized to have a talk with the insurgents. Refusing to give up, Usui swims across the river. Impressed by Usui's perseverance, the boatman promises that he will take him back across the river when he returns.

Usui's perseverance pays off. To his surprise, the old man speaks Japanese, although his Japanese is tainted with the peculiar Korean accent and mispronunciations of Japanese words. Usui's anxiety over the hostility he expected from the old man subsides as he learns that not only can the old man speak Japanese but also he receives his Japanese guest with both generosity and dignity. Even when the old man is showing the blood-stained clothes his daughter was wearing when she was killed, he graciously struggles to hold his emotion in check so as not to upset his Japanese guest too much. The old Korean and the young Japanese warm to each other. Usui's goodwill is finally transmitted to the old man and it is thus translated. But who translates it? Is there any genuine translation involved in the interactions between the old man and Usui? The Korean host is courteous enough not to be too critical, and the Japanese guest is willing to be critical enough of Japanese colonial rule. The reader might momentarily forget that Usui was contemptuous of the backwardness of Koreans in the region. The Korean and the Japanese understand each other and they agree with each other. Neither miscommunication nor any points of contention lie between them. They are in sync. No translation is called for. Finding his services are not required, the translator retreats into silence. Thus, the story is also about the erasure of translation.

As the story proceeds, it takes an unexpected turn. Having been well treated with good food and drink, Usui retires to sleep in a room provided by the old man. Awakened in the middle of the night by a strange sound, he sees a dark shadow entering and checking his possessions. The shadow soon leaves, but Usui recognizes it as the old man. Usui starts to suspect that the old man's hospitality is a ruse to lure him into a trap. He curses himself for naively believing that he can build solidarity with Koreans by transcending differences in language, culture, and ethnicity. His suspicion grows into paranoia and he concludes that, from the beginning, his friend Hong has colluded with the old man to harm him. In the end, it turns out that the old man is probably rummaging through Usui's possessions to find out if Usui is a spy from the Japanese police. The old man is a known anti–Japanese activist and must be alert to any possible police intrusion. Usui knew about the old man's anti–Japanism from the beginning, and that is exactly why he wanted to talk to him. Thus, Usui's commitment to a genuine encounter with the insurgent turns out to be much more fragile than it first appeared.

When these mutual suspicions and misunderstandings arise, the translator is clueless and helpless. He fails to interpret the old man's real intentions behind his suspicious actions or to mediate between the colonizer and the colonized. He is as much scared and suspicious of the old man as Usui is. He is a failure at his task as a translator, mistrusted by the station manager in the beginning, found ineffective in persuading the boatman, and unnecessary for mediating between Usui and the old man. Moreover, he fails to resolve misunderstandings between the two when they need his intervention most. It is Usui himself who later realizes that he misunderstood the old man's stealthy visit while the translator is still debating whether to escape from the old man's house. Thus, the story pivots on the failure of translator and translation.

What does the ultimate failure of translation in the story reveal about the colonizer's anxiety over translation? Why is the translator mistrusted and translation obviated in the story? Why is translation erased at the moment when the insurgent anti–Japanese Korean and the sympathetic colonizer Usui open their hearts to each other? As argued below, I suspect that the anxiety of colonizers over translation relates to the idea of translation as a supplementary mediation between the addresser and addressee. In the ideal situation of transparent communication, the addresser and the addressee speak the same language. The presence of a translator hints at the impossibility of transparent communication and exposes the uncertainty of the univocal signification of the addressor's authorial voice. To execute colonial power over the mundane lives of the colonized, the colonizer has to rely on language to convey thoughts, intentions, and orders to the colonized. However, most of the colonized cannot understand the colonizer's language. Thus, translation is called for at the service of colonial rule. Nevertheless, the need for translation reminds the colonizer of his vulnerable dependence on translation for communication with the colonized. As discussed below in more detail, translation highlights the materiality of language because it centers on differences between languages. That materiality frustrates the transparent signification of the colonizer's authorial voice, the voice of the authoritarian regime of colonial rule. In short, in the mindset of the colonizer, the need for translation suggests that despite the intricate network of military and administrative apparatuses at his service, his authorial voice is still vulnerable to the misunderstandings and refusals of understanding by the colonized in the course of signification and translation. In that sense, the erasure of translation in the story "Recalcitrant Korean" resonates with the colonizer's desire to reclaim his absolute authority over transparent communication and reconfirm his authorial voice. The colonizer's desire dictates that his voice should be heard and understood without adulteration. From that perspective, translation inevitably fails because it cannot help but adulterate the authorial voice in the process of translation.

The story brilliantly shows that even a sympathetic Japanese like Usui is still entrapped in such authorial and authoritarian subjectivity of the colonizer. Usui does not desire to encounter the other who refuses to understand his good will. In other words, Usui fears translation as an occasion in which the self faces the other, who might challenge the univocal signification of the self's authorial voice. Thus, the translator is mistrusted, and translation obviated. The thankless job of a translator is taken up by a nameless Korean in the story.[8]

In principle, a colonial translator need not be from the colonized. A colonizer can be a translator if he or she is proficient enough in the language of the colonized. As a matter of fact, as the first chapter of this book shows, the translation of Korean historical and literary classics into Japanese by Japanese translators simultaneously shaped and confirmed the ways in which Koreans and Korean culture were represented. Nevertheless, there are virtually no depictions of Japanese figures who translate between Japanese and Korean in colonial literature.

The lack of bilingual Japanese figures in colonial literary texts reflects a colonial reality in which Japanese was privileged not only by the colonizers but increasingly also by the colonized themselves, a point I will discuss further in Chapter 5. Whereas, as seen in the case of Hosoi Hajime, the main focus of Chapter 1, quite a few Japanese Korea experts engaged in textual translation (*pŏnyŏk* in Korean/*hon'yaku* in Japanese), it was Koreans who were relegated as colonial functionaries/translators to the task of verbal translation (*t'ongyŏk/ tsūyaku*) for mundane matters. The dearth of Japanese functionaries/translators is also inferred from the following quote from a column published in the newspaper for the Japanese colonial police in Korea.[9] The column's author laments the lack of enthusiasm among Japanese colonial officials to learn Korean.

> Officials are not interested in Korean language study, and accordingly they cannot do their work without translators as some argue that there is no need for learning Korean because Korean children have been taught Japanese at elementary school for the last twenty years. This is a precondition for taking the first wrong step in ruling Korea.[10]

Although indicating that there were few Japanese functionaries/translators in colonial Korea, the quote also begs further questions about translation and, its implication in and resistance to colonial domination. The author of the column does not suggest that Japanese colonial bureaucrats should learn Korean to replace Korean translators. Instead, he urges that Japanese colonial bureaucrats should do their work without translators. What does this dismissal of translators tell us about? Why does the author not see that the realization of his suggestion for Korean language study will eradicate neither translation nor translators but only turn Japanese colonial bureaucrats themselves into translators, who translate between Japanese and Korean? Does this rejection of translation and translators not echo the uneasiness of the colonizers about translation as revealed in the literary texts examined above? From where does this desire to eradicate translation come?

A clue to a rather prosaic answer can be gleaned from the above discussion on Nakajima's story "Landscape with Policeman: A Sketch of 1923." Korean functionaries/translators are suspected of either sabotaging or muddling communication between the colonizers and the colonized. Unlike the Korean functionary/translator, the bilingual Japanese bureaucrat does not mediate between the colonizers and the colonized. He himself is a colonizer. Above all, is it not obvious that he represents no one other than his own authorial voice? Such reasoning, however, does not exhaust colonial translation, which flows in both directions between the languages of the colonizer and the colonized. Not only would the bilingual Japanese bureaucrat still have to translate for his fellow colonizers from Japanese to Korean but, more important, he would also have to render Korean-language texts both textual and verbal into Japanese.

It is necessary to push the discussion further to take it as a point of departure for rigorously examining translation and its relationship to colonial domination. The conventional understanding of translation, which Roman Jakobson designated as translation proper, posits that translation is above all a linguistic practice of rendering an authorial voice expressed in one language into another, whether the voice is inscribed in a written text or enunciated verbally by a speaker. What makes translation distinct from other linguistic practices is the interval between the language in which the authorial voice is originally expressed and the language to which it is transferred. In essence, then, there is no difference between textual translation (*pŏnyŏk/honyaku*) and verbal translation (*tongyŏk/tsūyaku*). In the course of translation, the authorial voice is fixed onto a meaning in a different language, which has its own sets of semantic and syntactic patterns and rhetorical modes. Without the difference between languages translation intends to transcend, translation is not distinguishable from interpretation or rewording, which Jakobson called intralingual translation because of its affinity to translation.[11]

The cognate relationship between translation and interpretation turns attention to another interval, which inheres not only in translation but also in any act of reading and listening, the interval between the authorial voice and its signification. The authorial voice cannot present itself instantly and transparently because it materializes only through language and because that very materiality compromises the spirit of the voice. In other words, to be addressed to the other, the authorial voice needs to first be transformed into a series of sounds or letters. Even in the case of monologue, the voice cannot materialize outside of language. Put differently, the voice comes only as a sign that supposedly corresponds to its meaning. However, as long as the voice can be expressed only as a sign, it does not remain univocally tied to a fixed meaning. As Jacques Derrida elucidated, signs are invested with meanings that can be expressed only by other signs.[12] If meanings are generated through the relationship between signs and the authorial voice comes only as a sign to be signified, then there is always slippage between the authorial voice and its signification. Unlike in the case of interpretation or rewording within one language, the authorial voice is initially expressed in one language and its signification is eventually enacted in another in the course of translation. Because of differences between languages, the interval between the authorial voice and its signification is much more pronounced in the case of translation than that of interpretation or rewording.

The authorial voice exceeds the limits of what Derrida called voice, which is supposed to be the pure medium of interior monologue immediately and transparently present in the consciousness of the subject.[13] As Derrida demonstrated in his critical interpretation of Edmund Husserl, desire for the presence of transparent and immediate meanings figures in the voice, the idea of the pure medium of interior monologue. Although the authorial voice is already contaminated by references to the external world, the solipsistic voice is silent, prior to utterance, and insulated within the solipsistic interiority of the subject. Only in the instance of solitary speech is a perfect match between a signifier and a signified possible. Such an absolutely clear signification within the subject's interiority, however, communicates nothing to the other because an immediate and transparent meaning present to the subject's consciousness is not transmissible to the other, who is external to the interior selfhood of the subject. In other words, any attempt to engage with the other accompanies the adulteration of the subject's solipsistic voice.

With the above exposition of translation in mind, let us return to the Japanese colonial police newspaper column in which the author does not acknowledge that what he recommends Japanese colonial bureaucrats do is translation. As suggested above, despite the desire for the erasure of translation manifested in the column, the Japanese bilingual bureaucrat could not break free from the position of a translator. His work would inevitably entail rendering Korean texts, both textual and verbal, into Japanese. In such a case, he would obviously be engaging in translation in its common sense meaning. Then, what about the other way around in linguistic transactions? Is he translating when speaking or writing to the colonized in Korean? The question is deceptively simple. Is it not too obvious that he is speaking rather than translating when enunciating in Korean? Put differently, unlike in the case of translation in the usual sense, both the authorial voice and its signification coincide in the same person when the Japanese colonial bureaucrat is speaking or writing in Korean. Thus, it appears that the answer to the question should be negative: The Japanese bureaucrat's linguistic practice of speaking or writing in Korean fails to qualify as translation.

The seemingly simple question merits further examination, however, because it pertains to understanding the desire for the erasure of translation revealed in colonial discourse. In a situation in which a Japanese writer fluent in Korean is rephrasing his own Japanese-language work in Korean, the consciousness of the subject splits into the speaker (or writer) and the interpreter even though it is the same subject who has written the work in Japanese and is rephrasing it in Korean. To be more exact, the consciousness of the subject is punctuated with the split into one who wrote the original work and the other who is interpreting it, and the two are distanced or spaced in the Derridean sense by time. This split is all the more pronounced because of the presence of the text, the work, which is being rendered in a different language.

Does this split of the subject not inhere in the Japanese bureaucrat's speech in Korean? As discussed above, the work in which the authorial voice of the past is inscribed marks the interval between the speaking and translating subjects within the same person. Because there is no visible work of the authorial voice from the past in the case of the Japanese bureaucrat speaking Korean, the split of the subject is likely to go unnoticed.

To make the point more concretely, suppose that the interval between the authorial voice inscribed in the work and its interpretation enacted in translation is progressively narrowing and converging to such a point that the voice is almost simultaneously signified in a foreign language as soon as it is presented to the subject's consciousness. No matter how miniscule this interval may be, because it implies the split of the subject, it cannot be eradicated completely because the authorial voice materializes only as a sign and an interval necessarily remains between the voice and its signification even when the subject is speaking to himself. The split of the subject inheres in any enunciation, whether it is speaking or translating. The materiality of language constantly frustrates its immediate and transparent signification. Because the materiality of language is spotlighted by differences between two languages in the course of translation, the act of translation accentuates such a split of the subject, which often goes unnoticed in monolingual practices.

Translation is a paramount instance in which the subject encounters the other from within as well as without. As examined above, demand for translation presupposes an other who does not share any common ground with the self for understanding. At the same time, translation highlights the split of the subject, which hardly comes to light when the self speaks its native tongue, supposedly under its total command. Does the desire to erase translation glimpsed from colonial discourse not amount to a yearning for transparent communication and fear of facing the split of the subject, then? Because the presence of the translator brings to attention the impossibility of the self's control over the other in conversation, and translation calls the putative unity of the subject into question, translation can be said to undermine the epistemological and ontological foundation of an individual colonizer's subjectivity, which is often uncritically extended to the national subjectivity of colonizers.

As discussed earlier, however, the collusion between colonialism and translation depicted in the Korean and Japanese literary texts suggests that translation as conventionally understood can also reconfirm the ethnic and linguistic identity of the enunciating subject by reifying the boundaries of the languages between which translation is taking place. The Japanese poet, critic, and early Tolstoy translator Kitahara Hakushū's preface to the Korean translator Kim Soun's 1929 Japanese-language anthology of Korean folk songs *Chōsen Minyoshū* (Collection of Korean Folk Songs) illustrates the ways in which the concept of translation works simultaneously to denaturalize and reconfirm the unified subjectivity of the individual as well as national self.[14] In the earlier part of the preface, Kitahara Hakushū in effect deconstructs the unified subjectivity of the Japanese by historicizing its emergence. However, his deconstructive move dissipates into oblivion as his discussion on translation proceeds with an effort to recover the unity of the Japanese national subjectivity in the end.

As discussed further in Chapter 4, during the colonial period, Kim actively introduced Korean literature and culture to Japan through translation. The success of his Korean folk song anthology earned him prominence as the most authoritative Japanese-language translator of Korean literature and enabled him to go on to translate and publish modern Korean poetry. This anthology is still in print 80 years after its initial publication.

Kitahara Hakushū begins his preface with a memory of Korea when he was a child in his hometown of Yanagawa, which is in Fukuoka prefecture on the island of Kyūshū, the part of Japan closest to Korea. Children in his hometown used to call Korea "Kara," a name that conjures up a sense of intimacy and nostalgia (*shitashiku natsukashimareta*) for him. From time immemorial, even in the era when Japan was "closed," the region had close trade and cultural relations with Korea. Village fishermen often sailed to the shores of the Korean peninsula to fish and Korea appeared often in the village elders' stories. Some of the fishermen fathered mixed-blood children with Korean women and their wives burned with jealousy. Kitahara Hakushū's memory of the virility of the men from his village, which could function as a metaphor for Japan's colonial expansion, ironically leads him to realize that the culture of his home region has descended from miscegenation between the cultures of ancient Japan, Korea, China, the South Pacific islands, and the Netherlands, which had a trading base in nearby Nagasaki during the Tokugawa period.

Kitahara Hakushū's recognition of the cultural miscegenation of his home region makes him differentiate the collective identity of his people, whom he addresses as the first person plural "we," from the national subjectivity of Japan. He goes on to point out that even though both the Tōhoku region of northern Honshū and his home region supposedly belong to the same country, Japan, the Tōhoku region was more alien than Korea to people in his home region who were brought up with their regional folktales and language deriving from the mixture of such different foreign cultures. Hakushū historicizes the process of the unification of Japanese culture by observing that Japanese folk songs and children's songs transcending regional limits gradually emerged only after the implementation of the "alternate attendance" policy of the Edo period and the ensuing expansion of trade between distant regions during the Tokugawa period.[15]

What catches our attention in Hakushū's discussion is the double-edged function of "translation" in his discussion, simultaneously denaturalizing and reconfirming the putative unity of Japan. Hakushū perceptively argues that Japanese folk songs and children's songs are actually translations of regional songs. Because the folk songs would not have been understandable to people from other regions if people had continued singing them only in their regional dialects, the songs were translated into standard Japanese. From this observation, Hakushū inferred that the putative unity of Japanese culture was constructed not least through the process of translation of regional differences as variations of one uniform people and culture. Although Hakushū did not go into detail about how the unified subjectivity of the Japanese behind this translation process might arise, the Japanese national subjectivity and the idea of homogeneous national culture emerged, as many Japan historians have pointed out, only after the new Meiji government had implemented educational, economical, and political institutions to integrate various social and local segments into the unified consciousness of the Japanese in the process of building a modern nation state in Japan in the late 19th century.[16]

In his *Origins of Modern Japanese Literature,* the Japanese critic

Karatani Kōjin insightfully points out that Japanese writers' translation and internalization of Western literary works made a decisive impact on the formation of modern Japanese literature. His examples are Futabatei Shimei's translations of Ivan Turgenev and Mori Ogai's translations of a variety of European literary works.[17] In contrast to such "external translation" from Western culture and literature, Hakushū is calling attention to the importance of "internal translation" from various localities within Japan in the construction of modern Japanese culture. Needless to say, it became feasible to make a clear distinction between "external" and "internal" only after translation drew boundaries between the unified space designated as Japanese culture and others outside.

By calling attention to the aspect of translation that violently renders regional differences as mere variations of one uniform culture, Hakushū inspires the reader to glimpse traces of regional differences that had been suppressed through translation in the process of constructing a homogeneous national culture. However, Hakushū's discussion suddenly reverses course and proceeds with his reconfirmation of the unified national subjectivity of the Japanese. In this case, too, it is the notion of translation that enables him to postulate the unity of Japanese subjectivity. Even though the culture of Hakushū's home region became integrated into the unified Japanese culture only through the process of translation, Hakushū argues that, because people in his home region are also Japanese, it was not impossible for them to internalize the Japanese spirit and tradition, which seeped into written language as well as lyrics of the songs from other regions. It seems as if he believes the unified Japanese subjectivity preceded the construction of homogeneous Japanese national culture through translation. Hakushū's reasoning is, of course, circular because it suggests that the preexisting homogeneity of the Japanese had laid down the foundation on which the homogeneous Japanese subjectivity was built through the construction of homogeneous national culture.

In Hakushū's ensuing discussion, however, the idea of a unified Japanese culture registers most clearly in contrast to Korean culture. Hakushū sees Kim's translation of Korean folk songs into Japanese as a commendable feat bridging a much wider gap in language and national character than the translation of regional folk songs into standard Japanese and their dissemination to other regions of Japan. Here, when Hakushū refers to a linguistic practice transcending a gulf between Korea and Japan, translation is ironically understood to reify boundaries between Japanese and Korean cultures and languages. In contrast to the case of translating regional cultures within Japan into standard Japanese where the practice of translation suppresses difference, the act of translating Korean folk songs into Japanese plays up the difference between two nations. According to Hakushū, the lyrics of the Korean folk songs tend to be more acerbic, cynical, and melancholy because they developed from "the particular domestic situation of Korea." The implication is that because the Korean people were misruled by an incompetent and despotic ruling class, they tended to express anger, cynicism, and sorrow in their folk songs. In Hakushū's view, Chinese influence was also so strong over the formality and vocabulary of Korean folk songs that it had a negative effect on them.

Despite his emphasis on the difference between Japanese and Korean folk songs that ensures the homogeneity of Japanese culture in contrast to Korean culture, Hakushū's profuse praise of Kim's translation betrays his uneasiness toward the lack of difference he expected to find in the Japanese translations of Korean folk songs. In Hakushū's eyes, Kim's expert translation made Korean folk songs too "Japanese." Kim's mastery of Japanese poetic sensitivity and diction was to such a degree that his translations evoke uncanny feelings of repulsion. Here again can be seen Hakushū's forced maneuver at reconfirming the homogeneity of the language and culture enclosed within Japan. As noted above, Hakushū asserted in the beginning of his preface that people in his home region in Kyūshū felt closer to Korea than to such distant regions within Japan as Tōhoku. As cultures of different regions within Japan were integrated into Japanese national culture through translation, Korean culture grew alien even to people like Hakushū, who had previously felt close to Korea. Hakushū, however, seems to have entirely forgotten the supposed intimacy with Korea of which he reminisced. Through Kim's skillful translation, Korean folk songs, part of now defamiliarized Korean culture, return as something uncannily similar to Japanese folk songs and eerily familiar to Hakushū.

As Hakushū himself recognizes earlier in the preface, the defamiliarization of Korean culture to people in Hakushū's home region at least came as much from the homogenization of culture in Japan since the Tokugawa period and especially since the Meiji Restoration as from the deteriorating domestic situation in Korea or from Chinese influence over Korean culture. When Hakushū treats Japanese culture as a unified body of social practices particular to Japan and distinct from those in Korea, his perspective has already shifted from the one rooted in his regional identity to one based in the Japanese national subjectivity. As can be seen in his anxiety over the lack of expected difference in Kim's Japanese translations of Korean folk songs, the unified body of Japanese culture and the Japanese national subjectivity can be posited only in contrast to Japan's other, whether it is the West or its colonies like Korea. Instead of critically contemplating his anxiety, Hakushū holds up Kim's mastery of Japanese vocabulary and poetic diction to reprimand contemporary Japanese poets for their indifference to Japanese literary tradition as they rush to imitate the Western poetic style. Thus, Hakushū ends up reconfirming the homogeneity of Japanese culture and language supposedly inscribed in Japanese literary tradition.

What eventually undermines Hakushū's initial insight into the fragmented nature of national subjectivity is the fact that, for him, the difference of the other the self encounters in translation is not absolute. As seen above, translation for Hakushū is the site where difference is either suppressed, as in the case of the regional folk songs translated into standard Japanese, or stressed, as in the case of the Korean folk songs translated into Japanese. The difference Hakushū recognized in both cases is appropriated to posit the self-sameness of the Japanese and that of Koreans.

As the Korean poet Kim Suyŏng, who is the focus of Chapter 5, shows, translation can also be a site at which the self-sameness of national subjectivity is brought into question because an act of translation continuously pushes the translator to doubt whether he or she can master the mother tongue, let alone the foreign target language, an anxiety over the very underpinnings of a sense of belonging to linguistic, national, and cultural communities. In short, translation can be an occasion in which the self encounters the otherness of its own mother tongue. The self's encounter with the otherness of its native language can constitute a first step toward an ethically and politically arduous position for critical reflection on the self's relationship with its own language, culture, ethnicity, and country. As I argue to varying degrees throughout this book, particularly in Chapters 2 and 5, such a self-reflective position is ethical and political because it can eventually open up an alternative way of associating with others who are presently excluded from communities defined by their sameness.

1. Translation and the Community of Love

Hosoi Hajime and Translating Korea

In the preface of his 1924 anthology *Chōsen Bungaku Kessakushū* (Collection of Korean Literary Masterpieces), the Japanese editor and translator Hosoi Hajime explained the importance of his Japanese translation projects of classical Korean literary works by recalling a resolution he made at the time of the March First Independence Movement five years earlier. According to his recollection, when he heard the disturbing news about Koreans uprising against Japanese rule in the colony, Hosoi had the epiphany that his mission in life would be to bring Japan and Korea together into genuine unity, and that to achieve that unity, the Japanese (*naichijin*, or the people of Japan proper) needed to understand (*rikaisuru*) Korea (*Chōsen*). In Hosoi's view, understanding Korea meant knowing completely both the merits and the faults of the Korean people.[1]

Hosoi warned his readers that it would do no good for the Japanese to dwell on Koreans' defects without respecting them for their strengths and empathizing (*dōjōsuru*) with them for their weaknesses. Hosoi went on to advise readers that there is no better way to understand the mind of a nation (*kokka minzoku*) than knowing its literature because, he reasoned, the best of human feelings (*ninjō*) is "distilled" and "crystallized" into literature.[2] Hosoi contended, furthermore, that literature helps not only comprehend the zeitgeist (*seishin*) of the period when it is written but also helps to trace the origins of the national character (*kokumin seikaku*).

What stands out in Hosoi's preface is the priority he gives to literature and to language in interpellating "the Japanese" and "the Koreans" as colonizer and colonized. Korean literature is prioritized as the cultural repository in which the national character of the colonized is manifested, whereas the Japanese language is privileged as the marker of the colonizer in that those Hosoi is addressing as the Japanese are distinguished as speakers of vernacular Japanese. Certainly, it is nothing new to see a body of literature written in a vernacular language as belonging to that language community, which, in many cases, is understood to coincide with a nation. Nor is it unheard of to regard such national literature as the locus in which national character is manifested. For example, Hosoi's assumption resonates with 18th- and 19th-century European romanticist discourse on culture and nation that privileged literature and language as the culmination of culture and the manifestation of national spirit. The view that each nation has a unique literary tradition first emerged in 18th-century Europe.[3] Since then, the idea of national literature has prevailed and is echoed by such commonsensical expressions as American literature and Irish literature. In Japan, such pioneering works on Japanese literary history as *Nihon Bungakushi* (History of Japanese Literature) of 1890 affirmed the phonocentrism inherent in the valorization of vernacular language by privileging Japanese phonetic language over Chinese script as the essential element of Japanese national literature. Mikami Sanji and Takatsu Kuwasaburō, the authors of *Nihon Bungakushi*, further harnessed literature to national character by defining "national literature" (*kokubungaku*) as the literature that possesses the "essential qualities inherent in each country" (*hōkoku ni yorite sono koyū no tokushitsu*).[4]

Despite its banality, Hosoi's view on the national character of the colonized and their literature merits attention precisely because such banality testifies to the generic mode of colonial discourse in which differences between the colonized and the colonizer are laid out. Colonial discourse abounds with emphases on cultural differences between the colonized and the colonizer, but, ultimately, the difference of the colonized always serves to explain their supposed inferiority. Japanese colonial discourse on Korea was no exception. When flipping through the pages of Japanese publications on Korea during the colonial period (1910–1945), one can easily find descriptions of backward customs and degenerate national character attributed to Korean culture.

Even though I use such expressions as "Korean culture" and "Japanese representation of Korean culture" in this book, I do not believe that there exists a genuine national culture as such prior to representation. The way in which a social practice is "nationalized" and thus associated with Japanese culture or Korean culture is already ideological. As discussed below, such national identities as Korean and Japanese are schematized to exist in their own right only through the intricate and incessant mechanism of identification that operates in legal, educational, and other social institutions. Needless to say, "ideological" in this context should not be taken to mean false or fallacious. As Louis Althusser points out, "ideology" refers to the representation of social relations that is indispensable in the construction of subjectivity.[5]

Hosoi was one of the most active Korea experts in Japan during the early years of Japanese colonialism in Korea. Hosoi was born on February 10, 1886, in Fukuoka. He and his sister moved to Tokyo after the death of their parents. Hosoi then entered a vocational school to study radio communications, where he became alerted to labor issues for the first time. In the fall of 1906, Hosoi became a reporter for *Nagasaki Shinpō,* a newspaper based in Nagasaki near his birthplace in Kyūshū. He organized a socialist study group, which was disbanded, however, by the authorities soon after, and he was forced to resign from his newspaper job. Branded a socialist, Hosoi could not find work and so, partly for this reason, he went to Korea in 1908, looking for employment. He was working as a journalist in Korea when the country was annexed by Japan and, in 1911, he cofounded the *Chōsen Kenkyūkai* (Association for Research on Korea) with Kikuchi Kenjō and Ōmura Tomonojō. Returning to Tokyo later that same year, he went to work for the prestigious Japanese newspaper *Tōkyō Asahi Shinbun* (Tokyo Asahi Newspaper). Hosoi founded a journal called *Rōdō to Kokka* (Labor and the State) and called for cooperation between workers and capitalists. After the March First movement in 1919, he went back to Korea and worked there as a journalist, with financial support from Saito Minoru, the governor general in Korea at that time. After the Great Kantō Earthquake in 1923, Hosoi set out on a lecture tour around Japan addressing the Japan–Korea relationship and, around the same time, he also began advocating Pan-Asianism in earnest through publication and public speeches.[6]

By the time his *Collection of Korean Literary Masterpieces* was published in 1924, Hosoi had already spent 17 years introducing classical Korean literature, history, and culture to Japanese readers through translation and publication.[7] The list of Hosoi's publications is extensive and includes not only translations of classical Korean writings but also such original works as his 1911 *Chōsen Bunka Shiron* (Treatise on the History of Korean Culture) and his 1921 *Senman no Keiei: Chōsen Mondai no Konpon Kaiketsu* (Administrating Korea and Manchuria: The Fundamental Solution to the Korean Problem).

Despite his entreaties that the Japanese should recognize both the merits and shortcomings of Koreans, Hosoi's texts brim with negative descriptions of Korean national character that serve to explain why Korea deserved to be colonized. When read side by side with the treatises on nation, culture, and literature by Korean intellectuals of his day, Hosoi's texts are helpful for bettering our understanding of the Korean discourse of cultural nationalism that developed in the 1910s and 1920s primarily in response to the negative portrayals of Korean culture by the Japanese. The assumptions about national character on which Hosoi based his arguments were shared by both Japanese and Korean intellectuals of the time. The colonized intellectuals responded in one of two ways: They either refuted the colonizers' negative characterization of their nation by glorifying their history and culture or they appropriated the grammar and terminology of colonial discourse on the inferiority of their nation to make a case for building a modern Korean national culture to replace their failing tradition. In any case, as examined in the discussion below about a treatise on Korean literature by Hosoi's contemporary, An Hwak, Korean nationalist intellectuals also subscribed to the belief that the national character of a people existed in a verifiable way and that their national literature reflected the spirit of the nation.

At the same time Hosoi justified Japan's colonization of Korea on the basis of difference, he also earnestly called for harmony between Japan and Korea and saw his translation projects as efforts to bridge the gap between the two peoples by facilitating Japanese understanding of Korean national character and culture. Although advocating a more benevolent policy toward Koreans and denouncing heavy-handed measures taken by the Japanese colonial government, Hosoi insisted that the difference between the colonized and the colonizer necessitated an unequal relationship. In Hosoi's view, Japan as the big brother should not hesitate to chastise Korea when necessary to guide it to the right path. At the same time, Hosoi wanted to build a genuine community of both the Japanese and Koreans through mutual understanding, which would complement and stabilize the political unity of Japan and Korea brought about by colonization. Love (*ai*) was the principle Hosoi came up with to realize simultaneously his hope to bring harmony to the colonizer and the colonized and his desire to maintain a rigid hierarchy in the relationship between the two.

This chapter treats Hosoi's writings on Korea with a focus on his concepts of national character, literature, translation, and love. First, I examine the ways in which translation as both a linguistic practice and a trope enabled Hosoi to schematize the national character of the colonized and the colonizer. As mentioned above, Hosoi construed his translation projects of Korean writings as an effort to foster Japanese understanding of Korean national character and culture. It is interesting to note, however, that Hosoi simultaneously revealed his distrust of translation as "unreflective imitation" and "copying" inferior to the original. Despite the seeming contradiction, both his high regard and mistrust were derived from the conventional view of translation as representation of an original.

By examining Hosoi's texts on national character and literature in relation to the Korean nationalist intellectual An Hwak's treatise on the same topics from the same period, in this chapter I also show how the collective subjectivities of the colonized and the colonizer are simultaneously asserted and schematized as they are associated with traits of each nation. I pay special attention to the familiar argument found in both Japanese and Korean discourse that the literature of a people reflects its collective spirit, its national character.

Finally, drawing on G. W. F. Hegel, I parse Hosoi's demand for both the Japanese and Koreans to love one another to realize their unity. In later works on family, civil society, and the state, Hegel shifted his focus from love to the importance of law as the principal underpinning of communal bonds because he realized that love alone cannot keep a community united. However, even in his 1821 *Elements of the Philosophy of Right*, Hegel upheld love as the basis of the family. Reading Hosoi with Hegel is helpful in understanding why Hosoi chose to allegorize the unity between Japan and Korea as a familial one in his treatises on Japanese colonial rule over Korea, emphasizing the importance of love in the colonizer's relationship with the colonized. Because love can work as the principal bond only within a family, as Hegel realized, Hosoi's insistence on love as the primary bond between Koreans and the Japanese could hold only if the political community of the Japanese empire was imagined as a family.

The colonizer's emphasis on benevolent affections in the relationship with the colonized is not unique to the particular historical moment of Japanese colonial domination in Korea, however. As lucidly expressed in Rudyard Kipling's 1899 poem "The White Man's Burden," Western colonialism has also been justified as the manifestation of the colonizer's benevolence and affection for the colonized. By reading Hosoi's treatises on Japanese colonial rule over Korea through the lens of Hegel's ideas of love, family, and community, it is possible to see an affinity between Hosoi's emphasis on love and the general tendency of modern colonial discourse that insists on the colonizer's benevolence and affection for the colonized. Hosoi's concept of love ultimately failed to bind Japan and Korea together, however, despite his hope that it would overcome the difference between the colonized and the colonizers in language, culture, and ethnicity. To the contrary, as discussed below, his insistence on love only revealed that the community of the colonizers itself was already fractured.

TRANSLATING NATIONAL CHARACTER

Hosoi's first major work was his 1911 Japanese-language survey of Korean cultural history and literature. *Chōsen Bunka Shiron* (Treatise on the History of Korean Culture) appeared in the new colony only a year after annexation. Although the title suggests that it delves into various aspects of Korean culture in history, it focuses mainly on what is today usually called classical Korean literature, providing not only a chronological outline of representative literary, political, and religious works of premodern Korea but also biographical information about prominent writers who represent each period, many of whom were Buddhist monks and Confucian literati.[8]

The book was the first of its kind in Japanese, if not in any language. In the preface, Hosoi confessed that, when writing the book, he balked many times at the sheer amount of primary materials stored in Kyujanggak, the royal library of the Chosŏn dynasty. While admitting that his study was far from perfect, he expressed "a modest wish" that it would lay the foundation for further study on Korean literature and religion.[9] *The Treatise on the History of Korean Culture* was quickly adopted by the prominent Japanese scholars Yoshida Tōgo and Tomizu Hirondo as a textbook at Tokyo Imperial University and Waseda University, respectively.[10]

In the beginning of the preface of *The Treatise on the History of Korean Culture*, Hosoi remarks that one cannot help agreeing that "two thousand years of Korean history" has reached its miserable conclusion. He goes on to write that "if we (*warera*) were placed in the position of a third party without any relation to the Korean nation (*Chōsen minzoku*), we could afford just to heave a sad sigh over its pitiful end as if reciting an elegy about it." He reminded his readers that "since Japan and Korea have merged into a family, and twelve million people of the Korean nation have become the infant children (*sekishi*) of His Sacred Majesty (*seijō*) and brothers of the Japanese, the Japanese should guide them onto the right path to assimilation (*dōwasuru*)."[11]

Hosoi seems almost to lament that he cannot afford to yield to his sentimentality and leisurely write a sad poem over the tragic ending of the Korean nation instead of writing a bulky book on the history of Korean culture, but the "we" he references has a pressing reason to act to achieve the colonial project of assimilation. Hosoi worries that assimilation will take time, maybe as long as hundred years, because of the "pitiful" Korean national character he finds manifested in Korean history. He argues that "Korean politics changed as capriciously as a prostitute's heart, its literature was nothing but imitation and failed to develop any originality, and its religion remains limited only to superstition."[12] In short, just as the lack of principles characterized Korean politics prior to colonization, Hosoi judged its culture as lacking originality. Hosoi observes that because the ruling *yangban* class of Confucian literati despised fiction and theater as the expression of vulgar emotions, those literary genres existed mostly by and for the lower classes, and most works in those genres were written in the vernacular Korean script. Many of them emerged first as translations of such famous Chinese works as *Xīyóujì* (Journey to the West) and *Sānguó yǎnyì* (Romance of the Three Kingdoms).[13]

Japanese colonial discourse on Korean culture often centered on the argument that throughout history Koreans had slavishly imitated Chinese civilization. For Hosoi, however, Koreans could not even copy Chinese civilization correctly. He argued that they missed the essence of Confucianism and only clung to its fossilized formalities. Neo-Confucianism (*Chujahak* in Korean/*Shushigaku* in Japanese) flourished briefly during the late Koryŏ dynasty (918–1392), but it ossified into the ideological support for a cruel regime during the Chosŏn period, in which warring factions of the ruling class meticulously cited passages from the Confucian canon about rules of propriety and ceremony to denounce their political enemies. Political rivalries often escalated into ruthless purges and persecutions, taking a heavy toll on the nation, he concluded. Hosoi also harps on the toadyism of Koreans and traces this perceived tendency to worship the powerful to the time of the unification of the three ancient kingdoms by Silla in the seventh century. The Chosŏn dynasty's loyalty to Ming China exemplified the extremes of such a tendency. Hosoi goes on to argue that both the ruler and his officials had held on to toadyism, obeying the powerful country (that is, China) abroad while oppressing their own people at home. Hosoi argues that the Korean people submitted to such tyrannical rule and turned to superstitious religious practices as a means of escape from suffering and privation.[14] In contrast to his relentless criticism of the Korean ruling class, Hosoi showed sympathy toward ordinary Koreans, who, in his view, had been victimized by the oppressive rule of the *yangban* elite.[15] Nevertheless, in the end, Hosoi did not spare any Koreans, oppressed or oppressor, from his generalizations of Korean national character. He reasoned that the instability of their society was what made Koreans "shady and scheming, and obsequious and obdurate."[16]

Thus, Hosoi asserts that Koreans are doomed to failure and emphasizes that twelve million Koreans truly deserve "our" sympathy. To rescue Koreans from their dismal fate, Hosoi concludes that the "we" (the Japanese) need to educate them with noble ideals.[17] The "we" as an advanced nation should embrace these Koreans in the newly annexed land and come in peace as "a companion and teacher."[18] To achieve this goal, Hosoi reminds his readers, his study is intended to trace the genealogy of Koreans' thinking and analyze their culture. Hosoi asserts that to understand sentiments and customs of a nation, it is essential to examine its native literature (*sono kuni koyū no bungaku*) because human emotions distilled into literature, which not only captures its zeitgeist but also controls and cultivates the nation's character throughout history.[19]

The way Hosoi asserts a strong correlation between national literature and character suggests that he took the validity of this strong correlation for granted. To fully grasp his view on national character and literature, it is necessary to read his essay "*Kosho Kobun o Tsujite Mitaru Chōsenjin no Shinsei*" (The Korean Mind Seen Through Its History and Literature), which appeared a decade later, in 1921, in *Chōsen* (Korea), the Japanese-language journal published by the government general in colonial Korea.[20] In this article, Hosoi explains how national character takes shape throughout history and how it is reflected in literature. According to Hosoi, just as an individual has a personality, a nation has a national character that reflects the totality of its people's personalities and constitutes the national spirit that determines the rise and fall of that nation. Citing the French racial theorist Gustave Le Bon, Hosoi states that the personality of an individual is shaped not only by upbringing, formal education, and socialization but also by genetically inherited physiological and mental characteristics. These genetic characteristics are not determined within a generation but developed and inherited from one generation to another. Thus, tying his thought on national character to a pseudobiological theory, Hosoi concludes that because a people inherits its ancestors' acquired physiological and mental characteristics, individuals are inseparably connected not only to their parents but also to the entirety of their ancestors and ultimately their race (*shūzoku*). In short, for Hosoi, the national character is shaped by what the nation has inherited from its ancestors, and individuals are not isolated beings but rather exist to pass the collective characteristics of their ancestors on to their descendents.[21]

Hosoi goes on to argue that experiences of trial and error throughout history are what add up to culture, which in turn informs and conditions the people's knowledge and patterns of behavior. In other words, for Hosoi, not only does generational inheritance explain how an individual is connected to his or her "genus," in other words, the nation, but generational inheritance also explains how the ethos a nation acquires at one point in history is passed down from one generation to the next and is deposited in the nation's culture. Thus, a pseudoscientific theory of race was fused with culturalism in Hosoi's reasoning. Hosoi was clearly influenced by Social Darwinism, which gained wide currency among East Asian intellectuals during the late 19th and early 20th centuries and provided a "scientific" framework to normalize competition between nations and to justify patriotism and imperial expansion. Needless to say, this fusion of racial theory and culturalism was not unique to Hosoi.[22]

For Hosoi, surveying Korean writings of the past enabled his Japanese readers to see how transparently the texts exhibited Koreans' negative national character. In other words, the inevitable decline of the Korean nation was retrospectively confirmed by this Korean historical and literary canon. For example, drawing on such texts as *Pyŏngjailgi* (The Records of the Namhan Castle in 1636) and *Mongminsimsŏ* (Admonitions on Governing the People), Hosoi recounted how a Korean official deserted his post to selfishly save his own father as the invading Qing army was advancing and showed how corrupt provincial magistrates during the Chosŏn period exploited the people beyond imagination.[23] In Hosoi's account, those were telling signs of Koreans' abominable national character.

Hosoi did not find his evidence of Korean character only in nonfiction documents, however. As mentioned earlier, he considered Korean literature no more than imitations of the Chinese originals. He deemed such Korean adaptations of Chinese stories to be low-quality romantic fiction, which provokes either "sensual stimuli" or "a long sigh of resentment." Hosoi reasoned that because the literature of commoners ought to express their thoughts and emotions and that the Korean people had suffered from oppressive rule, one might expect that Korean literature would produce works on a par with the Japanese kabuki play about the Edo-period street tough Banzuiin Chōbei whose story, in Hosoi's judgment, expresses the indignation and hopes of Japan's common people.[24] He did mention *Hong Kildong chŏn* (Story of Hong Kildong) in which the eponymous hero leads a band of bandits and punishes corrupt officials and monks. He ultimately dismissed the tale, however, as just "derivative of Nezumikozō."[25] The fact that the Korean tale preceded the famous early 19th-century Japanese thief by more than two hundred years did not restrain him from making such a sweeping dismissal. In his view, Korean literature was worthy of attention only as indisputable evidence for Koreans' lack of originality and creativity

In Hosoi's essay "The Korean Mind Seen Through Its History and Literature," as in colonial discourse in general, the colonized can be known only through difference from the colonizer. To embrace the colonized, the colonizer must understand how the colonized is different and how this difference results from their respective national characters. The historical experience of the colonized shapes their culture and national character, which is reflected in their literature and history, and translating the colonized's historical and literary writings is instrumental in fostering the colonizer's understanding of the colonized on both levels of cognitive and empathetic capacities. In other words, the assumption behind Hosoi's translation projects was that reading the history and literature of the colonized through translation enabled the colonizer to both know about and empathize with the colonized. Needless to say, Hosoi had no doubt that the colonizer's empathy should and would be reciprocated by the colonized in the end. Thus, for Hosoi, translation was central to forming a genuine community of the Japanese and Koreans, which would complement and stabilize the political unity between the two peoples.

It is noteworthy, however, that, in spite of his commitment to his translation projects, Hosoi also slighted translation as an unworthy act of copying parasitically dependant on the original. Hosoi's disdain for translation can be glimpsed when he dismissed Korean literature as the adaptation of Chinese literature and proof of Koreans' lack of originality. Even though Hosoi used adaptation (*hon'an*) instead of translation (*hon'yaku*) in "Korean Mind Seen Through Its History and Literature," he understood adaptation as resulting from a lack of originality. Furthermore, he also used translation to indicate unreflective imitation of the original in other places. When, for example, Hosoi was criticizing Japan's failure to win over Koreans in his policy recommendation to the Japanese government, he denounced early Japanese colonial policy as a verbatim translation of a Western model that did not fit the case of Japanese colonialism in Korea.[26] Moreover, he reasoned that Koreans had resented the reform policies foisted by Japan on the Korean government before annexation because they were a translation of Japanese law that did not take traditional Korean customs into account.[27] He also dismissed socialist and other radical strands in the Korean independence movement as mere translations of Western ideas.[28] Here was Hosoi's conundrum: While assuming that his translations of Korean classics would render Korean national character transparently into Japanese for Japanese readers, he was suspicious of translation as a slavish copying of the original.

Hosoi's high regard for translation as the path to understanding the national character of Koreans did not necessarily conflict with his disregard for translation as copying of the original, however, because both his high regard and his suspicion were derived from the idea of translation as representation of the original. In Hosoi's view, Japanese translations of classical literature could convey the meanings of the texts because they represented the original. However, so long as a translation merely represents an original, it never exceeds it. Not only does a translation fail to go beyond its original but also it is inevitably inferior to it because it is a parasitically dependant copy of it. In Hosoi's eyes, the new colonial situation in Korea required a new original policy, not a copy of the Western colonial policy. In a similar vein, he denounced the radical ideas embraced by Koreans because as copies of Western radical ideas, they did not fit Korean society.

KOREAN APPROPRIATIONS OF NATIONAL CHARACTER: AN HWAK'S "KOREAN LITERATURE"

As mentioned earlier, Hosoi's view on literature and national character was not unique. Not only Japanese but also Korean intellectuals of Hosoi's time shared the view of literature as a mirror of national character. When juxtaposed with Korean nationalist discourse on Korean national character and literature, Hosoi's arguments are even more instructive for understanding the rise of the cultural nationalism of the colonized in response to the colonizer's representation of their culture. In response to the colonizers' negative characterization of their nation, the colonized intellectuals either attempted to disprove it by glorifying their own history and culture or they rejected their own traditional culture by ascribing to it the blame for their nation's decline. In either case, they appropriated the grammar and vocabulary of Japanese colonial discourse on the Korean national character found in Hosoi's writings.

An Hwak's 1915 essay "*Chosŏn ŭi Munhak*" (The Literature of Korea) is a good example of a Korean nationalist response to the Japanese characterization of Korean culture and literature.[29] One of the pioneering nationalist intellectuals, An (1886–1946) devoted his life to studies in a wide range of fields including literature, language, history, music, fine art, and martial art. He is credited with writing the first book-length Korean-language study on Korean literary history, *Chosŏn Munhaksa* (History of Korean Literature), published in 1922, 11 years after Hosoi's *Treatise on the History of Korean Culture.*

"The Literature of Korea" was one of the earliest conscious attempts to define literature (*munhak*) in Korea. In the essay, An defines literature as writing expressive of aesthetic sentiment. He further argued that literature impresses the human spirit and presents its ideals.[30] Like Hosoi, An deems the literature of a nation to be the mirror of that nation's culture and, echoing Hosoi, he asserts that, to examine the civilization (*munmyŏng*) of a people (*inmin*), it is more fruitful to survey the rise and fall of that nation's literature than changes in the political arena because literature rules the internal feelings of the people whereas politics govern the external world. However, for An, literature does not only passively represent the national character and culture. It can also actively remedy the ills of the nation. He thus goes beyond Hosoi by implying that the task of national literature is to revive the ideals of the nation and lead to reform in its politics.

An's evaluation of the Korean literary tradition certainly sets him apart from Hosoi. In contrast to Hosoi, who dismissed Korean literature as a mere copy of Chinese literature, An stresses the difference between Korea and China. Even though he acknowledges that Korean literature was under Chinese influence, he insists that it is no parasitic copy of Chinese literature. He points out that Koreans had developed distinct conventions of writing in classical Chinese and stresses that even the Korean literature written in classical Chinese had retained a unique style different from that of Chinese literature. He pointed out that Koreans had also invented their own Chinese-character compound words such as *singsing* (fresh), *p'aekjŏng* (butcher), *chŏmshim* (lunch), and *kaekchu* (broker).

An based his positive evaluation of Korean literary tradition on his idiosyncratic observation that literature is inherently pessimistic to a certain degree. For him, literature not only seeks ideals but also simultaneously yearns for liberation even from such ideals. Thus, An declares, the pessimism inherent in literature stems from these opposing desires, and he goes on to argue that traditional Korean poetry was more advanced than its European counterpart because it had expressed this pessimism for hundreds of years, whereas European literature veered toward pessimism only during the 19th century, after years of chaos during which "Hellenic" and "Hebrew" thought had tangled.[31]

An admits, however, that Korean literature failed to develop on a par with modern European literature and blames that failure on Chinese influence.[32] In his eyes, having been entrapped in Confucianism for four thousand years, Chinese literature demonstrated only a superficial intellect and imagination as it harped on a banal morality of praising good and denouncing evil.[33] Taking his argument a step further by criticizing Confucianism itself, An holds Confucianism responsible for the decline of the Korean nation. In his view, then, because Confucianism cherished tradition and rejected progress, it finally turned into lifeless, fatalistic conservatism. Furthermore, An argues, by fastidiously insisting on correct manners and rituals and ruthlessly persecuting heretical views, Confucianism incited factionalism (*sasaek tangjaeng*).[34]

An calls for the construction of a new literature to replace the traditional literature that was written in classical Chinese and under Confucian influence.[35] He worries, however, that the construction of a new literature is not an easy task to accomplish because Koreans are malleable, unreflectively affected by foreign influences. In his view, then, Korean history testifies that Koreans were gullibly swayed by such foreign influences as Buddhism and Confucianism and quick to forfeit their native spirit. More specifically, An expresses concern that Korean writers might be too willing to follow the lead of European literature in constructing a new literature.

An's concerns about the putative malleability of Koreans eerily echo Hosoi's characterization of them as lacking originality and slavishly imitating Chinese civilization. An warns that if Korean writers and poets only imitated foreign literature marveling at new trends, as their predecessors had done Confucianism and Buddhism, the unique character of Korea would perish.[36] He expresses concern that the defects in foreign nations that were reflected in their literatures might rub off on Korean writers and poets, who would then transmit them into Korean literature.

> Drawing on French literature, one might become lured into its defects of frivolity and anarchistic tendency. Studying Spanish literature, one might become inclined to selfishness and isolationism. Admiring the ethos (*kip'ung*) of the English and Germans, one might become infected by their arrogance. Attempting to test Americans' fairness, one might experience their treachery. Taking a peek at the Russian character (*t'ŭksŏng*), one might be surprised by their debauchery and lack of focus. Praising the sensitivity of the island people (Japanese),

> one might mimic their deviousness and cruelty and feel dizzy about their pessimistic idea of nature.[37]

An concludes his essay with a Social Darwinist view, calling for the construction of new Korean literature as a contribution to the revival of the Korean nation. In An's view, races (*injong*) and nations (*minjok*) were in competition (*kyŏngjaeng*) that was taking place primarily in the realm of politics. On the other hand, he emphasizes that it is also competition between the character of one nation and that of another. Because each nation drew on its own national character (*minjoksŏng/ minzokusei*) in competition with others, An reasons that the result of such competition comes down to how to succeed in the dissemination of native thought and the appropriation of foreign ideas. Literature is one realm in which this can happen, and An urges anyone with a hand in literature to contribute to building a new literature.

Where Hosoi treated Korean literature as only a cultural repository that made the defective national character of Koreans manifested, An emphasized the establishment of a new Korean literature that would contribute to the revival of the Korean nation in the future. Thus, where Hosoi dwelled on historical and literary works of Korea, looking back to the past, An called for the construction of the new literature of Korea and looked forward to the future. Despite the difference, however, An's essay is typical of how Korean nationalist responses to Japanese colonial discourse shared significant assumptions with it. For both Hosoi and An, literature existed only as particular national literatures reflective of each nation's collective character. Although they differed on their positions on Japan's colonization of Korea, they were also in agreement that the Korean nation was easily swayed by foreign influence.

THE COMMUNITY OF LOVE

Continuing political disturbances in Japan and Korea in the decades following the publication of his literary history diverted the main focus of Hosoi's activities from publishing translations of dusty old books to writing policy suggestions in the face of pressing realities in the colony. The first such political disturbance was the March First movement in Korea, a series of mass demonstrations that broke out and spread across the colony in March 1919. The Japanese colonial authorities heavy handedly suppressed the Korean protests, and thousands of protesters were imprisoned, wounded, or killed. The event prompted Hosoi to write

Administrating Korea and Manchuria, blaming Japan for its failure to earn Korean consent to colonial rule by criticizing the cruelty of Japanese settlers toward Koreans and the forced imposition of Japanese laws and institutions on Korean society.[38]

In this pamphlet, Hosoi blames the poor performance and oppressive nature of Japanese rule in Korea on Japanese national character, identifying three characteristics of the Japanese nation that were proving obstacles to Japan's success in the colony. First, the Japanese tend to be aggressive and wrest others' possessions away from them. *Wakō* (piracy) in the 16th century was, according to Hosoi, one notable example of such a national tendency in history. Second, the Japanese tend to be insular, a tendency exacerbated during the Tokugawa period when Japan closed itself to other countries. Third, since the opening of the country to the West, the Japanese had grown to idolize the West.[39] In Hosoi's judgment, Japan's success or failure in its colonial rule in Korea depended on whether it could overcome the shortcomings in its own national character as well as whether it could understand Koreans and their culture.

The great Kantō earthquake in 1923 and the massacre of Korean immigrants in its aftermath pushed Hosoi to reformulate his idea of benevolent colonialism further.[40] Since his 1911 *Treatise on the History of Korean Culture,* he had emphasized the importance of Japanese understanding of the Korean national character and culture that he had launched his translation projects to foster. Understanding in this context refers both to cognitive capacity, which produces knowledge, and to emotive capacity, which engenders empathy. In earlier writings, Hosoi assumed a seamless connection between the two, but after witnessing Koreans' continuing resistance to Japanese rule and Japanese brutality and oppression against Koreans, he realized that his stress on the importance of knowledge of the colonized's culture was not enough to lead the Japanese to embrace Koreans as their compatriots and get Koreans to reciprocate Japanese "good will." He recognized that intellect and emotions are not necessarily unified in understanding in a dialectical fashion. Hosoi set out to underline the importance of feelings vis-à-vis intellect because he realized that only when the colonizer went beyond the cognitive level and reached the emotive level of understanding would he embrace the colonized and overcome the differences in language, culture, and history. What Hosoi came up with to enable the necessary leap from intellect to feelings was love.[41] For him, love entails knowing and empathizing with the other. Love is, in that sense, a higher form of knowledge, a dialectical sublimation of intellect and feelings. Love incorporates difference between self and other only to transcend it and eventually bind them in genuine community. In other words, Hosoi envisioned that, although love would not immediately eradicate difference between Japan and Korea, it would eventually lead the two peoples to become one as love transcends difference. Through love, the self and the other would merge into one, as "we."

After the earthquake, Hosoi began in earnest to call for mutual support and love between the Japanese and Koreans. For example, in a short essay published immediately after the earthquake, "*Naisenjin Ketsugō no Kitan*" (Beginning of Union Between the Japanese and Koreans), Hosoi blames a lack of mutual support and love for the disappointing performance of Japanese colonial rule in Korea.[42] When Korean youths resorted to "nihilistic violence" or "civil disobedience" in protest against Japanese rule and showed their obliviousness to their own responsibility for the decay of their nation, the Japanese responded to the protests with oppressive measures. Hosoi laments that there was no sign of harmony and reconciliation between the two peoples and that this hatred and confrontation can only lead to mutual annihilation.

In the terrible destruction by the earthquake and the ensuing massacre of Koreans, however, Hosoi saw a ray of hope. He reported that some Japanese had risked their lives to help Koreans in the face of threats from vigilante groups. For Hosoi, these commendable Japanese personified such ideal characteristics of the Japanese nation as sympathy, benevolence, and courage. He did not refer back to the negative aspects of the Japanese national character he had denounced in *Administrating Korea and Manchuria*. After the earthquake, for Hosoi, what was at issue was not so much casting off the Japanese negative national traits as reclaiming the ideal characteristics of the nation, which not many Japanese held to anymore, unfortunately. In his 1925 book *Chōsen Mondai no Kisū* (The Destiny of the Korean Problem), Hosoi equated the much-heralded spirit of Japan (*Yamato damashi*) and the way of the warrior (*bushidō*) with this virtue of mutual support and love.[43] As proof, he presented what he termed as the first principle of bushidō, that the samurai should possess sensitivity to the fleeting nature of things (*mono no aware*), an aesthetic value much touted in Japanese nativist discourse. Hosoi argued that if a person possessed this sensitivity to nature, he would surely be considerate and thoughtful and willing to help others with love. Thus, Hosoi's circular reasoning was that genuine Japanese national character is marked by the virtue of mutual support and love because it is the national character of the Japanese manifested in the spirit of Japan and the way of the warrior. In this manner, he sought to construct a Japanese subjectivity to support the colonial mission of assimilating the colonized while avoiding excessive violence.[44] This does not mean that the genuine identity of the Japanese nation preceded the construction of the Japanese subjectivity as a colonizer. National identity is, of course, never static. It exists only through ongoing processes of individual self-identification with the nation and, in this sense, coincides temporally with mechanisms operating in spheres ranging from culture to law that interpellate an individual as a national subject. Although status as a subject of a state is instrumental in forming identity, national identity cannot be reduced to that status alone, as shown by the example of the Korean "imperial subjects" within the Japanese empire.

Hosoi's texts on national character show the ways in which such identification operates. As examined above, Hosoi continually identified certain traits as Japanese and others as Korean national character. In other words, the Japanese as well as Korean nations were schematized as tangible and self-evident entities. Furthermore, in Hosoi's texts, the interpellation of "we, the Japanese" as benevolent colonizers bore on the construction of Japanese national subjectivity and, needless to say, paralleled the construction of Korean subjectivity as a helpless colonized nation.

In "Beginning of Union Between the Japanese and Koreans," the aforementioned essay Hosoi wrote immediately after the great Kantō earthquake and ensuing massacre of Koreans, he advises Koreans to give up their hopes for independence and urges the Japanese to return to their ideal national character. He argued that however much Koreans try to achieve independence, Japan will not allow it to happen. Hosoi recommends instead that Koreans develop their society by training technicians, improving their living standards, and, above all, acquiring a national character as well as individual personalities suitable to the modern world. To refute Korean demands for independence, Hosoi allegorizes the relationship between Korea and Japan in a parable of a woman and her savior and patron. Before annexation, Korea was like an old woman who could not survive on her own. Through annexation, she was transformed into a newborn baby and now, 13 years later, is like a 13-year-old girl. Hosoi likens Koreans' yearning for independence to a 13-year-old girl's demands for the freedom to love (*ren'ai*) the man of her choice. Just as a sensible parent would not let an adolescent girl choose who is right for her, Hosoi argued, Japan cannot allow Koreans to decide what they want to do.[45]

It is noteworthy that although Hosoi feminized Korea, he did not portray Japan as her male lover. Thus his story went against a convention of colonial romance that represents the colonizer and the colonized as a man and a woman in love. Furthermore, Hosoi seems to have consciously preempted a possible allegorization of the Japan–Korea relationship as an amorous one. His allegory of Japan as a patriarch who volunteers to rescue and protect a feminized Korea as an adopted family member makes it clear that the two are not in a conjugal relation because the woman Korea is either too old or too young. This model of an adoptive family reflected Hosoi's desire to create love and at the same time maintain hierarchy in the relationship between the Japanese and Koreans. I will return to this allegory later to explain Hosoi's idea of love through Hegel's discussion of love, family, and the state.

A way of placing Hosoi's concept of love in the context of his overall colonial project is offered by the text of a speech that was published in 1926 in the Japanese-language journal of *Chōsen Shakaijigyōkai* (Korean Social Work Association), a quasi-governmental social work organization supervised by the colonial government. As the title "*Gojosōai no Taigi to Chōsen Mondai*" (The Great Significance of Mutual Support and Love, and the Korean Problem) suggests, the speech offered a sustained argument for mutual support and love as the key to the success of Japanese colonial rule in Korea.[46] The article deserves attention not only because it gives a succinct outline of Hosoi's thought and highlights his idea of absolute love but also because it is a reminder of Hosoi's importance as a propagandist for Japanese colonialism. In 1924 alone, he gave more than 250 public lectures about Korea in Japan and southern Korea, attended by a total of 128,000 people.[47]

Hosoi began his speech by reflecting on the aftermath of the great Kantō earthquake. According to Hosoi, more people died of hunger in its aftermath than from the earthquake itself, and there were even cases of mothers strangling their babies to protect them from starving to death: Without loving support, even a person who survived an earthquake and ensuing fires might die anyway. Survival depends on the mercy of those who distribute food and shelter after a disaster. Hosoi then promoted mutual support and love as the foundational principle of genuine community while at the same time denouncing the individualistic tendencies he found prevalent in Japan, prioritizing individual freedom over the unity of the community. For Hosoi, the individual is connected to the community both diachronically and synchronically. The individual's existence results from that individual's own ancestors, thus making filial piety one form of the mutual support and love on which the community is based. Furthermore, genuine love for one's own self should not be averse to mutual love. One should cultivate personality so that love for oneself does not conflict with love in the community. According to Hosoi, converging in harmony at the heart of the communal spirit are love for oneself, filial piety, and loyalty to the state.

Hosoi then illustrated how his concerns about Japanese national character were connected to his vision of mutual support and love between the Japanese and Koreans. As national character is the sum of individual personalities, the individual represents the nation. The way a Japanese person interacts with a Korean, for example, affects the ways in which Koreans understand the Japanese nation as a whole. One individual's good deeds are more effective at bringing Japanese and Koreans together than a political slogan like "harmony between Japanese and Koreans." Koreans would see the Japanese national character in such an individual deed and judge whether the Japanese would be trustworthy as the older brother to whom they could turn in a time of difficulty.[48]

Hosoi admitted, however, that in contrast to quite a few commendable Japanese individuals who dutifully fulfilled their colonial moral imperative as benevolent colonizers, there were a number of Japanese who failed to live up to the ideal national character of Japan. He reported that while traveling in Korea he had himself witnessed a telling incident. He was in a bus going from Pusan to Tongnae in the southeastern part of the country when the bus had to stop because an oxcart was blocking a narrow country road. The Japanese bus driver got off and punched the Korean ox driver on the cheek. Appalled by the sudden violent act, Hosoi asked the bus driver why he hit the Korean, and the driver angrily retorted, "These days gooks (*yobo*) won't listen if you're a nice guy." Hosoi implored the Japanese to realize that Japanese "imprudence and indiscretion" (*seikyūtanryo*) and "arrogance and inconsiderateness" (*gōmanmushiryo*) provoked Korean violence.[49]

Despite numerous discouraging incidents like the one with the bus driver, Hosoi did not abandon his hope for harmony between the Japanese and Koreans. The basis of his hope rested on occasions in which good intentions were ultimately understood by the other no matter how impossible it might seem at first glance. He asserted "individuals from two belligerent countries can meet heart to heart, and foreigners who do not speak my language nevertheless can understand me."[50] For Hosoi, even when the other and the self do not speak the same language, the good intentions of the self can and should be conveyed to and reciprocated by the other without the mediation of translation. Hosoi went on to say that even a dog and its master can understand each other when the master is affectionately patting the dog on the head. Hosoi asked, then, how could Koreans not understand the Japanese if the Japanese embraced them as their younger brothers? Although he initiated his translation projects to help the Japanese understand Koreans and their culture, he argued that genuine understanding would transcend language without the mediation of translation. In other words, for Hosoi, genuine understanding between the self and the other would render translation unnecessary.

Even though his reasoning bordered on racism and fell right into overbearing paternalism, Hosoi nevertheless called on the Japanese to reflect on their attitude toward Koreans because Koreans' hatred of the Japanese would persist as long as the Japanese treated Koreans in unjust and heavy-handed ways. Hosoi's idea of love, however, did not rest on equality between Japanese and Koreans. He believed that the Japanese should be like an elder brother to Koreans, whose culture and society lagged behind, and should lead them to become equals with the Japanese themselves in the future. In that sense, Hosoi's ideal community of the Japanese and Koreans would not be based on solidarity among equals but rather modeled after patriarchy or hierarchical fraternity between siblings.

To further persuade his fellow Japanese to "love" Koreans despite such troubling moral defects of the latter's national character as laziness, deceptiveness, and vainglory, Hosoi historicized these moral defects. According to Hosoi, Koreans suffered unprecedented oppression under the rule of the yangban elite during the Chosŏn period. If the Japanese had likewise been under such oppressive rule for so long, they, too, would have developed moral defects. Koreans were made lazy. Since corrupt officials took away wealth that people worked hard to accumulate, they lost the desire to work. Over-taxation was another example of the ruling elite's abuse of power. There were cases in which the military levies were imposed even on dead men and unborn children. Koreans had to resort to deception to survive such heavy taxation and corrupt bureaucracy. They never had any government help to address their grievances. The powerful always won in court no matter how horrible were wrongs they did. Koreans suffered in a world without love, hope, and support. Because they had never been loved, they tended to behave conceitedly once someone showed them a bit of affection. If treated with genuine love, "they would open their hearts and respect, trust, and thank the person as if he were a god (*kami no kotoku*)."[51] Thus, for love to be the remedy to mend the fissure between the colonizer and the colonized, the colonizer's love should be returned by the colonized. Hosoi did not and could not allow the colonizer's love to go unrequited because his idea of love as the principal communal bond would crumble if he saw that the colonized might not reciprocate the colonizer's love. The colonized should do exactly as the colonizer expected them to. In other words, Hosoi's colonial moral imperative could not acknowledge the alterity of the colonized.

Another aporia haunting Hosoi's text is that his call for love failed to recognize the fragmentation inherent in any kind of community. His argument for love between the colonized and colonizer assumed uniformity in the communities of the colonized and colonizers because he called for love not between individuals but between the collectivities of colonizer and colonized. According to his colonial moral imperative of love, Japanese should love Koreans not as individuals but as members of an ethnic community. The love Hosoi called for does not exist between people as singular human beings. It transpires only between members of one ethnic group and those of the other. In other words, Hosoi's love presupposed the uniformity of each ethnic group whom he urged to love each other. In Hosoi's arguments, it was national character that produces uniformity in each ethnic community. Contrary to his intentions, however, his text reveals that the community of the Japanese was already fractured. In the essay, Hosoi admits that despite Japan's true national character, there were a number of Japanese who lacked the spirit of mutual support and love: arrogant colonial settlers who harassed Koreans, unscrupulous businessmen who exported substandard commodities, thus ruining the reputation of Japanese goods abroad,[52] and selfish refugees who perished on a burning bridge after the great Kantō earthquake because they refused to yield to those heading in the opposite direction.[53] For Hosoi, love was required not only to bind the Japanese and Koreans, but also to recover unity among the Japanese whose own community had disintegrated because of materialism and selfishness. In other words, not only did Hosoi's text constantly differentiate between colonizer and colonized even though he was calling for the ultimate assimilation of the latter into the former, it also inadvertently exposed the absence of a unified community of the colonizer.

READING HOSOI'S INSISTENCE ON LOVE THROUGH HEGEL'S ACCOUNTS OF FAMILY

To fully appreciate the issues at stake, it is necessary to do more than merely trace aporias in Hosoi's texts. As mentioned above, from the beginning of his career as a Korea expert, Hosoi worked to foster Japanese understanding of Korea, and his efforts were shown in his translation projects. Understanding in this sense meant both knowledge about and empathy toward Korea. As he saw Koreans' hatred of Japan persist and Japanese contempt for Korea go on unchanged, Hosoi realized that knowledge about the colonized and their culture did not necessarily lead to empathetic feelings toward them. Especially after the great Kantō earthquake, this realization led him to underline the importance of sentiment, as seen in his emphasis on love.

Hosoi's emphasis on sentiment is found especially in his criticism of the Japanese colonial authorities' blind reliance on law. One of the most serious problems for Japanese rule in Korea was, in Hosoi's view, the failure of Japanese colonial bureaucrats to take account of difference between the Japanese and Koreans. Colonial bureaucrats tried to give Koreans what they deemed to be desirable without considering the differences in customs, tradition, and language between the two peoples. Koreans could not become Japanese overnight even though Japan implemented reform policies through its colonial administration. Needless to say, Hosoi did not advocate autonomy for the colonized. In his view, the Koreans did not know what they needed. Instead, he argued that even with perfect law and impeccable theory, the colonizer would still fail at governing another people if he ignored the aspect of "human emotion" (*ningen no kangeki*).[54] It was still the colonizer's responsibility to provide for the needs of the colonized.

At this juncture, I want to interject Hegel's account of love, law, family, and community to further grasp Hosoi's argument. I make this argument because Hosoi's prioritization of love over law echoes the criticism of Kantian ethics Hegel developed in his early writings on Christianity. In his 1799 essay "The Spirit of Christianity and Its Fate," Hegel deemed love the essence of Christianity and aligned Kantian ethics with his depiction of Judaism, which, in his view, erroneously privileged law over love.[55] Viewing Immanuel Kant's moral imperative as a heartless universal law dictated by an intellect cold to human feelings, Hegel upheld love as the ultimate principle establishing unity between intellect and emotion, which Kantian philosophy had kept separate. Not only did Hegel view love as a higher form of knowledge unifying intellect and emotion, but he also regarded it as the principle of communal unity in which the self and the other are sublated into a "we" through which competing individual desires and duties are overcome. Hosoi's notion of love parallels

Hegel's views in that it also underpins harmony between knowledge and empathy in understanding and constitutes the foundation of a genuine community between the Japanese and Koreans.

As if preemptively warning against rash attempts at building secular communities like society and state on the principle of love, Hegel declared that communities of love could survive only in isolation from the secular world in which individual desires and duties inevitably clash and are never reconciled through love alone. That is why Jesus told his disciples to retreat from "the profane world" and leave their families behind.[56] Hegel suggested that it is no longer tenable to retreat from this world to build a community of love. The ethics of love is too lofty to be relevant to communities in this world. It cannot effectively bind people who do not share the same faith. As a community expands beyond a small group of believers, the communal bond based on love diminishes.[57] In later writings, Hegel declared that love is no longer an attribute of the state by asserting, "There, one is conscious of unity as law; there, the content must be rational, and I must know it."[58] There is little room for love as the principal communal bond in the state in which the law is what binds the people together. This is exactly why such secular ideologies as nationalism and patriotism require quasi-religious elements to ensure that the nation and the state are represented as sacred communities deserving of reverence and demonstrations of love. In other words, the quasi-religious aspects of nationalism and patriotism compensate for the lack of the communal bond of love in the secular communities of a nation and the state.

The problem of love as the principle of communal unity can be summed up in the following question: What if the other does not reciprocate the love offered by the self? The self cannot force the other to reciprocate its love because love is the opposite of dominance. Because love does not tolerate dominance, it presupposes a nonviolent relationship. The problem of love hinted at by Hegel points to one pitfall in Hosoi's conviction that the colonizer's love must be reciprocated by the colonized in the end. Hosoi's call for love does not allow the colonized the right to refuse to reciprocate the colonizer's love.

As his thought developed, Hegel further shifted his focus from love to mutual recognition as the basis for ethics, but he did not renounce love entirely. Instead he assigned it to the family as the basic unit of community, which, in his view, provides the foundation for the highest level of community: the state.[59] At the core of the Hegelian family are the husband and the wife, whose conjugal relationship constitutes a union between two independent individuals based on love. Each feels incomplete alone and becomes complete only in union with the other. The service of particular need of an individual "is transformed, along with the selfishness of desire, into care and acquisition for a communal purpose, i.e. into an ethical quality."[60] The marriage partners voluntarily surrender their independent personalities to the conjugal union.[61] Love involving this gentle mutual recognition is in stark contrast to the violent struggle between the self and the other for recognition delineated by Hegel in his famous master–slave trope.[62] Furthermore, Hegel dissociated marriage from the contractual relationship that Kant considered necessary to ensure equality between the conjugal partners because Hegel believed it leads to objectification of human beings.[63] From Hegel's perspective, by degrading human beings to the level of things, Kant's view of marriage as a contract debases the conjugal union in which husband and wife should become one through love.

Thus, the husband and the wife in Hegel's account of the family are partners, bound together by love, on an equal footing. The Hegelian family, however, is the 19th-century bourgeois family with its gendered division of labor. Hegel believed that men and women were different by nature: He held that men are active and rational and women are passive and emotional.[64] Under this theory, men participate in the world external to the family through their work while women's sphere is the domestic one. The man as husband and father is in control of family property in Hegel's view. Thus, a tension arises between Hegel's acknowledgment of equality between husband and wife as the conjugal partners and his differentiation between them in regard to their tasks and areas of authority. Where equality between man and wife was presupposed in love as the condition constitutive of the conjugal union, hierarchy is maintained in the relationship between the parents and the children. Parents have the right to discipline their children to bring them up properly so they develop "the self-sufficiency and freedom of personality." Hegel believed that the family naturally dissolves when the children come of age and leave to form their own families. He held that marriage can also be dissolved by divorce if the conjugal partners find the relationship antagonistic and irreconcilable.[65]

Hegel's accounts of love, family, and community are helpful for reconstructing why Hosoi did not follow the conventions of colonial romance in his allegorization of Korea and Japan as a 13-year-old girl and her patriarchal guardian. As mentioned above, in his 1923 essay, "Beginning of Union Between the Japanese and Koreans," Hosoi allegorized Korea as a young girl who wanted to be free to choose her lover against the will of her guardian. I have already highlighted how Hosoi presented the relationship between Japan and Korea not as an amorous one between a man and a woman but as a familial one in which Japan served as the paternal guardian for the girl Korea. Hosoi slighted love (*renai*) as amorous feelings when he likened Koreans' longing for independence to a 13-year-old girl's yearning for unhindered romantic love. For him, such love is a frivolous emotion that dissipates as passion burns away. True love is not contingent on capricious passion. Only the institution of family brings stability to an amorous relationship, as seen in Hegel's account. Marriage, the core of the family, however, presupposes equality between the two parties who volunteer to subordinate their independent personalities to the conjugal union. If the annexation of Korea was the result of illegitimate force, it could not be allegorized as marriage.

The widely circulated story about the eminent liberal Japanese politician Ozaki Yukio's 1920 meeting with the prominent Korean social activist and journalist Yi Sangjae is indicative of the difficulty faced by the colonizer in allegorizing a colonial relationship as a conjugal one.[66] Ozaki was one of the many Japanese politicians who visited Korea after the March First movement to investigate the political conditions in the colony. One of the Korean leaders from whom Ozaki sought an opinion was Yi. When Ozaki remarked that "Japan and Korea are like a married couple. Even if the husband makes a small mistake, won't it be too harsh for the wife to rise against him?" Yi replied, "Surely, you're right. But what if they are not a legitimately married couple and actually were forced to marry?" What is implied in Yi's riposte is that Korea and Japan were not only on an unequal footing but that their union was illegitimate because it was forced onto Korea against its will. As Hegel argued, marriage should not be arranged especially against the will of the female partner.[67] Furthermore, it can be annulled if the marital relationship falls apart irrecoverably. In other words, the trope of marriage can do disservice to colonial discourse, which assumes the inevitability of colonial rule and justifies the hierarchical relationship between the colonizer and the colonized because marriage can be dissolved and is based on the presupposition of equality between the conjugal partners. Hosoi's concern for Korean women's suffering under Korean men's oppression also suggests that he would agree with Hegel on a more equal relationship between husband and wife.[68]

Thus, it would not be too far-fetched to argue that because Hosoi detected the problems in the widely used trope of marriage for representing the Japan–Korea relationship, he could not help but choose as his metaphor the relationship of parent and child.[69] As seen above, unlike the conjugal relationship, the relationship between parents and children is hierarchical even in the Hegelian family even though it also hinges on love. What is more problematic about Hosoi's allegory is that Korea is represented as a family member adopted into the extended but organically unified familial community of the Japanese nation.[70] When discussing national character, Hosoi had regarded a nation as an extension of blood ties by arguing that an individual belongs to a nation through ties with his ancestors and descendents. To obviate any contradictions in this pseudo-familial connection to the nation, a view not unique to Hosoi, he might have chosen marriage as a more convincing trope for the union of Japan and Korea.[71] As discussed above, however, the implied equality between the conjugal partners in the trope of marriage ruled marriage out as an effective metaphor for the hierarchical unity between Japan and Korea. Accordingly, Korea ended up being allegorized as an adopted child instead.

Hosoi's allegory makes Japan a fatherly or brotherly guardian who treats his child with benevolence but does not hesitate to discipline her for her own good. It is also implied that such benevolence should and would be reciprocated by the child with respectful obedience. In the same 1926 essay in which the allegory is presented, Hosoi even echoes Hegel's idea of the natural dissolution of the Hegelian family, hinting that Korea might be granted autonomy when it reaches maturity under the guidance of Japan.[72] Unlike in the Hegelian family, however, it is not specified when the family naturally dissolved in Hosoi's allegory. Its dissolution is postponed indefinitely. By the time he delivered this speech, "The Great Significance of Mutual Support and Love, and the Korean Problem," Hosoi had firmly concluded that Japan and Korea must become one family and should stay united as a family against the white race who had conquered "nine-tenths of the world."[73]

It is clear why Hosoi's justification of Japanese rule over Korea relied on the schematization of the relationship between the Japanese and Koreans as a quasi-family. As the logical extension of Hosoi's privileging of family and love on the basis of Hegel's view of the family, civil society, and the state, it can be said that there was nothing more effective than family as a metaphor of the foundation on which the genuine unity between the Japanese and Koreans can be imagined. Hosoi could not identify such a foundation in either the state or civil society. As described by Hegel, civil society was the economic realm in which individuals compete in pursuing self-interest. As discussed earlier, Hosoi himself lamented the disintegration of the communal sense in Japan because of selfishness and materialism he found rampant in Japanese society. Consequently, for him, civil society could not be a privileged arena in which harmony between the Japanese and Koreans would be realized.

Nor, in Hosoi's view, could the Japanese state alone constitute a substratum on which the harmony between the Japanese and Koreans could be built. The Hegelian state, placed above the family and civil society, constitutes the ethical entity under which the sectarian schisms of civil society are sutured and individuals are harmoniously connected to the community. In contrast, the Japanese state failed to realize genuine unity between the Japanese and Koreans because its ruthless application of law to the colony only alienated the colonized further.

On the other hand, as the family plays the important role of the ethical foundation for the state in Hegel's thought, it also figured prominently in Hosoi's thought as the metaphor of an imaginary sphere in which the persistent conflicts between the Japanese and Koreans were destined to come to an end and the two peoples were brought into harmony by the power of love.[74] Love is the key to understanding Hosoi's endeavors to bring the Japanese and Koreans into harmony. The love Hosoi advocated was the colonizer's benevolent caring of the colonized. Hosoi launched his translation projects of Korean classics to foster the Japanese understanding of Koreans and their culture, arguing that if the Japanese could understand through the translations of Korean literary and historical classics that the defects of Korean national character had come from Koreans' historical experience of oppressive rule by their own ruling class, the Japanese would empathize with Koreans and embrace them as their new brothers and sisters. In Hosoi's view, knowledge and empathy unified in understanding would lead to building a genuine community of colonizers and the colonized because Koreans would reciprocate Japanese empathy with loyalty to the Japanese state. It goes without saying that this genuine community would still hinge on the hierarchical relationship in which the Japanese would guide backward Koreans toward progress. In sum, at the heart of Hosoi's translation projects of Korean literature and history lay the colonizer's desire for knowledge about and recognition from the colonized. The desire went unfulfilled because of the continuing mutual hatred between the Japanese and Koreans. Hosoi's notion of love as the spiritual bond of a genuine community of colonizers and the colonized alike grew out of his concerns over diehard antagonisms between Koreans and the Japanese, which understanding alone would never curb.

In that sense, Hosoi's figuration of the relationship between Japan and Korea as a quasi-family based on love revealed that attempts were made primarily within the arena of culture to overcome political conflicts brought about by Japan's colonization of Korea precisely because they could not be resolved within the realm of politics so long as colonial domination continued to exist.

2. Treacherous Translation

The 1938 Japanese-Language Theatrical Version of the Korean Tale Ch'unhyangjŏn

As the war with China dragged on following Japan's initial military successes in 1937, the Japanese colonial authority stepped up the total mobilization of colonial Korea for the war effort. The importance of Korea came to be spotlighted because of the large size of its population and its geographical proximity to China and Manchuria. Consequently, interest in Korea and the Asian continent grew in Japan. Modern Korean literature for the first time drew substantial attention from the Japanese literary establishment. Quite a few Japanese literary luminaries, including Yasuda Yojūrō, Hayashi Fusao, and Kobayashi Hideo, went to Korea on their way to Manchuria and met writers and poets in the Japanese colony and the occupied territories. Korean literature of the day, including short stories and poetry, also came to be translated into Japanese. The bulk of Korean-language literary works, however, remained unknown in Japan. It was in that context that the Japanese-language theatrical play based on a traditional Korean story *Ch'unhyangjŏn* (The Tale of Spring Fragrance)[1] was staged at the Tsukiji Theater in Tokyo in early 1938 and later that year was performed in Japanese in Korea as well.

This chapter examines the 1938 staging of *Ch'unhyangjŏn,* a love story derived from a Korean folktale, and the ensuing controversy. In particular, the staging of the play in Korea provoked heated debate over the issue of translation. As part of the controversy, Korean and Japanese intellectuals tackled such issues as colonialism, nationalism, and culture. I use this concrete historical case to criticize the very influential view that the ideal model of translation is an equal exchange between two languages. I argue that such a view was inscribed both in the logic that the colonizers used to justify the colonial translation and in the thinking of the colonized who resisted it. In other words, I focus my criticism on the view of translation as equal exchange. To achieve this goal, I employ the arguments of Karl Marx, who astutely critiqued symmetrical reciprocity in equal exchange, and those of Emmanuel Levinas, who stringently insisted on the asymmetry of the ethical relationship between the self and the other. I read Marx through Levinas to reveal the ethical aspect of Marx's political economy and Levinas through Marx to explicate the implications of Levinas's ethics for radical politics in order to criticize the idea of equal exchange based on reciprocity, which is not only inherent in the conventional view of translation but also prevalent in the colonizer's justification for colonial dominance.[2]

TRANSLATION AND COLONIAL DISCOURSE

As Naoki Sakai has argued, translation can reify boundaries between two languages by leading to the assumption that each language is externally independent and internally unified.[3] If one person were to encounter another who is speaking a language absolutely foreign to him, that person cannot even tell whether the verbal sounds the other is making are semantically and syntactically comprehensible verbal expressions or merely a series of idiosyncratic exclamations incomprehensible to anyone else or even imitations of animal sounds. If, say, a second stranger approached the person and informed him that the sounds in question belong to, say, a local version of the Zoque language spoken by a handful of people in Ayapan, Tabasco, Mexico, and she happens to be one of the very few outsiders who have learned the language and that she is willing to translate what the man is saying.[4] Only after she offers her account of what language the man is speaking and serves as an intermediary with him in dialogue do the incomprehensible sounds coming out of the man's mouth register as a language, one identified as a dialect of the Zoque language. The first person cannot even begin to locate the boundaries between the man's language and his own until the translator steps in and represents him in language. A hypothetical situation like this one, which appears unlikely to occur, however, shows the way in which translation makes it possible to schematize the difference between incomprehensibility and comprehensibility in language as boundaries between languages. In other words, only after the initial absolute foreignness of what the man is enunciating is tamed through translation as the relative foreignness of language is it possible to envision boundaries between known and unknown languages. Furthermore, once boundaries between the two languages are demarcated, the foreign language can be imagined as internally homogeneous and externally autonomous equal to other known languages. Put differently, although it is often taken as a given that human language is divided into different languages with clearly demarcated boundaries, the idea of language split into such separable, and thus countable, units as Russian, English, Korean, and so on cannot make much sense unless linguistic boundaries are schematized through translation.

By forcing attention to the differences between languages, translation in the conventional sense thus reifies the autonomous, homogeneous language communities the differences between which it is intended to bridge. Such reification tends to position the two language communities on the same plane. In other words, the assumption that there exist internally unified and externally independent languages leads to a second assumption, that there exists an equal relationship between the languages and communities associated with those languages. Translation from that perspective is nothing less than reciprocal exchange between two languages and language communities. The ideal translation in this sense, as George Steiner claimed in *After Babel,* is exchange without loss of meaning or aesthetic value.[5]

However, as Tejaswini Niranjana has argued, the idea of translation as equal exchange tends to be oblivious to, and thus becomes complicit with, the hegemonic domination inscribed in the very process of translation. She asserts that Steiner's view of the ideal translation as exchange without loss is not only futile but also treacherous in the colonial context because it masks the unequal power relationship that sets the conditions for colonial translation. Whereas Niranjana focuses her criticism of colonial translation on the problems concerning the representation of the colonized and their culture by a process of translation that is always permeated by unequal power relationships, I call attention to the homology between translation and colonial discourse.[6] As briefly mentioned in the preface, both translation and colonial discourse are simultaneously based on the difference between the colonized and the colonizer and intended to overcome it. Even though Steiner urged translators to try to reach the ideal of exchange without loss, he nonetheless admitted that it cannot be realized. The ideal cannot be reached because of the inerasable difference between languages, just as the abolition of colonial discrimination cannot be achieved because of the unyielding difference between the colonized and colonizer in colonial discourse.

As Homi Bhabha has argued, the denial of difference between the colonizer and the colonized coexists and works together with the acknowledgement of that same difference to perpetuate colonial domination.[7] As a consequence, colonial discourse is haunted by the ambivalence that results from the simultaneous recognition and denial of difference between the colonized and the colonizer. My acknowledgment of this simultaneous denial and recognition of difference is not, however, simply a reiteration of the criticism of the Manichean opposition between the colonized and the colonizer, overdosing on the notion of ambivalence in colonial discourse that Bhabha valorized as subversive disruption of colonial domination. In other words, my argument is not to slavishly follow an abstruse theory abstracted from the experience of European colonization. As Oguma Eiji has documented well by drawing on scholarly writings, newspaper and journal articles, and memoirs by Japanese people about the Japanese colonies, Japanese colonial discourse also oscillated between the acknowledgement and disavowal of the difference between the Koreans and the Japanese.[8]

As slogans like "harmony between Japan and Korea" (*nissen yūwa*) and "Japan–Korea as one body" (*naisen ittai*) imply, Japanese colonial assimilation (*dōka*) policy was theoretically directed at the amalgamation of Koreans and Japanese, but in practice, it entailed unilaterally forcing Koreans to "become" Japanese. Enforcement of the assimilation policy intensified after the beginning of the Sino-Japanese War in 1937. As mentioned above, the Japanese state needed to secure support from Koreans for its war effort because of Korea's geographical proximity to China and Manchuria and its large population.[9] The assimilation policy, however, could not eradicate the differences between Koreans and Japanese. According to its logic, discrimination could come to an end only when all differences between the colonized and colonizer disappeared. Existing differences between the colonized and the colonizer served to legitimize discriminatory practices.

The unreachable promise of erasing difference between the colonized and colonizers is ubiquitous in colonial discourse. Colonial domination relies on the difference between the colonized and the colonizer, which in turn serves to justify the colonial hierarchy and discriminatory practices. Simultaneously, however, colonial discourse asserts that the difference between the colonized and the colonizer will disappear in the future, along with discrimination, when the colonized finally succeed in becoming assimilated into the colonizer. But the erasure of difference is delayed forever. Accordingly, colonial discourse is plagued by ambivalence because it oscillates between the colonial practice of fixating the identity of the colonized on their difference from the colonizer and the gesture of eradicating the difference, which justifies colonial discrimination. In short, colonial discourse depends on the dual operation of emphasizing and denying the difference between the colonized and the colonizer. On that point, colonial discourse and translation are homologous. Translation recognizes differences between languages and cultures and simultaneously intends to bridge them. Colonial discourse thus operates homologously with translation as understood conventionally.

The place of equal exchange in the conventional definition of translation is also homologous with the strategy of colonial discourse, which never fails to render the relationship between the colonizer and the colonized as something reciprocal and beneficial to both. Colonial discourse never stops describing pairs placed in lopsided power relations as symmetrically reciprocal. It portrays the colonial relationship as reciprocity by insisting that colonial development benefits the colonized and by disregarding the violence and injustice on which economic and social development under colonial rule rests. It works to convince the colonized that colonial violence, injustice, and discrimination are somehow bearable in exchange for the virtues of a modern market economy and the social institutions that colonial power introduces. The dignity, justice, and autonomy of the colonized are (de)valued to the point they can be traded for the colonizers' investment in modern infrastructure and the introduction of capitalism.

For example, there have been numerous scholarly and nonscholarly arguments made that Japanese colonial rule significantly advanced the economy in Korea. One of the most memorable instances of such an argument was a statement made by Kubota Kan'ichirō, the chief Japanese delegate at the diplomatic talks between Japan and South Korea in 1953. Kubota told his Korean counterparts that the contributions made by Japan to the economic development of Korea during the colonial period cancelled out any demand from the South Korean government for compensation for Japan's colonization of Korea.[10] In other words, what colonial discourse continues propagating, even in the postcolonial era, is that colonial domination offered equal exchange between the colonizers and the colonized! As Marx pointed out, it is not two parties equal in economical, political, or cultural power that establish equal exchange. On the contrary, it is the equivalents in the act of exchange that posit the two parties as equal to each other.[11] Thus, what should be problematized is the insistence on symmetrical reciprocity in colonialism and equal exchange and not the impossibility of symmetrical reciprocity or the unattainability of exchange without loss in translation.

Marx offered a sharp critique of the presumption of symmetrical reciprocity.[12] In *Grundrisse,* he pointed out that circulation of exchange values relates to the two most important ideological concepts of bourgeois society, freedom and equality based on symmetrical reciprocity.[13] Put simply, the parties to an exchange come of their own volition into a relationship of exchange on equal terms because it is assumed that the relationship is beneficial to both of them. Deriding French socialists of his day who regarded exchange and exchange value as "a system of universal freedom and equality" and blamed capital for disrupting equal exchange, Marx argued that the emergence of capital in the development of the system of exchange is "merely the realization of equality and freedom, which prove to be inequality and unfreedom."[14] Marx cogently suggested that it is pointless to privilege exchange and exchange value as the source of equality and freedom over capital because exchange value will inevitably turn into capital, whereas labor for production will develop into wage labor.[15] Thus he criticized the bourgeois ideology of equality and freedom premised on symmetrical reciprocity in equal exchange for operating in agreement with the inequality and unfreedom inherent in the relationship between capital and wage labor.

As is well known, in his *Critique of the Gotha Programme,* Marx clarified his criticism of symmetrical reciprocity in exchange by proposing his famous dictum, "from each according to his ability to each according to his need."[16] What one takes is not to be determined by what one gives but rather by what one needs. For Marx, justice is not served by symmetrical reciprocity mediating equal exchange on which the bourgeois ideas of freedom and equality rest. Rather, justice can be achieved only when such symmetrical reciprocity is liquidated in favor of unlimited care for the demands of others. This in turn establishes an inevitably asymmetrical relationship between the self and others. Certainly it is an ethical imperative that obliges one to give up symmetrical reciprocity and give in to the demands of others who need more than they can provide one in the relationship.

The ethicality of Marx's critique of symmetrical reciprocity comes into clearer view when read side by side with Levinas on the responsibility of the self for the other. In conversation with Philippe Nemo, Levinas argued that "the intersubjective relation is a non-symmetrical relation. In this sense, I am responsible for the other without waiting for reciprocity, were I to die for it. Reciprocity is his affair."[17] Levinas thus insisted on the self's unceasing concern for the other, even while realizing that the other cannot be reduced to an object that can be appropriated by the self for its own interests. In contrast to the ethical relationship of asymmetry, symmetrical reciprocity presumes that the other and the self are equal to each other in the relationship and thus interchangeable. It presupposes that the other is the same as the self and thus denies the singularity of the other as well as of the self.

In other words, an individual is put into an unceasing cycle of equal exchange with others in which that individual tries to maximize his or her benefit in symmetrical reciprocity based on the assumption that the others are also trying to get the most out of exchange. As a consequence, symmetrical reciprocity does not allow for the absolute otherness of the other. Put differently, equal exchange based on symmetrical reciprocity pivots on the cunning calculation that one does to benefit from the relationship in proportion to what one contributes to it. This symmetrical reciprocity does not take into account the unlimited responsibility imposed on the self toward the other. According to Levinas, such a situation is unethical.

Special importance is accorded to language in Levinas's ethics. Throughout his two most important works, *Totality and Infinity* and *Otherwise Than Being*,[18] Levinas hinted that language is itself the relationship with the other, who is foreign to the self. The essence of language is not the transmission of ideas between interlocutors but is instead what indicates "the irreversibility of the relationship between me and the other."[19] It is worth repeating in a discussion on the ethicality of language that, in *Otherwise Than Being*, Levinas made a distinction between the two aspects of language, what he called the *saying* and the *said*. As discussed in some detail in the preface, the said refers to the content, idea, and theme of discourse.[20] On the other hand, saying describes the event in which the self is summoned to approach the other in discourse.[21] Although Levinas admitted that the saying can be manifested only in the said, he clearly prioritized the former over the latter because it is the very condition of possibility of discourse as an ethical relationship. The self's freedom is constrained in language by the other. The self is helplessly exposed to misunderstanding and the refusal of understanding by the other, which it cannot control.[22] Despite the uncertainty presented by the saying, the self is responsible for engaging in dialogue with the other. Thus language is ethical practice in the relationship with the other. As I will discuss below, this essence of language as ethical is what I intend to emphasize in dealing with the problem of translation, which surfaced in the controversy over the Japanese-language version of the popular Korean romance *Ch'unhyangjŏn* staged by the Japanese theatrical company *Shinkyō* in 1938.

AMBIVALENT TEXT AND TREACHEROUS TRANSLATION

Ch'unhyangjŏn is believed to have been first developed as *p'ansori* traditional one-man opera and later transcribed into written form. The oldest extant text of *Ch'unhyangjŏn* is a classical Chinese verse, seven characters per line, written by Yu Chinhan in 1754, reportedly after listening to a *p'ansori* performance of the story.[23] Although the text has been presented in numerous versions, its main storyline can be summarized as a love story between Ch'unhyang, the daughter of a *kisaeng* (courtesan), and Mongnyong, the son of the local magistrate in a southwestern city called Namwŏn during the Chosŏn period. They fall in love and secretly marry despite the difference in their social positions. Fate separates them when the hero's father is transferred to a new position in the capital. The new local magistrate, Pyŏn Hakto, is enthralled by Ch'unhyang's beauty and tries to make her his concubine, but she refuses out of loyalty to her husband and endures harassment and even torture and imprisonment at Pyŏn's hands. Meanwhile Mongnyong, having passed the civil service examination and taken the post of the king's secret inspector, returns to Namwŏn to save Ch'unhyang, and the story ends happily.

Ch'unhyangjŏn's popularity grew during the colonial period.[24] From the mid-1930s on, theatrical performances of the story were increasingly frequent on the stage in Korea.[25] Thus it was not surprising when the *Tōkyō Haksaengyesuljwa* (Tokyo Students' Art Theater), a Korean student theatrical company based in Tokyo, staged the Korean dramatist Yu Ch'ijin's Korean-language play of the story in Tokyo in 1937.[26] After seeing it, the playwright and director Murayama Tomoyoshi (1901–1977) was impressed by the story and decided to stage his own theatrical version in Japanese.[27] Murayama was one of the leading figures in the *Puroretaria Engekidōmei* (Japan Proletarian Theater League). In 1934, Murayama had proposed the consolidation of various leftist theatrical companies that had been weakened under the government pressure into one progressive theatrical company, and that year he founded *Shinkyō Gekidan* (Shinkyō Theatrical Company). Until it was closed by the government in 1940, Shinkyō continued to stage realistic plays with social agendas and consequently maintained its reputation as the premier leftist theater company in Japan.[28]

In an article published in the journal *Chōsen oyobi Manshū* (Korea and Manchuria) just before his play was first staged in Japan in 1938, Murayama explained why he chose to stage a Japanese-language version of the story.[29] First, Murayama wanted to present Korean culture to the

Japanese people as what he regarded as one of the maternal bodies (*botai*) of Japanese culture. Second, he specifically selected *Ch'unhyangjŏn* from among Korean literary works because it was the most popular and thus most representative literary creation of Korea. Third, he hoped to entertain Koreans living and working in Japan and expected many of them to see the play. He claimed that because the story contained the soul of Korea, he would attempt to depict the Koreanness (*Chōsenteki na mono*) of the story as precisely as possible.[30]

Murayama asked the writer Chang Hyŏkchu to write a Japanese-language script.[31] There were good reasons why Murayama chose Chang. First of all, Chang was familiar with the story because he was also planning to stage *Ch'unhyangjŏn* in cooperation with novelist Yuasa Katsue, although the project stalled and did not come to fruition.[32] Furthermore, Chang was the most famous Korean writer in Japan who worked in the Japanese language in the 1930s. He made his literary debut in Japan when his novella *Gakidō* (The Path of Hungry Ghosts) won second place in the *Kaizō* literary award competition of 1932. The story described the hardships faced by Korean peasants under the Japanese rule. The Akutagawa literary award had not yet been founded, so at the time the *Kaizō* award was a rare and competitive venue for newcomers to gain access to the literary establishment.[33]

Chang studied various versions of the story, including a *changgŭk* (Korean opera) version.[34] From the beginning, however, he emphasized that the script would be his own and not merely a translation of some existing text.[35] After finishing his script, he published it in March 1938 in the Japanese literary journal *Shinchō* (New Tide).[36] Murayama felt that Chang's script lacked dramatic tension and made his own revisions with the help of Yu Ch'ijin, whose Korean-language play he had originally been inspired by.[37] It is interesting to note that Murayama also took the liberty of introducing elements of *kabuki*, long promoted as one of the most Japanese forms of stage art, into the play even though he had pledged that he would present the Koreanness of the story as faithfully as possible.[38] He also experimented with cross-gender casting in the play, probably following Kabuki practice in which male actors play female roles. However, Murayama reversed the conventions of *kabuki* by casting a female actor for the role of the hero. Actress Akagi Ranko was cast as the hero Yi Mongnyong, and Ichikawa Haruyo, a movie star of the Nikkatsu studio, as the heroine Ch'unhyang.[39] Other male roles were played by male actors. Incorporating elements of *kabuki* was an important innovation, Murayama explained, which opened up new possibilities for modern theater.[40] His decision provoked controversy: One reviewer argued that *kabuki*-style acting infused into the play made it difficult to locate "Koreanness," and another regarded it as a symptom of the commercialization of the Shinkyō theatrical company.[41]

Nonetheless, reviews of Murayama's staging of Chang's play were mostly favorable, but for varying reasons. Both the government and critics of the government appreciated the success of the play for utterly different reasons. For example, Hirata Isao, the thought prosecutor notorious for his role in the *tenkō* (ideological conversion) of the Communist Party leaders Sano Manabu and Nabeyama Sadachika, wrote a review in the magazine *Teatoro* (Theater) reflecting the essence of the government response. Although praising the play primarily for "keeping away from ideology and offering a fantasy," Hirata maintained that, by incorporating elements of the kabuki style into a modern drama, the play contributed to the further development of the Japanese traditional performance art. More important, he extolled the performance as an effort to promote the harmony between Japan and Korea and did not forget to mention the importance of Korea in the current situation of the Sino-Japanese War.[42]

Alongside Hirata's review, *Teatoro* published another review by Fuse Tatsuji, the lawyer famous for his efforts defending leftists and Koreans. Fuse read an allegory of the plight of the colonized into the play. Calling attention to the discord between responses from the Korean and Japanese audience members, he found that certain scenes evoked tears from the Korean audience but laughter from the Japanese. He encouraged Japanese audiences to ponder the meaning of anger and tears of the Korean audience and insinuated that the emotions of the Korean audience were related to the colonial reality in which they were caught. He continued to imply that Ch'unhyang's determined faithfulness to her husband in the face of threats from the local magistrate signified more than one woman's loyalty to her lover. In the end, he suggested that Ch'unhyang was elevated to a heroic character to reproach an unjust authority.[43]

The diverse and even conflicting views presented by the reviews suggest that the play itself was a text haunted by ambivalence, allowing viewers to read various subtexts into it. Critical intellectuals and government officials both surely saw the play, with its exotic costumes and *kabuki*-style acting, as a departure from Shinkyō's reputation as a leftist theatrical company, and one review criticized it for the same commercialism Hirata, the thought prosecutor, praised it for.[44] However, in the tradition of leftist theater, the play still retained certain scenes, including Korean peasants suffering from unjust rule, which could be interpreted as political messages. It thus allowed viewers to see the play as criticism of the Japanese colonial rule if they stretched their sensitivity to colonial injustice enough to juxtapose the play with the colonial realities under which the colonized were placed.

After a successful 20-day run at the Tsukiji Little Theater in Tokyo in March and April, the performance toured Osaka and Kyoto. According to Murayama, many in the audience in these cities were Korean. Later that same year, *Shinkyō* launched a tour of Korea, marking, as Murayama proudly claimed, the first time a Japanese theatrical company had performed for Korean audiences in Korea.[45] The play was performed by Japanese actors, in the Japanese language, for colonized Korean audiences, and Murayama expected it to promote cultural exchange in theater between Japan and Korea.[46] Akita Ujaku, a dramatist and writer who went to Korea with *Shinkyō*, wrote in the Japanese-language Seoul newspaper *Keijō Nippō* (Seoul Daily) that the company wanted to perform in Korea not just because it had been successful in Japan but because it was desirable to show Koreans the results of the "cultural blending between the two peoples."[47]

In contrast to mixed reviews in Japan, the response from Korean reviewers was uniformly unfavorable, skeptical, and even hostile. In the criticisms of the Korean critics Chang's script was derided as a poor translation that failed to measure up to the original story. In a Japanese-language review printed in a Japanese-language journal, *Chōsen* (Korea), the philologist Sin T'aehyŏn harshly criticized the play for failing to deliver an "accurate" representation of Korean customs and culture. He ascribed Chang's inadequate interpretation of the story to his lack of background knowledge about *Ch'unhyangjŏn*.[48] In the Korean-language newspaper *Chosŏn Ilbo* (Korea Daily), the literary critic Yi Wŏnjo also disapproved of Chang's "translation" of the original language of *Ch'unhyangjŏn*. Yi saw *Ch'unhyangjŏn*'s particular value resulting from the *p'ansori* form in which it was narrated. Because *Ch'unhyangjŏn* in written form had been transcribed from songs performed before audiences, it retained the meter of the original verses. Thus he argued that the value of *Ch'unhyangjŏn* had everything to do with its language, and held that Chang's rendering of the story neutralized the musicality of the original *Ch'unhyangjŏn*, which he credited for its artistic value.[49]

Chang responded by adamantly claiming that his script was his own creation, not a translation. Chang correctly acknowledged the multiple origins of the story.[50] He pointed out that there were a number of different versions of *Ch'unhyangjŏn*, including *p'ansori* and *changgŭk* versions as well as those in written form.[51] Chang explained that initially he tried to translate the story word by word from existing written versions but found it impossible to preserve the charms of the original tale. As a consequence, he decided to write his own modern *Ch'unhyangjŏn,* borrowing only the storyline, characters, and setting. By emphasizing the difference between his own and previous versions of *Ch'unhyangjŏn,* Chang attempted to establish a case for his claim that the script was his own creation and not a translation of another's original. He also insisted on the heterogeneous origins of the story to argue that there was no single reference point for his script and that it was not a translation parasitically dependent on the original text.

If Chang's claim was not unreasonable, neither was the Korean critics' insistence that his script was, in fact, a translation. Inasmuch as Chang asserted on several occasions that he wrote the script with the intention of introducing Korean culture to Japanese audiences, what he did with *Ch'unhyangjŏn* was to present the story to those who did not share the language and culture as well as to those who regarded it as their own.[52] In other words, he translated an original story that was deemed representative of Korean culture into another language so that it could be understood by Japanese audiences. As long as Chang's script was connected to the original story that supposedly represented authentic Korean culture and customs and as long as Chang's intention with the script was to show Korean culture and customs to Japanese people who did not know much about them, Koreans regarded the play as a translation in a negative sense, as a secondary, parasitic copy of an original. Korean critics took issue with Chang's representation of the original story because they deemed it to be an inaccurate translation.

EQUAL EXCHANGE AND TRANSLATION

The problems of translation as equal exchange and its collusion with colonial domination surfaced in a roundtable discussion among Japanese and Korean intellectuals convened in Seoul as the Japanese-language *Ch'unhyangjŏn* went on stage there in late October 1938. The Japanese present included Murayama and Akita from *Shinkyō,* a Keijō Imperial University professor of Chinese literature named Karashima Takeshi, and Furukawa Kanehide, the director of the publication censorship department of the Government General. They were joined by the writer Hayashi Fusao, who was visiting Korea on his way to Manchuria and northern China. Koreans on the panel included Chang, the poet Chŏng Chiyong, the literary critic and poet Im Hwa, the writer and Posŏng College professor Yu Chino, the literary critic Kim Munjip, the writer Yi T'aejun, and the dramatist Yu Ch'ijin, who had helped Murayama revise Chang's script.[53]

Convened under the title "*Chōsen Bunka no Shōrai*" (The Future of Korean Culture), the roundtable discussion had not been intended to be about the play, but the play quickly became the central topic of discussion. The Koreans argued in unison that *Ch'unhyangjŏn* could not be translated and that, once translated, its value was lost and it was not *Ch'unhyangjŏn* anymore. Hayashi countered by asking them whether they were suggesting a total denial of translation. Karashima shrewdly tried to maneuver the discussion in a different direction, taking up a point made previously by a Korean participant who commented that professional writers in Korea faced economic difficulties because of the small market for literary works there. He said that if Korean writers had their works translated into Japanese, they would find a bigger market among Japanese readers. However, Karashima's economic argument failed to divert the Korean participants from continuing to return to the problem of translation. The Koreans insisted that, in the course of its translation into Chang and Murayama's play, *Ch'unhyangjŏn* had lost its inherent value because it was impossible for it to be expressed in Japanese. In response to the persistence of the Koreans, Murayama admitted that Japanese might feel the same way about an English translation of *Manyōshū,* the thousand-year-old verse collection Japanese nationalist scholars considered the essence of Japan, but he also argued that a Japanese translation of *Ch'unhyangjŏn* was necessary because Japanese people could not read Korean. In response, Kim Munjip bluntly suggested that the Japanese-language *Ch'unhyangjŏn* was staged not for cultural but rather for political reasons.[54]

Having kept silent to this point, Yi T'aejun abruptly posed a question to the Japanese participants: He asked them whether Korean writers should keep writing in Korean or whether they should instead create literary works in Japanese. Akita and Murayama, following Karashima, adhered to a purely economic logic. They argued that because the number of Japanese-language readers was greater than that of their Korean counterparts, it might be better for them to write in Japanese because they would have access to a larger market. Akita added that if they had difficulty writing in Japanese, they surely could get their works translated into Japanese, but Hayashi urged the Koreans to pen their writings directly in Japanese. Murayama offered a compromise that Korean writers should create literary works in Japanese while reserving the Korean language for whatever expressions they deemed untranslatable.[55]

The Korean intellectuals showed two levels of concern regarding colonial translation in the discourse centered on the staging of the Japanese-language *Ch'unhyangjŏn*. On one level, they were wary of any misrepresentation of Korean culture and customs to the colonizer. On another level, they were even more suspicious of translation as an interim stage in the total assimilation of Korean culture into Japanese. The first level of concern troubling the Korean intellectuals addressed the colonized's mistrust of translation as representation of their culture and literature, and eventually of themselves. Translation framed as representation, they intuited, does not do justice to the original. The original is inevitably distorted in representation. In other words, the colonized complained about the inevitable difference of any translation from its original. *Ch'unhyangjŏn* could not be expressed in languages other than Korean. In the eyes of the Koreans, the translation of *Ch'unhyangjŏn* was not a complete exchange between Korean and Japanese. Something valuable was lost in translation that was so essential to the story that *Ch'unhyangjŏn* was no longer *Ch'unhyangjŏn* without it. Difference in the medium of expression condemned translation to the secondary and inferior position with respect to the original. The exchange transpiring in the course of translating *Ch'unhyangjŏn* was not an equal exchange. In short, their resistance to the translation pointed to their aversion to an unequal exchange. The Korean intellectuals insisted that any translation of *Ch'unhyangjŏn* and of Korean literature in general was impossible because it could not guarantee equal exchange between the two languages. They sensed that the questions surrounding the translation at issue, the one by Maruyama and Chang being staged in a colonial city in the colonizer's language, were not just linguistic or literary but rather political. They did not flinch from declaring their suspicions that the staging of the Japanese-language play they considered a translation of a Korean original they knew and loved had much to do with the current political situation of the Sino-Japanese War, which required the total mobilization of the colony for Japan's war effort.

The debate over the Japanese version of *Ch'unhyangjŏn* did not stop, however, at the colonizer's imposition of, and the colonized's resistance to, translation. The Koreans' aversion to translation indicated their instinctive understanding of the collusion between colonialism and translation, which provoked the second level of their concern over colonial translation. Just as translation may be intended to bridge the differences between two languages and cultures but cannot help but point out those very differences, so, too, colonialism aims at the erasure of difference between the colonized and the colonizer while simultaneously retaining discriminatory practices against the colonized marked with the difference it claims to eradicate.

The Koreans, as the colonized, knew well that the erasure of difference between them and the Japanese meant the extermination of their difference from the colonizer, not the other way around. In other words, when it comes to the intention of a colonial power to erase difference between the colonized and the colonizer, the burden of change and assimilation falls on the shoulders of the colonized. It is the colonized, not the colonizer, who must adapt to colonial expectations. In the realm of literature, the biggest difference between the colonized and the colonizer is language. If the erasure of difference was to take place in the realm of literature, then it would be tantamount to the extermination of the Korean language itself. Thus the roundtable debate concerning *Ch'unhyangjŏn* and translation evolved into a discussion of Koreans' creative writing in the Japanese language. In short, the second level of concern plaguing the colonized intellectuals was the problem of Koreans writing in Japanese. Koreans were faced with a fundamental threat to Korean-language literature: If Korean writers and poets wrote their works in Japanese, there would be no need for translation. The erasure of difference would lead to the condition in which exchange—translation—would become unnecessary. Koreans were being doubly trapped in a situation from which there was no exit. They resisted translation because they thought that it could not ensure equal exchange between a translation and the original because of differences between languages and cultures, and they sensed the looming end of the Korean language should the even-worse condition emerge in which translation was no longer necessary.

In response to the Koreans' protests, the Japanese did not stop arguing that the translation was equivalent to the original and the product of a necessary exchange. The Japanese intellectuals admitted that the translation was different from the original even though translation was intended to emulate that original to the point of becoming the same, as if that had been ever possible. The Japanese intellectuals hinted that even if the valuable quality to which the Koreans clung was lost in the course of translation, it was not without compensation. In reaction to the colonized's protest against translation, the colonizers presented the logic of economy. They argued that if Korean writers produced works in Japanese, or at least had their works translated, they would be able to reach more readers. Korean writers who could not make ends meet by selling their writings in Korean were likely to be better off if they found a market for their works among Japanese-language readers because they were more numerous than readers of Korean and clearly had an interest in the colony and its culture.

Below the surface of this logic, which is economic in the conventional sense, lurks another layer of the logic of economy that propagates exchange based on symmetrical reciprocity between the colonizer and the colonized. In other words, the translation, even though it is an imprecise representation of the original, is presented as something exchangeable for mercenary gain. The colonized are placed as one party of exchange on the same plane with colonizers who force translation on them as a transaction in a literal sense. Even if exchange without loss is a tantalizing but unrealizable possibility in the transmission of a text from one language to another, it can only be realized extratextually. Put differently, the loss that transpires in the course of translation of the text is compensated for with material gain outside of the text. Such material compensation is equivalent to the alleged loss in value of the original text. In other words, the Japanese found a way to seduce the Koreans into commencing a cycle of exchange premised on symmetrical reciprocity one way or another.

Even if the colonized's culture and language are placed on the same plane as the colonizer's by the ruse of the equal exchange of translation, the colonized do not become equal to the colonizer in political, economical, and cultural power. Equal exchange in translation rests on symmetrical reciprocity, which requires constituting equivalence between two languages. As Marx pointed out, it is not two individuals on equal terms who establish equal exchange. On the contrary, the equivalent value of the commodities exchanged posits the owners of those commodities as equal in the exchange.[56] By forcing the colonized into equal exchange—through translation in the case of the roundtable discussion on the future of Korean culture—the colonizer demanded that the colonized recognize their relationship as symmetrical and reciprocal.

My argument has so far only interpreted the implications of the colonizer's insistence on symmetrical reciprocity in his relationship with the colonized despite the asymmetry necessarily resulting from colonial domination. However, in the spirit of Marx's famous 11th thesis on Feuerbach,[57] the point is to propose what the colonized can do in response to radically challenge the legitimacy of that colonial domination. Before offering any suggestions, however, it is necessary to examine the surge of interest in Korean cultural tradition among intellectuals during the 1930s to situate the debates surrounding the staging of the Japanese-language *Ch'unhyangjŏn* in the intellectual atmosphere of colonial Korea of that time.

CULTURAL NATIONALISM AND RESISTANCE TO COLONIALISM

Debates over the staging of the Japanese language *Ch'unhyangjŏn* took place against a backdrop of surging interest among intellectuals in Korean cultural tradition. The two most influential Korean-language newspapers, *Chosŏn Ilbo* (Korea Daily) and *Tong-a Ilbo* (East Asia Daily), spearheaded this rise in interest during the 1930s. In January 1935, *Chosŏn Ilbo* ran a series of articles by such experts in Korean culture as Yi Pyŏnggi, Kim T'aejun, and Yi Hŭisŭng addressing Korean classical literature and literary traditions.[58] The presumption of the series was that Korean society could maintain its unique culture by carrying on its traditional arts in the face of a flood of cultural influence from the West and Japan. *Tong-a Ilbo* also published articles discussing the establishment of a Korean national literature (*minjok munhak*) based on its traditions.[59] Preserving Korean cultural tradition had also been the center of discussion in national literature debates of the 1920s in Korea as nonsocialist, nationalist intellectuals advocated a national literature (*kungmin munhak*) by stressing the essential importance of Korean cultural tradition in literary writing.[60] The advocates of national literature argued that the leftist writers' emphasis on class conflict served to bring pernicious schisms into Korean society. The nationalist intellectuals believed that a national literature would awaken the consciousness of the Korean nation in the face of ever increasing pressures to slavishly follow Japan's imitation of Western culture.[61]

However, there was a significant difference between the 1920s national literature debate and the revival of interest in Korean cultural tradition in the mid-1930s. As the Korean scholar of literature Hwang Chongyŏn points out, the 1920s debate emerged as a response by Korean nationalist intellectuals to the menacing rise of the Proletarian Literature Movement. The revival of interest in Korean cultural tradition in the 1930s, on the other hand, was a response to Japanese colonial rule. In that sense, it is noteworthy that it coincided with the demise of the Proletarian Literature Movement. In the atmosphere of ruthless suppression of any political resistance including the communist movement, Korean intellectuals turned to cultural tradition as a rare forum in which they were allowed to imagine Korea's autonomy from Japan.

Korean cultural nationalism in the 1930s was, however, also a response to the economic boom triggered by Japan's takeover of Manchuria in 1932.[62] The Korean bourgeoisie saw the subsequent establishment of the state of Manchukuo as an economic opportunity. The editorial of *Chosŏn Ilbo* published on April 10, 1932, reflected this perspective, identifying the establishment of the state of Manchukuo as one of the conditions that would foster the economic development of Korea.[63] Japanese aggression in China did in fact help Korean enterprises flourish. For example, the Korean spinning and weaving company Kyŏngsŏng Pangjik, run by Kim Yŏnsu, invested substantially in Manchuria.[64] The company also benefited greatly from the economic boom of the Sino-Japanese War in 1937.[65] *Tong-a Ilbo,* which, along with *Chosŏn Ilbo,* instigated the Korean cultural revival of the 1930s, was owned by Kim's family.

From the perspective of the Korean bourgeoisie, Korean cultural nationalism served to counter the internationalism of Korean leftists that emphasized solidarity with the Chinese people against Japanese imperialism. Moreover, Korean cultural nationalism served to muffle the cry for class struggle from Korean workers by emphasizing the unity of the Korean nation over the class division of colonial society. Although Korean cultural nationalism could have been subversive to Japanese colonial domination by raising the national consciousness of Koreans, it did not pose a real threat because of a compromise the Korean bourgeoisie made with Japanese colonial domination. The Korean bourgeoisie gave up on political resistance to capitalize on Japanese expansionism in East Asia. In that sense, it is not too far-fetched to say that cultural nationalism was the ideology of the Korean bourgeois class.[66]

The zeal for Korean cultural tradition spread among Korean men of letters during the period. *Munjang* (Writing), the literary journal Yi T'aejun founded in 1939, devoted many of its pages to literary works expressive of affection for Korean cultural tradition. In such essays as *"Kojŏn"* (Classics), *"Kowan"* (Artifacts), and *"Kowan gwa Saenghwal"* (Artifacts and Daily Life), Yi himself expressed interest in and affection for Korean cultural tradition, which he considered to be rapidly disappearing from the daily life of the modern world.[67] In *"Ilpyŏnnakto"* (A Fragment of Paradise) and *"Tongbaeknamu"* (Camellias), the modernist poet Chŏng Chiyong, another participant in the roundtable discussion on the future of Korean culture, experimented with a quasi-traditional style of writing peppered with archaic words and redolent of the rhythm of classical Chinese writing. He also tried his hand at imitating *naeganche,* the writing style of women of the Confucian literati class in the Chosŏn period.[68] Yu Chino, another participant in the roundtable discussion, had dabbled in Marxism as a university student in the early 1930s and written stories dealing with social issues, but later turned to writing such short stories as his 1938 "*Ch'angnangjŏnggi*" (The Story of the Clear Water Pavilion), which described a disappearing world of tradition.[69] The cultural nationalism Koreans expressed in the roundtable discussion about the Japanese language play *Ch'unhyangjŏn* thus reflected a more general interest in Korean cultural tradition in the 1930s.

The Korean cultural tradition that these Korean men of letters harked back to was, however, that of the ruling class of Confucian literati and not that of the peasants. This emphasis resonated with the Japan Romantic School's call for a revival of Japanese traditional culture. Following the government's crackdown on leftist movements in the early 1930s, the Japanese intellectuals affiliated with the Japan Romantic School voiced their concerns about the rapid ascendancy of mass culture accompanying the economic boom after World War I. The popularization of culture was most visible in the emergence of the so-called one-yen-per-book (*enpon*) multivolume sets of Japanese and Western literature that the Japanese publishing industry mass produced to target the general public. In the eyes of the Japanese intellectuals, mass culture reduced the worth of an artistic creation to its exchange value as a commodity. The views of Yasuda Yojūrō, who advocated a return to Japanese classical literature and denounced both Tokugawa-period commoners' culture and the mass culture of his contemporary Japan, were representative: He not only denounced modern Japanese authors for their failure to carry on Japanese literary traditions but also criticized such modern literary forms as novels and literary criticism as imported genres alien to the Japanese mind.[70] He went on to contend that the imperative task in the reassertion of Japanese literary tradition should be to recapture "the essence of Japanese poetry (*nihon shi no kokoro*) and its development in the history of Japanese literature."[71] Like the Japan Romantic School, the rising interest in Korean cultural tradition marked a more general intellectual trend of critical reflection on modernity in the 1930s and the 1940s.

Such contemporary Korean Marxist critics as Im Hwa criticized the surge of interest in Korean cultural tradition as regressive traditionalism. In a series of essays he wrote in 1936 under the name Im Insik for another Korean-language newspaper, *Chosŏn Chungang Ilbo* (Korea Central Daily), he denounced the interest as a reactionary mood that not only unscientifically glorified the past but also legitimized escapism.[72] The attacks on the Korean cultural revival did not come only from Marxists, however. Another prominent intellectual who was skeptical about Korean cultural tradition was Ch'oe Chaesŏ, who was trained in English literature and versed in English literary theories and who argued that cultural development in Korea should be instead anchored in European cultural traditions because Korean traditional culture could not offer any contribution to the development of modern culture in contemporary Korea.[73] As discussed in the following chapter, by the early 1940s, Ch'oe would become one of the most notorious collaborators with Japanese colonialism. An intellectual's position on the Korean cultural tradition revival cannot be understood as a barometer of willingness to collaborate with Japanese colonialism.

It is not easy to elucidate what modernity stood for in the eyes of Korean intellectuals. Although it was unquestionably associated with the West, as further examined in the following chapter, it was also related to Japan because modernization had come to Korea with colonization by Japan. In that sense, Korean cultural tradition was one of the few remaining arenas in which Korean intellectuals were allowed to imagine the autonomy of Korea with respect to Japan. Thus the preference for Korean cultural tradition by such Korean intellectuals as Yi and the contributors to his journal *Munjang* has been favorably interpreted by later readers as a form of subversive, though passive, opposition to Japanese colonialism.[74]

Nevertheless, the cultural nationalism of Korean intellectuals failed to pose any meaningful challenge to Japanese colonial rule in Korea even if it did attempt to secure an autonomous space for Korean culture within the Japanese empire. Thus, toward the end of the roundtable discussion, when Hayashi proposed that Korean writers and poets should volunteer to serve the Japanese military in China as war writers, Yu Chino welcomed the suggestion. Yu's agreement made for a stark contrast with his assertion that Korean writers should keep writing in Korean when he rejected Hayashi's forceful urging of the Korean panelists to produce literary works in Japanese. Yu's support for the Japanese war effort was met with no opposition from any other Korean at the roundtable.[75]

As demonstrated above, the Koreans at the roundtable were opposed to the translation of *Ch'unhyangjŏn* because they regarded it as unequal exchange. They adamantly maintained that something very important was lost in the course of translation. That something was the foundation on which they built their cultural nationalism. However, their cultural nationalism did not contradict their agreement to support the Japanese war effort. When the corps of writers that was to serve to "comfort" the Japanese imperial military (*kōgun imon sakkadan*) was organized in Korea in 1939, it included Chŏng Chiyong, Yi T'aejun, and Im Hwa, all roundtable participants. Nonetheless, my intention here is not to accuse these Korean intellectuals of being pro–Japanese collaborators. The three intellectuals were not particularly cooperative with the colonial government when compared with such infamous collaborators as Ch'oe Namsŏn, Yi Kwangsu, Hyŏn Yŏngsŏp, and Ch'oe Chaesŏ. I rather call attention to a specific juncture in which cultural nationalism coexisted with support for colonial expansion. My criticism targets how the roundtable participants mingled cultural nationalism of the colonized and collaboration with colonial expansion in their discussion of the Japanese-language staging of *Ch'unhyangjŏn* in Korea in 1938. I argue that the cultural nationalism and collaboration did not merely coexist but rather cooperated with each other in perpetuating the established regime of colonialism. By assuming a symmetrical relationship between the Korean and Japanese cultures and languages, cultural nationalism served to compensate for the political asymmetry between the colonized and the colonizer.[76] However, cultural nationalism was not a substitute for resistance to colonial domination. The Korean cultural nationalism manifested at the roundtable discussion echoes the ethnic identity politics of multiculturalism promoted under the current dominant U.S. ideology. Although ostensibly a gesture toward tolerance within the borders of the American nation, multiculturalism fails to challenge the unquestioning loyalty that the American nation state demands of individuals of every ethnic group, even in the face of the most obvious imperial aggression.[77]

Frantz Fanon once warned colonized peoples about becoming preoccupied with their own "authentic" culture and the colonizers' slights toward it. In Fanon's eyes, championing a native culture is ineffective unless it is tied up with political and social struggles against colonial domination. "It is around the people's struggles that African-Negro Culture takes on substance, and not around songs, poems, or folklore," as Fanon succinctly put it.[78] When cultural nationalism is divorced from politics, it stops short of challenging colonial domination. Furthermore, because the cultural nationalism of the colonized tends to focus myopically on creating autonomous space for native cultures within an empire rather than challenging regimes of colonial domination, it can blind the colonized to the colonial injustice inflicted on those outside their national community. In other words, cultural and linguistic nationalism tends to lead the colonized into callous indifference toward the colonial violence inflicted on other colonized peoples.

Assuming symmetrical opposition between Korean and Japanese cultures and languages, the colonized intellectuals' cultural nationalism worked to compensate for political asymmetry between the colonized and the colonizer by positing cultural parity between the two. In the history of the colonized peoples' struggles against colonial domination are examples of how cultural nationalism among the colonized has served to help mobilize political resistance by the colonized against the colonizer, but what must be kept in mind is that there have been cases throughout history in which cultural nationalism fails to challenge the legitimacy of colonial domination. Such was the case of the Korean intellectuals at the roundtable discussion who agreed to support the Japanese war effort while being alert to any encroachment on what they saw as autonomous space of their own culture and language.

One might be quick to protest that it is unfair to criticize the Korean intellectuals for their failure to dissent from Japanese expansionism in front of the colonial bureaucrat Furukawa Kanehide at the roundtable discussion. One might further point out that it was virtually impossible to raise a dissenting voice in general, especially during the last stage of Japanese colonial rule, without risking imprisonment and even death. However, the emphasis on the impossibility of voicing political dissent inadvertently points to the limitations of a cultural nationalism like the one expressed at the roundtable discussion. The cultural nationalism of the Korean intellectuals could be expressed only because the Japanese colonial authorities allowed it to be. As shown above, despite the presence of the colonial bureaucrat at the roundtable discussion, Korean intellectuals voiced their displeasure with encroachment by the colonizers on "their own culture" while silently agreeing to cooperate with the war effort.

TRANSLATION AS AN ETHICAL AS WELL AS POLITICAL PRACTICE

The 1938 roundtable discussion about the staging of the Japanese-language play *Ch'unhyangjŏn* in Korea offers a valuable point of departure for investigating further the issues of reciprocity and exchange in translation and colonialism. The Korean critics sensed that the translation of *Ch'unhyangjŏn* did not ensure an equal exchange between the original and the translation and between the Korean and Japanese languages. The refusal by these Korean critics pointed negatively to the fact that they also adhered to the ideal model of translation as equal exchange. In other words, they believed that translation should guarantee equal exchange between an original and any translation made of it. Because they thought that Chang's rendering failed to achieve equal exchange and, more important, that the original did not allow for such exchange, they rejected his *Ch'unhyangjŏn*. However, to envision a truly radical way of resisting colonial domination, it is necessary to be critical of the cultural nationalism of colonized intellectuals who are complacently fixated on "their own culture" but fail hopelessly to voice political criticism of their colonial master's expansion into other countries. In lieu of a conclusion to our discussion, what I will attempt to do in the rest of the chapter is to configure translation as an ethical as well as political practice with the help of Levinas.

As discussed above, Levinas continuously attends to the ethical aspect of language throughout *Totality and Infinity* and *Otherwise Than Being*. He insists on the ethical aspect of language as the possibility of dialogue between the self and the other and between one community and another that do not share common foundations for preestablished understanding.[79] In short, Levinas suggests that language enables the self to come into contact with the other, who is by definition foreign to the self. The engagement in dialogue with the other can be a traumatic experience because the self is vulnerable to misunderstanding and the rejection of understanding by the other, who does not share the logic and knowledge with the self. That is why Levinas describes the ethical aspect of language in terms of conversation between foreigners who do not share a common ground for understanding. Thus, dialogue between the self and the other who are foreign to each other is an event of translation. In Levinasian ethics, the essence of language cannot be the transmission of ideas between interlocutors. The essence of language is rather that it enables the self to engage in dialogue with the other, who is utterly foreign to the self. Language is the window through which the self approaches the other, and translation is the event of the self's encounter with other.

The idea of translation reformulated as an ethical practice requires the translator to humbly recognize that the task at hand is to encounter the other in language that ultimately cannot be tamed, controlled, or completely appropriated. The translator cannot be absolved from the responsibility for the other inscribed in the original. In other words, the translator's debt to the original cannot be paid off completely in an equal exchange because such a transaction is impossible in the asymmetrical relationship with the other. On the contrary, the translator is never free from the exacting relationship. While engaging with the other as inscribed in the original text, the translator realizes the foreignness within each of the two languages between which the translator moves. Languages are porous to the outside. The openness of and foreignness in languages are, however, concealed until, in the course of translation, the translator releases them from the shackles of the idea of languages as autonomous and homogeneous.

Levinas's insight is useful for formulating a critique of linguistic nationalism, which is inseparably connected to the idea of one national community the boundaries of which coincide with those of an autonomous and homogeneous language community. The cultural and linguistic nationalism of the Korean intellectuals is understandable if one remembers that Korea was put under the pressure of colonial domination that, in its last stage, sought to erase the Korean language itself from public spaces. However, it must also not be forgotten that, while attempting to keep intact the autonomous space for their language and culture, the Korean intellectuals wound up cooperating with Japanese colonial expansion into the Asian continent. Their refusal of translation thus was little more than a myopic obsession with their autonomous space of language and culture within the empire. Cultural nationalism as such certainly failed to acknowledge translation as an ethical and political practice that existed to be critical of colonial domination and to envision new ways of relating to the other. What colonized intellectuals should do with translation is thus neither reject it as unequal exchange nor yearn for equal exchange. The colonized should reconfigure translation in relation to the other by refusing the idea of equal exchange in language. Translation reconfigured as such is elevated to an ethical and political practice, thus implying fundamental criticism of colonial domination. Put differently, by disclosing the unethical nature of equal exchange and emphasizing instead the asymmetry of ethics, translation reframed as an ethical and political practice provides a radical criticism of colonial discourse that works homologously with a model of translation based on equal exchange and serves to propagate the idea of colonial domination as equal exchange in a reciprocal relationship between colonizer and colonized.

The relationship between the self and the other in Levinasian ethics should not be mistaken for the relationship with the other that is dominant in the tradition of Western thought that Levinas identifies as ontology.[80] Although the ego is solidified through the erasure of the otherness of the other in ontology, the self is vulnerable to the ethical call from the other.[81] In other words, whereas the ontological relationship with the other of ontology legitimizes the ego by sacrificing the alterity of the other, the other Levinas calls the self to face brings into question the legitimacy of that self in the ethical relationship. Thus, although the insistence on an ethical relationship between the colonized and the colonizer entails a clear demarcation between the two, it should not be regarded as a return to an old model of the Manichean relationship of ontology between the colonized and the colonizer on which rests both colonial domination and cultural nationalism. In other words, the ethical relationship between the colonized and the colonizer resists the constitution of the subjectivity of both the colonizer and the colonized as premised on such essentialist foundations as ethnicity, language, tradition, and culture. Not only does criticism of colonialism grounded in Levinasian ethics summon the colonizer to be vulnerable to the colonized's accusation of colonial violence but it also reminds the colonized of their responsibility to other colonized peoples as an other, existing outside of the self's supposed national community bound by ethnicity, language, tradition, and culture.

However, the unlimited obligation of the self to the other does not mean that the colonized are as ethically culpable to the colonizer as the latter is to the former because the colonizer is as much the other to the colonized as the colonized are to the colonizer. The Levinasian ethical relationship should not be mistaken for the equalization of ethical responsibility between the colonizer and the colonized. Such an argument bolsters a theory of equal exchange that the critique of symmetrical reciprocity disproves.[82] Ethicality built on asymmetry requires the self to be responsible for the other regardless of whether the other reciprocates that care or not. The critique of equal exchange offered by the concept of translation as a political and ethical practice thus does not offer the colonizer any excuses because it does not demand the same level of ethical obligation from the colonized and the colonizer and instead vehemently opposes any endeavor to dismiss the ethical obligation of the colonizer toward the colonized. Such ethicality emphasizes the insolvency of colonizers who forever fail to pay their debt to the people they have colonized. The theory thus denounces any attempt to posit the colonial relationship as reciprocally beneficial to both the colonizer and the colonized. The purpose of a critique of colonialism grounded in ethics is to criticize colonial discourse that relentlessly rehashes the logic of equal exchange between imperial aggression and defense of civilization, colonial exploitation and economic development, and free flow of capital and the spread of modern ideas and values.

3. The Location of "Korean" Culture

Ch'oe Chaesŏ and Korean Literature in a Time of Transition

Fourteen years after Japanese colonialism had come to an end in Korea, Ch'oe Chaesŏ contributed a regular column to the newspaper of Yonsei University where he taught English literature. In the column, he noted that his students had nicknamed him Reverend Dimmesdale, after the character in Nathaniel Hawthorne's *The Scarlet Letter,* because he seemed distant and hard to read.[1] He insisted that the nickname, however, was not apt because he did not share the sinister past of the novel's character. It is telling that, although his students only attributed the nickname to his aloofness, he was quick to distance himself from Dimmesdale's dark history. But despite his protestations, Ch'oe had a past so haunting that he once dolefully confessed that he had not seen a film since the Pacific War because movie going was a part of the youth he had buried along with his memories of the war.[2] How should this maneuver of simultaneously drawing attention to and distancing himself from the past be interpreted?

One answer can be found in the memoir of Yu Chino, a Korean intellectual active on the Korean literary scene during the colonial period and a member of the 1938 roundtable discussion on the Japanese-language staging of the Korean tale *Ch'unhyangjŏn*. Yu offered the following glimpse at the haunting past Ch'oe wished to consign to oblivion. In December 1942,

> Itō Norio, a thought prosecutor in Pusan, contacted me through a certain Mr. Ch'oe, who was the chief editor of a very influential literary journal at that time, with an invitation that since it had been a while he wanted to have dinner and talk over some bottles of Kanbotan, the quality [rice] wine of [the southeastern city of] Masan he bought on his way to Kyŏngsŏng [the colonial-era name for Seoul]. Even though the title "thought prosecutor" sounds threatening, Itō was an old teacher of mine from college from whom I took an introductory law course one semester. Besides, although he was a thought

> prosecutor, he had been demoted and transferred from Kyŏngsŏng to Pusan because he was known as a man of liberal or gentle nature if you wish. Therefore I accepted his invitation while wondering about it. . . . As I suspected, what Itō wanted to discuss was politics. Ch'oe, sitting next to him, expanded on what Itō said by asserting that the time had come for intellectuals like us without any personal ambition to consider the future of Koreans in the face of the current situation. Obviously, Itō and Ch'oe had planned this meeting in advance. . . . Mr. Chang Tŏksu stood up to leave, making an excuse that he had a previous engagement. Apparently he made up the excuse in order to escape. Ch'oe with an unpleasant look on his face grumbled "because he is a big shot" while glaring at the back of Chang who had turned to leave the room. Seizing my chance, I too stood up to leave. This time, he sneered at my back as I left and said in a quite loud voice, "you're a big shot, too, aren't you?"[3]

The "certain Ch'oe" in this anecdote was the same Ch'oe. In 1942, he was the editor of *Kokumin Bungaku* (National Literature), a Japanese-language journal that was the only literary periodical still in print in colonial Korea at the time this incident took place. At that time, Ch'oe was deeply involved in various cultural and literary propaganda projects directed at promoting the Japanese colonial policy of assimilation in Korea.[4] In Yu's account, Ch'oe is depicted as an arrogant villain who pressed his fellow Korean intellectuals to cooperate with Japanese colonialism against their will.

Ch'oe's enthusiastic embrace of Japanese colonial domination in the 1940s has bewildered scholars of colonial-period Korean literature. Ch'oe is credited with introducing the modern English literary criticism of T. E. Hulme, T. S. Eliot, I. A. Richards, and Herbert Read to Korea in the 1930s. Ch'oe emphasized the importance of intellect in literary criticism and argued that it was what unified the theories of these English literary critics despite discrepancies among their ideas. By applying Western literary theories to his analysis of Korean literature, Ch'oe attempted to bring the modernity he found in them to Korean literature. He believed that the future of Korean culture depended on the successful adoption of the Western cultural tradition, even though he considered the development of Korean society to be lagging, and thus impeding the growth of literary modernity.

Around 1940, Ch'oe began writing literary criticism that justified the Japanese colonial policy of assimilation, which was epitomized by the colonial slogan of the day "Homeland (i.e., Japan)–Korea as One Body" (*naisen ittai*). His criticism positioned Korean literature as a subset of Japanese literature, and he encouraged Korean writers and poets to contribute to a Japanese national literature, or *kokumin bungaku*. Ch'oe peppered his essays with the colonial ideology of assimilation, renouncing the modernity that was being "overcome" by Japan and declaring his loyalty to the Japanese state, even unto death. Thus in the eyes of Korean literary historians, Ch'oe's collaboration with the Japanese colonial authorities was not only a betrayal of his people but also a traitorous departure from his former advocacy of modernity and the intellect in literary criticism.

The enigma of Ch'oe's transformation from faith in the intellectual rooted in the Western literary tradition to an embrace of the cultural policy of Japanese colonialism makes his career a valuable window into the ideological topography of intellectuals in the final stage of Japanese colonialism's policy of assimilation in Korea. Not only did Ch'oe offer one of the most systematic theoretical justifications of colonial ideology in the realm of culture and literature in colonial Korea, but also he was able to proselytize his position in the Japanese-language publication *Kokumin Bungaku* (National Literature), the only literary journal allowed to remain in print by the early 1940s. By attempting to solve the enigma of his conversion, I hope to gain insight into the view of the colonized intellectual on collaboration.

More specifically, in this chapter, I closely read Ch'oe's 1943 Japanese-language book *Tenkanki no Chōsen Bungaku* (Korean Literature in a Time of Transition),[5] in which he set out to subsume Korean culture within Japanese culture and to call on Korean writers and poets to produce a national literature for Korean imperial subjects in Japanese that would serve to raise national consciousness of the Japanese empire among Koreans. I attempt to work through Ch'oe's defense of the assimilation policy of Japanese colonialism in Korea. The central chapters of Ch'oe's book pivot on his intellectual justification for positioning Korean literature as a subset of Japanese literature. Under the crust of his unabashed enthusiasm for Japanese colonial dominance in Korea lie more nuanced arguments for securing an autonomous space for Korean culture in the face of the assimilation policy of Japanese colonialism. However, I do not intend to rescue his writings from the sweeping denunciation of Korean nationalists by stressing that ambivalence, nor is it my intent to privilege ambivalence in Ch'oe's defense of Japanese colonialism as characteristic of the relationship between the colonized and colonizers or as the site of resistance to colonialism as brilliantly conjured up from colonial discourse by Homi Bhabha in his *The Location of Culture*.[6]

Instead, my aim is to analyze how Ch'oe's sincere intellectualism and his experiences as a denizen of everyday life in colonial society led him to collaborate with colonial domination. In doing so, I want to expose how the quotidian was turned into a space for the production and reproduction of colonial domination. I also pay attention to how his concept of history contributed to developing his argument. Echoing the Japanese philosopher Miki Kiyoshi, whose work was introduced into Korea by the Korean intellectual Sŏ Insik, one of the regular contributors to *Inmun P'yŏngnon* (Humanities Review), the Korean-language journal Ch'oe launched in 1939, Ch'oe argued that modernity originating in Europe had completed its historical task and that the world had entered a new historical era in which individualism and liberalism had rapidly become dysfunctional.[7] He called for a paradigmatic transition in culture and literature to reflect such a historical change. Ch'oe felt that the rise of totalitarianism and the ongoing war forced Korean intellectuals to face up to the reality that Koreans and the Japanese belonged to the same community formed by historical destiny and would have to band together to survive the violent worldwide conflict. He called for the establishment of a national literature to instill consciousness among Koreans of belonging to Japan.

Finally, by comparing Ch'oe's critical essays on literature, culture, and politics with his own translations, I examine the way in which the Korean-language originals and the translations into Japanese address a slightly different readership. Such minuscule differences between originals and translations, however, interrupt the transparent signification of such concepts as tradition, culture, Japan, and Korea, on which Ch'oe based his arguments in the essays. The difference reveals that the meanings of such concepts are undecidable in the Derridean sense. The undecidability embedded in the significations of the concepts ultimately disrupts Ch'oe's discursive strategy, which aimed simultaneously to include Koreans in the category of the Japanese nation and to establish an autonomous space for Korean culture within the empire of Japan.

In his reading of the works of Jean-Jacques Rousseau, Jacques Derrida observed that the French Enlightenment thinker described writing as a subordinate, but necessary, supplement to speech because writing partially restores what speech promises yet eventually fails to deliver.[8] According to Derrida, the term "supplement" is presented in Rousseau's writings in such a way that its meaning is undecidable between plentitude and deficiency, because a supplement simultaneously adds to and substitutes for what it supplements. It adds to something that is deficient to make it complete but it also fills in as a subaltern substitute for something that is already complete. Put differently, a supplement portends the full presence of what it supplements, yet ironically it also marks the lack of presence because presence depends on it to be complete. Thus, presence can be present only by proxy.

The implications of the concept of supplementarity extend beyond Derrida's reading of Rousseau's works to his critique of Western metaphysical thought, which, in his view, privileges presence. For instance, the question about how a human being experiences the external world lies at the center of the Western philosophical tradition. One major response to the question postulates that the thing in itself can never be directly accessed by the experiencing subject, and thus it is approachable only through its supplement, in other words, a representation of the thing. The representation is less than the thing in itself. Nevertheless, it is necessary because the thing in itself is not immediately available to the experiencing subject. By filling in for the thing in itself, the representation presupposes the presence of the thing in itself. Accordingly, hierarchy is embedded in the relationship between presence and its supplement. Presence is deemed original, pure, natural, and essential whereas a supplement is considered derivative, corrupt, artificial, and extraneous. Nevertheless, as discussed earlier, presence is present only as the aftereffects of its supplement. The original, pure presence is always deferred.

Through his deliberations on supplementarity in Rousseau's works, Derrida demonstrated his reading strategy, which is what has been branded deconstruction. It lays bare the ideology of what he termed transcendental reading. Transcendental reading is premised on the assumption that meaning can be exhaustively reduced to the transcendental signified outside the text, be that the authorial intent, the author's subconscious, or the extratextual context in which the author was located. The transcendental signified is indefinitely deferred, however, because, in signification, one signifier is replaced with another signifier rather than fixed onto the ultimate signified.

The notion of supplementarity manifests an occasion of undecidability, the kernel of Derrida's ethics and politics. As shown in the case of a supplement, the undecidable pivots on the dynamics of certain oppositions inherent in a text while simultaneously subverting the oppositional dynamics because of double meanings. Undecidability does not merely postulate the indefinite deferral of the transcendental signified. It also demands that when reading a text, the reader must choose with great care one possible meaning over another. Thus, instead of resulting in indecision, undecidability constitutes the very condition of the possibility of making a decision. Unless a decision arises from the ordeal of undecidability, it cannot be a genuine decision.[9] In other words, undecidability does not merely indicate the impossibility of meaning. On the contrary, it presupposes that there must be multiple plausible meanings among which the reader debates to make a genuine decision. Nevertheless, no matter how legitimate the reader's decision may be, the other possible meanings, which the decision left out, still haunt and disrupt the seemingly univocal signification of the text.

Needless to say, by engaging in a deconstructive reading of Ch'oe's texts, I do not deny the relevance of authorial intent and extratextual context. Undecidability itself would not work unless legitimate meanings were available through reading. Reading in turn cannot proceed without recourse to the authorial intent and extratextual context. Invoking Derrida's concept of supplementarity, I call attention to the undecidability inherent in Ch'oe's texts that is highlighted by the differences between the texts and his own translations of them. The undecidability merits our attention because it destabilizes the univocal signification of such concepts as culture, tradition, Japan, and Korea despite Ch'oe's authorial intention to fix them onto stable meanings.

Before venturing into examining Ch'oe writings on literature, culture, and politics, however, I will trace his early life to situate him and his thought in the history of Japanese colonialism in Korea.

A PORTRAIT OF THE COLONIAL INTELLECTUAL AS A YOUNG MAN

In 1943, Ch'oe wrote an essay that can be interpreted as a vindication of Korean intellectuals' lack of enthusiasm toward mobilizing behind Japanese colonial policies. In the essay, Ch'oe admitted that intellectuals have a tendency to skip political gatherings and, he added, when they do attend, they are always late. In addition, he contended that intellectuals are likely to argue at meetings, and even if they agree, they never fail to complain. However, Ch'oe attributed this uncooperative attitude to the intellectual temperament, ignoring any possibility that their actions might represent passive but deliberate resistance to colonial rule.[10] He reasoned instead that the temperament stems from intellectuals' pursuit of high principles and values that transcend the mundane life of ordinary people and their desire to help create a national culture for future generations. Although asserting that culture can be produced only when nation and art are perfectly harmonized, he insisted that intellectuals' laggard response to politics should not be deemed a remnant of liberalism, which he viewed as an obsolete ideology of the past. Instead, he implored critics to encourage the good side of men of letters, in other words, that which produces culture. Thus, Ch'oe asked for tolerance toward intellectuals who failed to enthusiastically cooperate with the colonial authorities.[11] Certainly, Ch'oe recommended that Korean intellectuals be more cooperative with the colonial authority and not support any political resistance. However, because Koreans, intellectuals or not, were forcibly mobilized for Japanese war efforts and every hint of political dissension was ruthlessly suppressed, Ch'oe's essay can be read as a gesture to protect his fellow Korean intellectuals from retaliation by Japanese colonial authorities. A rather sympathetic reading of this essay might allow for a shadow of the martyr in Ch'oe bearing the yoke of collaboration on his shoulders while saving other Korean intellectuals from the disgraceful task imposed on them by the Japanese colonial authority. In this part of the chapter, I will explicate this complicated mental terrain by piecing together anecdotes, personal memoirs, and essays by and about Ch'oe, as an example of the plight of intellectuals stranded in colonial society.

Ch'oe was born in 1908 in Haeju, Hwanghaedo, in the northwestern part of Korea. His father was a wealthy businessman-turned-farmer, and his family seems to have been more than affluent. It is said that his father's farm was so vast that the noise of the household never reached any of its neighbors.[12] He went to Keijō, present-day Seoul, to attend Keijō Second Higher Common School and, in 1926, he matriculated at the top of his class, bound for the Faculty of Letters at Keijō Imperial University.[13] Finishing its requirements in 1928, he entered the Department of English Literature at the university. Academically active and ambitious, he regularly wrote articles for the English department bulletin. Its editor-in-chief was Satō Kiyoshi, a Japanese professor in the English department. Ch'oe became one of Satō's most beloved disciples.

While at college, Ch'oe lived in a Japanese boarding house, made friends with Japanese classmates, and spoke in Japanese. He rarely spoke Korean on campus.[14] His only Korean friend, Hyŏn Yŏngnam (who later changed his name to Yŏngsŏp), was known to fellow students as an anarchist.[15] Ch'oe was well-known for his fluent English but he was extremely unpopular among Korean students because he socialized only with Japanese students and not with them. Once, some Korean students ganged up on him because of his "pro-Japanese" attitude, but it is not clear whether those "pro-Japanese" tendencies extended to a political allegiance. In the preface to his Japanese language-book *Korean Literature in a Time of Transition,* he wrote that since childhood he had held great affection for Japanese culture including the language, the Japanese-style room (*washitsu*), and the literature of the Meiji period, and that he had made many friends among the Japanese people. He confessed, however, that he considered his affection for Japan to be a matter of personal taste and not related to the Japanese state. He made this confession in the context of emphasizing the necessity for Koreans to embrace the Japanese state in the face of the historical transition following the outbreak of the Sino-Japanese War in 1937. Taking into account the context of the book, one might legitimately suspect that Ch'oe intentionally depicted his affection for Japan as apolitical to stress the contrast between a private, personal taste for Japanese culture and a public, political allegiance to the Japanese state. Such autobiographical statements must be subjected to examination against other relevant documents. An excerpt from the memoirs of one of Ch'oe's teachers at college, Takagi Ichinosuke, can serve that purpose. A prominent Japanese scholar of Japanese literature who taught at Keijō Imperial University for 14 years, from 1926 to 1940, Takagi met Ch'oe's college professor, Satō, when they studied in England on Japanese government fellowships, and the two remained friends. Knowing both Satō and Ch'oe, Takagi was close enough to the latter to witness this comic–tragic scene of the colonized man:

> [T]here was a student named Ch'oe Chaesŏ who was studying English literature. . . . After graduating, he became a lecturer and visited me quite often. While at college, he was regarded as pro–Japanese so much so that once he was even beaten up by other Korean students. However there was an incident during the New Year holidays when he came to my place late at night with an awful look on his face and with two or three bottles of beer dangling from his hands. He made threatening remarks like "no matter how much you professors brag about it, you cannot take away our Korean soul" and stomped out.[16]

What stands out in this latter anecdote is the sudden surge of nationalistic feeling from a young man whose previous sentiments had strayed the opposite way. Aided by alcohol, he may have been pouring out inner feelings that he had repressed while speaking only Japanese, socializing only with Japanese students, and making himself the most beloved disciple of the Japanese professor, while rarely befriending and therefore being detested by other Korean students.[17] However what is more relevant to our discussion is that Ch'oe's relationship with Japan was anything but transparent.

An essay that Ch'oe wrote in 1940 on James Joyce's *A Portrait of the Artist as a Young Man* offers some clues about what lay behind his affection for Japan and his aloofness from Korea.[18] Ch'oe calls attention to the protagonist Stephen Dedalus's alienation from his fellow students, who do not understand his cynicism about Irish nationalism and his ambivalent attitude toward English culture. The resentment of the students is succinctly summed up by the question that Stephen is asked by a classmate named Davin, which Ch'oe quotes in his review: "Are you Irish at all?"[19] This scene in the novel is superimposed on an autobiographical anecdote of Ch'oe being harassed by other Korean students in college for his lack of nationalistic zeal and for his affection for the Japanese culture and language. Ch'oe reasons that Stephen has to escape from parochial Irish culture and tradition to liberate the artist within. Ch'oe sees himself speaking for his own situation as well as for Stephen's. In other words, Korean tradition is an impediment to the cultivation of his artistic taste and Japanese language and culture are its vehicles.

Ch'oe's attitude toward Japan was too complicated to identify him as pro–Japanese if "pro–Japanese" carries political implications. My main concern, however, is not to defend Ch'oe from accusations that he was politically pro–Japanese starting in his college years. Ch'oe must have noticed that his personal taste for the colonizer's culture could not be dissociated easily from its political implications by his fellow colonized. Furthermore, if he identified with Stephen, whom Joyce is believed to have modeled on himself, his later actions were quite the opposite of those of Joyce. Although Joyce wrote in English, as Ch'oe wrote in Japanese, Joyce did not choose English literature over Irish literature or English over Gaelic, nor did he subsume Irish literature within English literature. Instead, he dismantled the putative unity of English, the colonizer's language, by hybridizing it with a variety of languages, as he did in *Finnegans Wake*. In other words, Joyce aimed to uproot English culture.[20] Ch'oe would harshly criticize such an uprooting as a negative characteristic of cosmopolitanism when defending Japanese colonial domination.

After his graduation from university, Ch'oe was forced to face the reality of colonial society in which the colonized were not only differentiated from the colonizers but also discriminated against, regardless of the extent to which they had accepted the colonizers' culture. Many years later he still recollected with bitterness how frustrated he was by the unfairness of colonial society, in which Japanese students with less talent easily moved ahead of him in society even though he had been always at the top of his class. This unfair treatment undoubtedly took place during his employment at the Keijō Imperial University. The scholarly life of teaching and academic writing was his first passion.[21] Ch'oe entered graduate school following his graduation from college in 1931 and was appointed lecturer in English at the university in 1933. He was one of the first graduates of the university to attain a teaching position there since its foundation in 1924. However, Ch'oe failed to win a permanent position and, in 1934, he moved to the Keijō College of Law, a government general-run school for bureaucrats, to teach English.[22] It was impossible at that time for Koreans to secure permanent teaching positions at Keijō Imperial University.[23]

Ch'oe's amicable relationship with his mentor, Satō, continued despite his failure to attain a position at Keijō Imperial University. With help from Satō, Ch'oe ventured into the Japanese intellectual world in December 1934 by publishing an article introducing the literary criticism of T. E. Hulme in the prominent Japanese journal *Shisō* (Thought). Ch'oe was, noted a postscript from the editor, the first Korean contributor to the journal in its more than 13-year history.[24] The following month, another article by Ch'oe, on the poetry criticism of John Dennis, appeared in one of the leading Japanese academic journals *Eibungaku Kenkyū* (Studies in English Literature). In other lectures and writings over the next several years, he introduced the literary criticism of Eliot, Richards, and Read as well as Wyndham Lewis to Korea.[25] His choices were eclectic, ranging from Hulme's neoclassical modernism to Read's psychoanalytical interpretation, but Ch'oe found a common thread in their emphasis on the importance of the intellect in criticism, and he lumped them together under what he called intellectualism (*chujijuŭi* in Korean; *shuchishugi* in Japanese).[26]

Ch'oe resigned from teaching in 1936 and started a publishing house that would become known for publishing the works of Korean writers as well as translations of such foreign novels as Pearl Buck's *The Good Earth* (1931).[27] Around the same time, he started writing reviews of Korean literary works. As he seldom spoke Korean at college and his literary theories were influenced by English critics, his writing reviews of Korean works marked a significant shift. Hyŏn mistakenly described him around this time as having been influenced by nationalism and socialism, but Hyŏn must have mistaken Ch'oe's emphasis on tradition and realism in his criticism of Korean literature for sympathy for nationalism and socialism.[28] In the late 1930s, Ch'oe came to emphasize the importance of morality in literary criticism. Drawing on Read, he argued that morality was the intuitive understanding of values through the intellect.[29] By stressing the importance of these two elements, he attempted to "restore judgment" to the field of literary criticism: It is necessary, he argued, to call for a literary criticism that would encourage literature capable of providing order for man in a chaotic world. He posited that intellect should hinge on (Western) cultural tradition and stressed that literature should be anchored in the living and historical experience of the people (*minjung*). He further argued that the writers should recognize that they are members of the community of the people, not isolated individuals. As discussed later, Ch'oe's emphasis on the living and historical experience of the people would later turn into a depoliticization of everyday life and mythification of history when he argued for the integration of Korean culture and literature into those of Japan. In any case, it should be pointed out that what Ch'oe meant by cultural tradition in this context was the European culture that had produced the Western men of letters he addressed in his critical writing.

Thus, as briefly mentioned in the preceding chapter, Ch'oe was skeptical about Korean intellectuals' own surge of interest in Korean cultural tradition during the 1930s. It was widely noted that Korean literary criticism fell into stagnation after the decline of the Proletarian literature movement, the wellspring of Korean literary criticism in the late 1920s and early 1930s, and, as discussed in the previous chapter, two major Korean-language newspapers, *Chosŏn Ilbo* (Korea Daily) and *Tong-A Ilbo* (East Asia Daily), initiated a call to reevaluate Korean cultural tradition.[30] That call was welcomed by intellectuals well beyond the ranks of conservative nationalists, but Ch'oe warned that such a revival would degenerate into an obsession with regressive tastes and their irrational reactionary implications. In particular, he pointed out that ancient treasures and literature alone could not constitute culture. To him, the issue was how Korean tradition could be made to contribute to the development of modern culture in contemporary Korea and eventually to world culture.[31] He believed that contemporary Korean culture should also be anchored in Western cultural traditions, whether Korean traditionalists liked it or not. In a similar vein, he was critical of Yi T'aejun and Chŏng Chiyong, who claimed to value Korean and "Oriental" sentiments over modern intellect in literature.[32] Ch'oe's skepticism about unreflective traditionalism should be seen in the context of his criticism about European totalitarianism, which he saw as based on regressive ethnic nationalism. He reasoned that the most important issue for European intellectuals of the day was how to defend the culture of Shakespeare and Goethe from the politically inspired barbarism that was driving intellectuals into exile and destroying cultural riches crystallized over centuries of strife and wisdom.

In 1939, Ch'oe founded a Korean-language literary journal called *Inmun P'yŏngnon* (Humanities Review), which soon became one of the most influential journals for intellectuals in Korea. He served as editor-in-chief and opened the journal to former socialists such as Kim Namch'ŏn, Im Hwa, and Yi Wŏnjo, who had gone through the infamous process of *tenkō* (ideological conversion) and to a group of intellectuals commonly known as the "philosophy of history" critics, including Sŏ Insik, Sin Namchŏl, Kim Osŏng, and Pak Ch'iu. By offering a new way to look at the relationship between Korea and Japan, the "philosophy of history" critics left a distinct mark on the mindset of Korean intellectuals in the late stages of Japanese colonial rule. Influenced by the Kyōto School conceptualization of world history promoted by Miki, Kōsaka Masaaki, and Kōyama Iwao, these Korean philosophers called for their countrymen to join Japan in "overcoming modernity," which, they saw, was fading out after the completion of its historical task. They welcomed the anticolonial and pro–Asian aspects of the so-called Greater East Asia Co-Prosperity Sphere discourse as a significant challenge to Euro-American hegemony over the world. As examined further below, Ch'oe grounded his justification for Japanese colonial domination in the theoretical foundation offered by the "philosophy of history" critics.

In 1940, Ch'oe himself started advocating Japanese colonialism in his journal. In those writings, he turned sharply away from his previous position stressing the significance of the intellect in literary criticism and the importance of European cultural tradition as the foundation of Korean cultural development. In 1943, he published the book that has been read in postliberation Korea as undisputable evidence of his traitorous collaboration with Japanese colonialism. A collection of literary criticism written in Japanese, *Korean Literature in a Time of Transition* was Ch'oe's justification for the assimilation of Korean literature into Japanese literature. This treatise would serve to condemn him to self-imposed silence for 10 years after the liberation of Korea and to the lifelong stigma of having been a pro–Japanese traitor.[33]

CONSTRAINED BY HISTORY, TAMED BY EVERYDAY LIFE: KOREAN LITERATURE IN A TIME OF TRANSITION

As mentioned above, in *Korean Literature in a Time of Transition,* Ch'oe called for the establishment of a national literature, which would inculcate Koreans with the Japanese national consciousness. What is most conspicuous about Ch'oe's discussion is that his conceptualization of a national consciousness did not rest on a primordial community of common blood. He emphasized that an awareness of common blood or of a community of everyday life alone is inadequate to produce literature because it transmits no value system that can infuse the creative spirit of the writer with concrete meanings and content.[34] He implied that national consciousness is not a feeling of belonging that stems from a primordial folk community but rather a sense of belonging to the people of a nation (*kokumin*) consciously mediated by the state (*kokka*). It goes without saying that to include Koreans in the category of the Japanese nation, Ch'oe, like other ideologues of "Japan–Korea as one body," had no choice but to emphasize that the notion of a nation should not be based on folk or ethnicity.

To understand his argument, it is necessary to clarify how Ch'oe defined national literature. Under total mobilization (*kōdo kokubō taisei,* literally "advanced national defense system"), the task of literature was to unify the nation and raise national morale. Japanese writers naturally subscribed to this theory when war broke out, but this had not been the case in Korea, which, Ch'oe argued, was handicapped by the mentality that national literature served only to instill a feeling of primordial community based on ethnicity or the folk (*minzoku*).[35] The Japanese, of course, automatically had such a sense of community as members of the Japanese ethnicity, but the task at hand, according to Ch'oe, was to awaken Koreans from that folk feeling of Korean nationalism to the reality that they were now subjects of the Japanese state. National literature was to serve that purpose.[36]

Ch'oe demanded that Korean men of letters should simultaneously write about Korea old and new; study Korean goodness, beauty, and sadness; and maintain Korean cultural particularity as part of the Japanese nation. It would not be possible for great national literature to be produced by the mere shallow impulses of discarding Korean tradition to bring alive the slogan of "Japan–Korea as one body." More was required.[37]

Ch'oe next tackled the debate over the use of "local color" by Korean writers. He argued that it is natural they do so in their creative writing, but he cautioned that emphasis on the particularity of Korea should not be abused. He underlined that Korean writers should not blindly imitate their Japanese counterparts in depicting the urban culture of Tokyo because blind imitation would result in degeneration of culture as a whole.[38] The future of Japanese culture should be sought in the totality of cultures rooted in each locality and should emerge from actual life in, and demands of, localities as they were becoming unified by the

Japanese spirit.[39] In that context and that context only could local color and culture make a meaningful contribution to national literature, but he warned that should local color overstep its boundaries and pursue the status of an independent entity, it would turn into an ideology of cultural independence, which, in Ch'oe's view, must be avoided at all costs. Love of a home province could be elevated to patriotism, but, should it grow out of bounds, it could undermine the balance of the whole. By falling into sentimentalism, it could become political and no longer in the realm of literature or culture. He warned that even if a writer were not using local color to fan an ideology of independence among Koreans, readers might interpret the work politically.[40]

Ch'oe's objective in his book, thus, can be summed up as positioning Korean literature and culture within the literature and culture of Japan. More than simply parroting the slogan "Japan–Korea as one body," he was locating a historical necessity arising not only in Japan but also in Europe for subsuming Korean culture within Japanese culture. The rise of such totalitarian movements as fascism and Nazism had sent the world into a seismic transition.[41] The old values of individualism, rationalism, and liberalism rapidly had become impotent in the face of the ontological conditions of human beings bound by nationality and ethnicity. Korean intellectuals were forced by worldwide historical change to realize that to survive the violent struggles among nation states, they did not have any choice but to embrace Japan as the state to which they belonged and to position themselves as a part of the Japanese nation. Thus, it was Ch'oe's analysis of historical developments and not ambition or cowering capitulation that led him to embrace Japanese domination in Asia. In that regard, it is noteworthy that Ch'oe believed an individual should sincerely embrace the realities of daily life rather than subsisting on the abstract ideals of socialism and liberalism, which he saw as the two aspects of cosmopolitanism that denied the essential importance of an individual's identity as part of nation and state.[42] Ch'oe regarded the rise of fascism and Nazism and the ensuing war in Europe and Asia as historical developments that made liberalism and individualism untenable.[43] Thus, he believed the world demanded a new intellectual framework to grapple with the turmoil of the 20th century. He assailed rationalism, liberalism, and individualism as the worldview of modernity, which offered no intellectual guidance for coping with the raging war that was ruthlessly consuming lives and the cultural achievements of humanity.

Ch'oe was not the only thinker critical of modernity in Korea during the late 1930s and the early 1940s. The "philosophy of history" critics, including Sŏ Insik, Sin Namchŏl, Kim Osŏng, and Pak Ch'iu, were drawing on the ideas of younger philosophers of the Kyōto School, such as Miki, Kōsaka, and Kōyama, to attempt to dethrone Europe from its position at the center of world historical development.[44] As mentioned earlier, it was Ch'oe who opened the pages of his journal *Inmun P'yŏngnon* to the Korean philosophy of history critics and thus provided them with a venue for publishing their ideas in the late 1930s. Like the Kyōto School philosophers, they criticized liberalism, rationalism, and capitalism and argued that the world crisis had been brought about by the rise of fascism, the emergence of the philosophy of life (*lebensphilosophie*), and the worldwide economic depression that had shown these European-derived dogmas to be bankrupt.[45] They saw themselves attempting to come up with a new world view to replace old intellectual systems. Ch'oe's critical writings in defense of Japanese colonialism drew on many of their concerns and problematics.

In "an age of total war in which nations enlisted their entire military, economic, and technological capacity to mobilize for survival," Ch'oe considered it futile to preach that human reason was shared equally among all individuals regardless of nationality.[46] He saw history as unfolding according to its own laws. Human beings were not active agents who created history but rather passive participants responding to historical changes that proceeded according to their own laws. Thus, he posited history not as collective events actively made by human beings but as an irrevocable force that moved on its own terms. In short, to Ch'oe, human beings could not actively change history for their own good but rather were relegated to passively responding to its vicissitudes. Individual human beings could not contest history; they had only to accept it. As the early 20th century was the period in which only the strong would survive, Koreans should cast their lot with a strong state rather than struggle to become independent. In fact, Koreans already belonged to a strong state, Japan, whether they liked it or not. Facing up to the fate already determined by history, the individual's task was to live with sincerity (*seijitsu*) under the conditions given. Living sincerely thus involved adaptation to the changing currents of history.

The analysis of history at the root of Ch'oe's argument was that writers should delve into the everyday life of the nation (*kokumin*) and ground literature in the concreteness of everyday life.[47] To some extent, this emphasis was a generic trait of the literature of ideological conversion (*tenkō bungaku*) produced by former leftists in Japan. Such goals of socialism as class equality and liberation from oppression were deemed too abstract to help ordinary people improve their everyday lives. Socialist activists were depicted as incompetents who could not even feed their own families, let alone save society from capitalist tyranny. For example, in his 1937 novel *Seikatsu no Tankyū* (Quest for Life), Shimaki Kensaku described a protagonist who is weary of the abstract ideals his colleagues spouted at college and is literally sick with a disease that he contracted in Tokyo.[48] As he commits himself to working on his father's farm in his hometown, he not only cures his disease but also discovers the true meaning of life. Shimaki's novel was very popular among readers. This tends to validate the thinking of the postwar critic Yoshimoto Takaaki, who has argued that the mass recantations of leftist intellectuals in the 1930s had more to do with their dawning awareness of their alienation from the masses than with state coercion. Yoshimoto contended that the mass conversion was inevitable because the leftists' dogmatic ideology had no applications to the everyday life of the people.[49] In other words, from Yoshimoto's perspective, the separation of socialist ideas from the life of the people mirrored the gulf between leftist intellectuals and the masses.[50]

Japanese conversion literature was not the only intellectual strain of the day that prioritized the concrete reality of everyday life. The contrast between the abstract ideals of leftist intellectuals and the concreteness of everyday life also constituted an important motif in the writer Kim Namch'ŏn's literary works in colonial Korea. Kim wrote stories describing leftist intellectuals' ineptitude at everyday life and their often frustrated endeavors to adapt to the real world.[51] Ch'oe praised one of Kim's short stories "*Tŭngpul*" (Lantern) for its prioritization of the concreteness of everyday life.[52] Ch'oe paid special attention to the main character's dedication to his family. The main character once demanded sacrifice from his family for his selfish literary pursuits. But later he realizes that he should give up his nebulous idea of literature for his family. Ch'oe stressed that the short story describes the journey of the main character from the abstract to the concrete, and argues that beauty is to be found in the daily life of a practical man. Introducing a scene in which the main character concludes a bedtime story for his children by saying, "I want to live," Ch'oe defined the main character as a man who exhausted his youth with abstractness, ideology, and rationalism but has now awakened to the importance of everyday life in his business, home, and family life. [53]

Ch'oe argued that the arena of the quotidian should be depoliticized. He urged other colonial intellectuals who did little while talking much about Korean independence or socialist ideals to find and work on their everyday lives. Thus Ch'oe posited everyday life as an apolitical space that the politics of resistance could not infiltrate.[54] Posing everyday life as an apolitical space was itself reactionary politics, however, because it neutralized any attempt to act out opposition to colonialism in everyday life. What the colonial intellectual was allowed to do instead was to carve out an autonomous space for Korean culture and literature within the Japanese empire in return for collaborating with the Japanese colonial authorities.

In Ch'oe's thinking, the space of everyday life was rigidly territorialized as a national space in which individuals live ordinary lives as members of their nation. While advising writers on how to write national literature that expresses the feelings of the nation, Ch'oe insisted that by breaking away from interiority, they enter "the everyday life of the nation" (*kokumin seikatsu*). He argued that only in the everyday life of the nation can writers empathize with their nation and learn what national sentiment is. Only by so doing can they write national literature, according to Ch'oe.[55]

THE AMBIGUOUS LOCATION OF "KOREAN" CULTURE

There are a number of contrasting and even contradictory polarities within Ch'oe's argument that distract the reader from looking directly at his idea of collaboration. As explicated above, Ch'oe called on Korean writers and poets to produce national literature to facilitate the assimilation of Korean culture into Japanese culture, but at the same time he argued that Korean literature and culture should remain distinct from Japanese culture and literature. He stressed an absolute belief in the Japanese spirit while often grounding his arguments in rational explanations of culture, literature, and the economy. He argued for a national literature to raise Koreans' political consciousness within the Japanese nation. Simultaneously, he set out to defend the autonomy of culture from politics by arguing that national literature should not degenerate into mere propaganda, and he insisted that rigid restrictions should not constrain literary creation. Finally, even though his focus was on Korea and Japan, he argued that his recipe for national literature was applicable to other nations because he saw the historical necessity for national literatures to emerge from historical events in Europe as well as in East Asia.

Those polarities, however, actually maintain the consistency of his arguments. The particularity of Korean culture and literature must be stressed exactly because it was being forcibly assimilated into Japanese culture and literature. He accepted the Japanese spirit on blind faith as a logical leap to compensate for the incompatibility between the colonial reality that Koreans were discriminated against and his demand that Koreans should nonetheless embrace Japan as their state (*kokka*). Writers and poets had no other choice but to cooperate with the Japanese colonial authorities, he posited, because their collaboration would be the only way to preserve a semblance of cultural autonomy from further encroachment by the colonial state. Ch'oe accepted that literature inevitably needs external support, just as "dahlia plants in the garden require staking." In this time of transition, what Korean literature needed most was strong support from outside. Cooperation with the colonial government was a way to achieve the strong external support for Korean literature to survive.[56] At the same time, Ch'oe proudly emphasized that his Japanese-language journal *Kokumin Bungaku* was the only literary journal being published in Korea at the time.[57]

In other words, the existence of the polarities in Ch'oe's writings attest to the compromises he had to make to defend the autonomy of Korean culture without politically opposing Japanese colonialism. At the core of his argument beneath the polarities was the idea that a national literature should be established to raise Japanese national consciousness among Koreans, but it is important to remember that the national consciousness he envisioned is not based on a feeling of belonging to a primordial community of folk, ethnicity, or race, but rather is based on the consciousness that one's fate is contingent on that of the state.[58] Consequently, the national literature he urged Korean writers and poets to produce was literature that enabled Korean readers to realize that they were subjects of the Japanese state and that both Koreans and the Japanese are in the same community of destiny because both belong to the Japanese state. However, Ch'oe not only urged Korean writers and poets to adapt to political change but also implored the Japanese to accept Korea as an integral part of Japan and Korean literature as Japanese literature.

Despite his efforts to position Koreans firmly within the Japanese state, Ch'oe believed he could preserve the particularity of Korean literature within the category of Japanese literature. For example, he did not hesitate even for a second to exclude the Japanese writer Tanaka Hidemitsu's work from Korean literature, even though Tanaka lived in Korea.[59] For Ch'oe, Tanaka's works were not connected to Korea because they have nothing to do with the lives of Koreans in Korea.[60] This rigid demarcation of Korean literature from that literature produced by Japanese writers coexists with his exhortation to subsume the former within the latter. It is not possible to understand Ch'oe's idea of collaboration without grasping this complexity.

At the center of Ch'oe's writings is the double desire of making Korea a part of Japan while simultaneously maintaining its autonomy. His discourse is marked by ambivalence about the location of Korean culture within the Japanese empire. In that sense, it parallels what Homi Bhabha has designated as the ambivalence of colonial discourse, deriving from its strategy of simultaneously disowning and acknowledging difference between the colonizers and the colonized. According to Bhabha, colonial discourse is dependent on fixing racial, cultural, and historical difference onto the colonized and then stigmatizing the resulting identity as inferior to that of the colonizer. At the same time, the colonizer professes that the colonized can be improved and civilized like him. Out of this ambivalence, Bhabha argues, emerges the "mimic man" who is recognizably the same but still different. In Bhabha's theorization, "the mimic man, by virtue of his partial and never complete representation, rearticulates the whole notion of identity and alienates it from essence."[61] Following Bhabha's framing of colonial discourse, one may view Ch'oe as an example of the mimic man, the colonial subject who is the same as, but still different from, the Japanese. A mimic man consciously and unconsciously spoke, wrote, read, thought, and behaved like a Japanese intellectual but was not Japanese. The ambivalence of Ch'oe as a mimic man undermines the fixed identities of the colonized and the colonizers on which the colonial regime leans, according to Bhabha. However, as should be clear by now, the ambivalence Bhabha has located in colonial discourse is not identical to the ambivalence in Ch'oe's writings. It is not the colonizer's fixating gaze but the colonized intellectual's own desire to be on the side of, but at the same time, to differentiate himself from, the colonizer that gives rise to ambivalence. I acknowledge that this colonized's double desire can be seen as a refracted form of the colonizer's gaze. Nevertheless, I insist that it is necessary to hold on to the difference between the colonized's double desire and the colonizer's gaze to gain insight into the colonized's acceptance of colonial dominance. As noted in the preface, I am not interested in appropriating this ambivalence as a site of resistance that subverts the Manichean world view on which colonial dominance depends. I intend rather to unravel Ch'oe's idea of collaboration from its entanglement with the unabashedly conformist rhetoric he used in his writings in defense of Japanese colonial domination and thus to map out the topography of the colonized intellectual's approach to colonial reality.

Ch'oe's project can be simply put as locating Korean culture as a subset of the culture of Japan. The end result that he aimed for was the demarcation of Korean culture as an autonomous space within the culture of the Japanese empire. In a way, Ch'oe inverted the strategy of colonial discourse that simultaneously excludes and includes the colonized. It is the colonized who differentiates his or her culture from the colonizer's while locating it within a new concept of culture of the empire, inclusive of both cultures of the colonized and the colonizer. In this context, it is important to remember that for Ch'oe, Japanese culture is not the culture of the Japanese folk (*Nihon minzoku*) but rather that of "Japan as a state" (*kokka to shite no Nihon*). If a literary work is identified as a part of Korean literature, then it is both Korean and Japanese because Korean culture is a subset of Japanese culture. However the converse is not necessarily true. Even if a literary work is recognized as Japanese literature, it is not necessarily regarded as Korean literature because Japanese literature includes all of the different literatures produced within the Japanese empire.

In sum, Ch'oe deprived Japan, the ethnic community interpellated as *Nihon* (or *Yamato*) *minzoku*, of its centrality and set out to "provincialize" (in Dipesh Chakrabarty's term) the Japanese folk as a part of the totality called the Japanese nation (*Nihon kokumin*), a newly configured political community that was open not only to Koreans and Japanese but also to Taiwanese and any other people within the Japanese empire. Using such reasoning, Ch'oe rejected Korean imitations of Tokyo culture because, to him, Tokyo designated nothing more than a specific locality within the Japanese empire. Its putative centrality as the capital of the Japanese empire did not override the particularity belonging to Korea. Moreover, by arguing that Korean literature was more than just one kind of local literature within Japan, akin to that from Hokkaidō or Kyūshū, Ch'oe insisted that it should be granted the special autonomy proper to its long literary tradition independent from Japan.[62] Opposing those who put Korean literature on a par with Kyūshū or Hokkaidō literature, Ch'oe asserted that Korean literature had more local particularity than its Kyūshū, Tōhoku, or even Taiwanese counterpart. He contended that not only was Korea different from Japan in terms of climate, character, and way of thinking but also it had a long literary tradition of its own. Moreover, he argued, it had different problems and demands. He contended that because Korean literature dealt with the reality and sentiments of everyday life in Korea, it would continue to be quite different from Japanese literature. He suggested it should occupy a position like that of Scottish literature in relation to English literature. Scottish literature is a part of English literature but it has its own character and has made many contributions to the latter. In contrast, Ch'oe pointed out that Irish literature, although it is largely written in English, has an anti-British cast. He insisted that Korean literature should not follow the Irish lead in relation to Japan.[63]

Never allowing himself to cry in despair that Korean literature was doomed to extinction or complete absorption into Japanese literature, Ch'oe proposed another vision: By retaining the originality of their own literature, Koreans should contribute to the construction of a new Japanese culture.[64]

The title of his book, however, poignantly betrays the aporia that haunts Ch'oe's view of the new Japanese national culture and literature as inclusive of local cultures and literatures within the empire. Ch'oe did not title his book *Tenkanki no Kokumin Bungaku* (National Literature in a Time of Transition) but rather *Tenkanki no Chōsen Bungaku* (Korean Literature in a Time of Transition). It goes without saying that without the modifier *Chōsen* (Korean), *bungaku* (literature) would be interpreted as *Nihon bungaku* (Japanese literature). To see the point, it suffices to recall that the Japanese critic Aono Suekichi had published a book of literary criticism titled *Tenkanki no Bungaku* (Literature in a Time of Transition) in 1927.[65] Certainly, the leftist politics that inspired Aono's literary criticism were in direct opposition to what Ch'oe expressed in *Korean Literature in a Time of Transition*, which stressed unwavering loyalty to the Japanese state.[66] However, I call attention to the fact that Aono did not modify the title of his book with the adjective "Japanese." In contrast, Ch'oe did need to specify which literature he was discussing. Otherwise, readers could not gauge from the title that the book (which was, after all, written in Japanese) was about Korean literature. One might rightly say that the Japaneseness of literature in Aono's book did not have to be specified because the book was delivered in Japanese. This instant correlation between the Japanese language and Japanese literature already points to the insurmountable difficulty that Ch'oe had to face in placing Korean literature within the sphere of Japanese literature. Korean literature could hardly be dissociated from the Korean language. As long as the Korean language was perceived to be distinct from, but on a par with, the Japanese language, the integration of Korean literature into Japanese literature could not be accomplished. Conversely, even though "Japanese literature" in this context referred to the literature of the Japanese nation (*kokumin*) rather the literature of the Japanese folk (*minzoku*), it still retained the connotation of the literature of the Japanese folk.

Thus, national language was central to establishing a relationship between Korean and Japanese literature in the framework of national literature. Although Ch'oe advocated the unique local color of Korean culture and literature within the culture of the Japanese empire, as discussed earlier, he expressed an unequivocal view that Japanese should replace Korean gradually as the medium of literary expression in colonial Korea.[67] If Japanese took the place of Korean as the literary language for Korean writers and poets, what would make Korean literature distinct from general literature—that is, Japanese literature—which was generalized enough not to carry any modifier, as in Aono's book title? While arguing that Korean literature as national literature should be part of Japanese literature, Ch'oe did not present any concrete ideas about how to put the principle into practice in creative writing other than emphasizing the importance of everyday life in which writers could learn the sentiment of the nation.

Regardless of Ch'oe's view on what would become of Korean literature, Korean language literature would linger until the Korean language was completely replaced by Japanese, as called for by colonial policy. Even though the number of literary works in Korean was steadily dwindling as more and more writers and poets wrote in Japanese under the pressure of the colonial authorities, the majority of writers and poets either continued to write in Korean or stopped publishing at once for various reasons. Their silence cannot be explained only by a nationalistic allegiance to the Korean language. First of all, there were discrepancies among Korean writers in their levels of Japanese fluency. As the literary historian Kim Yunsik pointed out, although most intellectuals in Korea were bilingual, only a small number of them were actually capable of producing literary works in Japanese.[68] For those Korean writers who were handicapped by their limited Japanese fluency, the replacement of Korean by Japanese as the dominant literary language meant the end of their literary careers. The Japanese colonial authorities and their propagandists like Ch'oe recognized that the complete replacement of Korean by Japanese was a long term project and would not be accomplished soon.[69] Accordingly, the journal *Kokumin Bungaku* that Ch'oe founded and managed continued to publicize as late as 1942 that it planned to regularly issue Korean-language literary collections even after it had decided to publish the monthly exclusively in Japanese and abandon its initial schedule of four issues per year in Korean and the rest in Japanese. In the announcement of the end of the Korean-language issues, Ch'oe argued that national literature in the genuine sense should be written in Japanese, but at the same time, he insisted that the journal's decision aimed not to put an end to Korean-language literature but instead to encourage intellectuals to take the initiative in the everyday use of Japanese. [70]

Thus, in Ch'oe's aspirations, "Korean literature in a time of transition" belonged to a liminal state in which Korean-language literature was gradually being replaced by a literature that was firmly integrated into Japanese literature through the exclusive use of Japanese as the medium of literary expression. It was only through translation that the difference between Korean literature in the present, which was primarily written in Korean, and the national literature that was to come in the future, which would be written exclusively in Japanese, could be instantly transcended. As a consequence, one form of transitional Korean literature advocated by Ch'oe was literature in translation from Korean into Japanese. As a matter of fact, as early as 1936, he had begun translating Korean stories into Japanese.[71]

Two chapters of *Korean Literature in a Time of Transition* were Ch'oe's own Japanese translations of two earlier essays he had originally written in Korean. In a sense, the translations can be seen as another example of his attempts to put his idea of national literature into practice. Ironically, however, minuscule differences between the original articles and the translations foreshadow the inevitable failure of his attempts. When reading the original articles and the translated chapters side by side, the reader can detect a subtle difference in the assumed readership between the originals and the translations. In lieu of conclusion, I show the ways in which such one difference destabilized Ch'oe's framing of Korean culture and literature under the category of the Japanese national culture and literature and interrupted his ultimate endeavor to establish an autonomous space for Korean culture within the Japanese empire.

TRANSLATING DIFFERENCE

Ch'oe wrote most of the essays included in *Korean Literature in a Time of Transition* in Japanese, but the first two chapters were his own translations into Japanese of articles he had first published two years earlier, in 1941, in his Korean-language literary journal *Inmun Pyŏngnon*. The first chapter, "*Tenkanki no Bunka Riron*" (Cultural Theory in a Time of Transition), was a Japanese translation of an essay that Ch'oe previously had published in Korean under a slightly different title, "*Chŏnhyŏnggi ŭi Munhwa Iron*" (Cultural Theory in a Time of Change).[72] In the essay, Ch'oe criticizes both the popular understanding of culture as the pursuit of the Western lifestyle and intellectuals' privileging of culture as an absolutely autonomous realm insulated from secular life and politics—the two tendencies he perceived to be dominant in Japan and Korea during the 1920s and 1930s. Ch'oe goes on to call for a new culture firmly rooted in the nation state to replace modern culture, which, in his view, would be based on rationalism, individualism, and cosmopolitanism.

The second chapter, *"Bungaku Seishin no Tenkan"* (Shift in Literary Spirit), was a critical essay in which Ch'oe traced the cause of the ongoing cultural crisis to the world historical transition that resulted from conflicts among nations and states in the late 1930s and early 1940s. Ch'oe argued that such a seismic change in history invalidated modern literature and its ideological underpinning—individualism—and called for a new literary spirit connected to the nation state. Its Japanese title was the literal translation of *"Munhak Chŏngsin ŭi Chŏnhwan,"* the title of the original Korean language essay.[73]

Ch'oe's criticism of modernity and cosmopolitanism in both essays was in tune with the dominant Japanese discourse of the late 1930s and early 1940s, which denounced the cosmopolitan tendencies in Japanese society of earlier decades.[74] The ascendancy of cosmopolitanism and its association with commercialism in interwar Japanese popular culture provoked anxiety among intellectuals over the Japanese national identity.[75] Because cosmopolitanism was based on a belief in universal culture, a growing number of intellectuals felt anxious about the potential threat that such universalism posed to the national subjectivity. Many Japanese intellectuals began to critically reflect on the universalist implications of cosmopolitanism for the Japanese national identity in reaction to the ascendancy of cosmopolitanism during the 1920s.

Whereas Japanese cosmopolitanism between the wars aligned Japanese civilization with that of the West on the basis of universalism, the growing anxiety over such cosmopolitanism led many intellectuals to perceive Japan as becoming culturally colonized by the West. On the other hand, both Japanese cosmopolitanism and anxiety over it did not take serious account of Japan's relationship with its colonies in their schemas of Japanese cultural identity with respect to the West. It would not be an unjustified exaggeration to say that Japanese intellectual discourse on cultural identity remained oblivious of Japan's colonies until the early 1940s, when the Japanese government needed support for war efforts from its colonies and pressed intellectuals to embrace the idea of the unity between Japan and its colonies.

In the early 1930s, the Japanese state stepped up persecution of the

Proletarian Literature Movement that had dominated Japanese literary circles since the 1920s. Under pressure from the state, a majority of leftist intellectuals recanted their political beliefs.

As briefly discussed in Chapter 2, following the ideological conversion (*tenkō*) of leftist intellectuals, those associated with the Japan Romantic School expressed their concern about the rapid ascendancy of mass culture accompanying the economic boom after World War I and its degenerative effect on society. The commodification of culture was regarded as a result of a modernization, which was equated in Japan with westernization. Therefore, anti–Western sentiments in Japan were embedded in criticism of the commodification of culture. More and more Japanese intellectuals ranging from the communist Takakura Teru to the cultural conservative Yasuda Yojūrō deemed Western modernity to be a threat to the indigenous tradition of Japan. They saw Japanese culture being colonized by modern culture, which they conflated with Western culture and commodification. The Japanese intellectuals came to regard the creation of literary works that confirmed the Japanese national identity as the only cure for the malaise of modern culture. This was what they called *kokumin bungaku*.

Since the Meiji Restoration, Japanese intellectuals had been educated in the tradition of the European humanities. However, many Japanese intellectuals began to think that modern Japanese culture was a mere copy of Western culture and came to believe that the copy could never match up to the original, let alone exceed it. Many Japanese intellectuals felt their culture was an inferior translation of the original text, and lamented that they had let their own tradition be subsumed in a copy of Western culture. Such critics as Asano Akira and Yasuda thus denounced modern Japanese literature since the Meiji Restoration as the product of parasitic intellectuals detached from the Japanese nation (*kokumin*). These intellectuals called on writers to create a new literature grounded in a conceptualization of a Japanese nation. As Japan's aggression in the Asian continent escalated into the war against America and Britain, Asano and Yasuda came to see the conflict as an opportunity to recover "the spirit of the opening of the nation."[76] However, the national literature debate cannot be dismissed as merely the expression of an absurdly fanatic nationalism. As discussed above, the anxieties of intellectuals of different stripes intersected at the point of trying to figure out how to cope with the loss of tradition and how to overcome the threat of modernity posed by the alien civilization of the West. The remedy they proposed was to anchor literature in a fixed foundation that could not be undermined by the incessant churning of modernity. Despite disparities in their arguments, those participating in the national literature debate agreed that Japanese literature should be based on *kokumin* (the people of the nation or the nation).

The concept of a national literature depended on the ability to define the nation. *Kokumin* is usually translated into English as "nation," while a similar term, *jinmin*, is translated as the "people" in general. However, the two words were used interchangeably to refer to the people of Japan during the Meiji period. As seen in the Chinese compound, *kokumin*, the word defines people in relation to the country or state (*kuni*) in contrast to *jinmin*, which lacks such a connection. As a consequence, more weight is placed on people than on the state in *jinmin*. That might be why socialists and leftists frequently used the word *jinmin* to describe the people in opposition to the established order and the government in such cases as *jinmin sensen* (popular front), *jinminshugi* (populism), and so on. In that sense, *jinmin* is the opposite of *kokka* (state) or *seifu* (government).

Another word often used in prewar Japan was *shinmin*. Although its literal meaning is closer to the English term "imperial subject," *shinmin* also referred to the people of Japan, because they all, under the Meiji constitution of 1889, were the subjects of the emperor. The term often appeared in imperial edicts. As the intellectual historian Yun Kŏnch'a has pointed out, even though such Meiji intellectuals as Tokutomi Sōhō popularized the term *kokumin* as opposed to *shinmin*, the Meiji state curtailed the liberal aspects of *kokumin* and interpellated the Japanese as the subjects of the state.[77]

According to the social linguist Kyōgoku Okikazu, *jinmin* was predominantly used in the early Meiji and was especially popular among those who were participants in the Freedom and People's Rights Movement. In contrast, *kokumin* gained currency beginning in the mid–Meiji period as the government tried to foster strong loyalty to the state, and more and more Japanese intellectuals gravitated toward nationalism.[78] It was at this same time that the Meiji intellectual Takayama Chogyū (1871–1902) called for the establishment of a national literature (*kokumin bungaku*) to revitalize the Japanese spirit. The nationalism of the mid–Meiji period turned on the predominant use of the concept *kokumin*.

There is another problematic word that must be clarified with respect to its relationship with the term *kokumin*. The English word nation can be translated into Japanese as either *minzoku* or *kokumin*. Whereas *kokumin* emphasizes the people's relationship with the state, *minzoku* gives more weight to the ethnic aspect of nation. The two terms, however, were used interchangeably throughout the 1930s and 1940s. Nonetheless, such Japanese scholars as the sociologist Usui Jishō endeavored to establish a more rigorous distinction between *minzoku* and *kokumin*. In April 1937, the prominent intellectual journal *Shisō* published a special issue on the concept of nation. In the issue, Usui characterized *minzoku* as a community based on culture while defining *kokumin* as the subjects of the state. In the same issue, the economist Yanaihara Tadao saw *minzoku* rooted in culture. And the historian Imai Tōshiki pointed to *minzoku* as the folk based on culture and *kokumin* as the nation subjected to the state.[79]

All of these efforts to distinguish *minzoku* from *kokumin* reflected the political reality of an empire within which not only the Japanese but also other peoples (*minzoku*) were subjects of the state. On the other hand, in his book *Minzokuron* (The Theory of Minzoku), Takata Yasuma (1883–1972) stated that *kokumin* was a modern form of *minzoku*. He argued that whereas *minzoku* was a passively formed community based on tradition, *kokumin* was an actively formed community based on the conscious goals and ideals held by its members. At any rate, there was a loosely shared assumption among Japanese intellectuals that *minzoku* was a cultural community based on tradition whereas *kokumin* was a political community associated with the state.[80]

Such categorization of nation as a political community raises questions about the Japanese national literature debate of the 1930s and 1940s. As briefly mentioned above, the discourse on national literature lacked any substantial deliberation on the colonized, who were not ethnically Japanese but nonetheless were politically subject to the Japanese empire. On the surface, the West was deployed in the debate as the other against which the Japanese nation is defined. The Japanese intellectuals who engaged in the national literature debate thought that modernity pushed Japan into discarding tradition and culturally colonized Japan. Because modernity was also associated with the West, the intellectuals' discourse on national literature was built on the dichotomy between the West and Japan.

Ch'oe's essays eerily repeated such Japanese criticism of modernity and cosmopolitanism, silencing significant differences between Japan and its colony Korea in their relationships with the West and with modernity and cosmopolitanism, which were after all introduced to Korea primarily through Japan during the colonial period. In that sense, Korea's relationship with the West from which both modernity and cosmopolitanism originated was even more complicated than Japan's. In the minds of most Korean intellectuals, modernity was associated not only with the West but also with Japan. To such Korean intellectuals as the modernist poet Yi Sang, Japan was another source of cosmopolitan modernism, not a mere copy of a Western cosmopolitan metropolis.[81] As a consequence, when Korean intellectuals denounced modernity and cosmopolitanism and advocated a return to tradition, the target of such criticism could be extended beyond the West to Japan as briefly discussed in the previous chapter.

The way in which the term national literature (*kokumin bungaku*) gained currency for the first time in Korea clearly suggests the difference between Japan and Korea. As discussed in the previous chapter, in reaction to the rise of proletarian literature in the 1920s, a group of non-socialist, nationalist intellectuals emphasized the importance of Korean cultural tradition in literary creation and called for a national literature. They believed that the rise of proletarian literature and its emphasis on class conflict undermined the unity of Korean society. The intellectuals also felt that a national literature would help raise Korean consciousness to withstand pressures to imitate Japan's mimicry of Western culture. Preserving Korean cultural tradition was at the center of their argument. Needless to say, in this case, nation referred to the Korean ethnic nation.

However, Ch'oe kept silent on such differences. He mentioned cursorily that the entirety of Japanese culture was in crisis, and so was Korean culture. He did not even attempt to deliberate similarities between Japan and Korea as non–Western societies whose traditions were being encroached on by menacing Western cultural influence disguised as universal culture as if he felt that such an emphasis on similarities between Japan and Korea would be redundant. Ch'oe seems to have believed the fact that Korea was politically part of the Japanese empire obviated any justification for his conflation between the colonizer and the colonized.

When Ch'oe called for a return to tradition in opposition to cosmopolitanism by following the dominant view of Japanese discourse on national identity, however, his emphasis on the importance of tradition suddenly destabilized his conflation between Japan and Korea. Although the interruption was momentary and compromised in the original text, its destabilizing effect on Ch'oe's overall conflation of Japan and Korea was much more pronounced in the Japanese translation of the essay. In the original Korean-language essay, Ch'oe wrote,

> If turning our eyes back onto ourselves, [we will realize that] we, having left the house of our tradition, have wandered on the grounds of the houses of others not like us. We mistook the extremely superficial imitation of the Western lifestyle for culture life (*munhwa*

> *saenghwal* in Korean; *bunka seikatsu* in Japanese). Even those who inwardly despised such vulgarization of culture saw the home of their heart in "the ether of cosmopolitanism" and wandered around without connecting to solid ground.[82]

Echoing Japanese intellectuals' poignant nostalgia for lost tradition as exemplarily expressed by the poet Hagiwara Sakutarō in his 1938 essay "Return to Japan" (*Nihon e no Kaiki*), Ch'oe called on his readers to embrace tradition by establishing a new culture rooted in the nation state.[83] However, he did not specify what or even which tradition his readers should return to, although his readers could conjecture that the tradition Ch'oe was talking about was Korean tradition, because it is fairly clear that he assumed all of his readers to be Korean.

Ch'oe often used the first person plural pronoun we (*uri*) throughout the essays. A *we* is ostensibly used to invoke an emotive as well as an intellectual community imaginarily formed between the author and his readers. Although any author can and must have a target readership in mind before and while writing, this we need not be imagined as a homogeneous community ethnically, racially, or even linguistically because texts can be translated into other languages. As mentioned earlier, it is quite clear that Ch'oe considered his readers of his original Korean-language essay to be Korean. For example, when criticizing the popular understanding of culture as the superficial imitation of the Western lifestyle, Ch'oe took *munhwa chut'aek* (*bunka jūtaku,* culture housing), the Japanese and Western mixed-style housing, as an example of such a misconception of culture:

> What mode of life has so-called culture life indicated since the Taishō period? What springs to our mind first is culture housing. *Since it is basically Japanese-West mixed-style housing, the Korean style must be added to it when we build it.* There must be a gas oven in the kitchen and a radio and a gramophone in the living room. Every member of the family, dressed principally in Western-style clothes, drinks coffee and black tea. The husband and wife go to the movies once a week and generally hold a liberal attitude toward their children's education, decisively turning against old customs and tradition, but they lack any discipline or principle in their life. Their only personality trait is cheap hedonism. Thus, the culture life is an extremely superficial imitation of the Western-style way of life at the service of cheap pleasure taken to an extreme. At the same time, the real facts of the culture life are the ignorance of, and pretended disinterest toward, real daily life and the more important aspects of tradition.[84]

As seen in his cynical caricature of the culture life presented above, Ch'oe addressed Koreans as "we," seeming to take it for granted that a community formed between him and his readers through the interpellation of "we," the first-person plural pronoun, was exclusive to Koreans as the Korean-style added to culture housing was inseparably connected to the we in the phrase in question.

Ch'oe faithfully rendered this part of the essay in his Japanese translation, with one significant exception. "Since it is basically Japanese-West mixed-style housing, the Korean style must be added to it *when we build it"* (*uri ŭi sonŭro chiŭlt'aeen*) in the original was altered in the translation to read "since it is basically Japanese-West mixed style housing, the Korean style is naturally added to it *on the peninsula* (*hantō no baai*)."[85] The we in the original text is erased in the translated passage, and instead it is replaced with the peninsula. Human subjectivity inscribed in the we is suppressed in the replacement, the peninsula, which is the name of a geographical object as seen from the Japanese archipelago. In that sense, through translation, Koreans are doubly objectified; first, they are deprived of the first person plural we; and second, they are metonymically replaced with an object, the peninsula, which also figures in the pejorative "*hantōjin*" or "peninsulars," the meaning of which can be made out only in opposition to "*naichijin*," the people of the Japan proper, in other words, the real Japanese people. In short, at this specific moment in the Japanese translation, Ch'oe did not take it for granted that his readers were Korean as he had in the original Korean-language text.

The community established between the author and his readers through the interpellation of we in the Japanese translation includes anyone able to read the Japanese text. The assumed readership includes the Japanese, who are signified in opposition to the peninsula, which in turn stands in metonymically for the Korean people. When readers juxtaposed this replacement and displacement of Koreans with Ch'oe's call for a return to tradition, they surely felt that the meaning of "our tradition" to which Ch'oe urged his readers to return is undecidable in Derrida's sense. To which tradition was he urging his readers to return? Because his readers were not limited to Koreans, it was unclear whether the tradition was Korean or Japanese, or even that of East Asia as a whole, which would subsume both.

Indeed, there is the possibility that the tradition might refer to something other than Korean tradition per se because the essays advocate the establishment of a new culture on the basis of the nation state with Japan being the state to which Koreans belong. In some of his essays originally written in Japanese, Ch'oe argued that Korean intellectuals should immerse themselves in Japanese cultural tradition by studying such historical and literary classics as the *Kojiki* and *Manyōshū*, as well as such works of the 18th-century "nativist learning" scholar Motoori Norinaga, including his *Kojikiden* (Commentary on the Records of Ancient Matters), *Naobi no Mitama* (The Rectifying Spirit), and *Tamagatsuma* (Wicker Basket). On the other hand, as mentioned earlier, Ch'oe urged Korean writers to continue writing about Korea, old and new, and to maintain the Korean cultural particularity. His treatises on Japanese national literature bristle with contrasting polarities, which actually work to maintain the consistency of his arguments that are at pains to carve out a space for Korean culture within the Japanese empire. The difficulty in determining the meaning of tradition certainly comes not least from Ch'oe's use of polarities. But there is a more fundamental issue implicated in the indeterminacy of the meaning of tradition.[86]

Strictly speaking, there would be no logical inconsistency even if Ch'oe had Japanese tradition in mind when he was calling on his Korean readers to return to tradition, because, in his framing, Korean tradition could be considered a subset of Japanese tradition inasmuch as Korean culture was deemed to be part of Japanese culture. As seen in his title *Korean Literature in a Time of Transition,* however, there remained ambivalence in Ch'oe's thinking on the relationship between Japan and Korea. Japan retained residues of the primordial community of Japanese folk rather than the community of the higher order, the Japanese state. It is not always clear whether the sign Japan signified the primordial ethnic community or the political community mediated by the state. In other words, Japan is an oscillating signifier whose meaning is undecidable. This undecidability interrupted Ch'oe's discursive project of subsuming the Korean people into Japan, the meaning of which was intended to be fixed onto "the Japanese state." In his attempt to ward off the undecidability, Ch'oe deployed nation (*kokumin*) as a sphere inclusive of both Koreans and Japanese to unravel the tenacious conflation of ethnic Japan and the Japanese state. The slippage between Japan as the ethnic group and another Japan as the political collectivity parallels the incongruence of the first-person plural we between the original Korean text and Ch'oe's own Japanese translation.

Korean (*Chōsen*) in the book title is itself haunted by undecidability. It is undecidable whether the adjective is related to Korea as a primordial community irrespective of the Japanese state or as an ethnic group bound by blood but firmly subsumed into the Japanese nation. The signification of Korea exceeds the meaning that Ch'oe deemed desirable. As mentioned above, in urging writers to moderate the use of Korean local color in their creative writing, Ch'oe warned that writers' emphasis on Koreanness might mislead readers into interpreting their works as signaling a political message of support for Korean independence. The warning marked his anxiety over the undecidability of Korean, which destabilized his framing of Korea as part of the Japanese empire politically as well as culturally and thus enabled his own advocacy of the particularity of Korean culture to register as a subversive message. In that sense, the book *Korean Literature in a Time of Transition* was ultimately an attempt to exorcise the undecidability of Korea by redefining Korean literature as an integral part of Japanese literature. Needless to say, the attempt was anything but successful as seen in the undecidability of the meaning of tradition.

The Korean in the book's title resonates with the undecidability of Japan, the meaning of which oscillates between Japan as the community of higher order inclusive of Koreans and other colonized peoples within the Japanese empire and as the primordial ethnic community exclusive to the Japanese people. Korean in the title simultaneously masks and traces the lack of transparent significance of Japanese as distinct from Korean. In that sense, Korean literature in Ch'oe's title is a Derridean supplement to Japanese literature.[87] As a Derridean supplement, it is distinct from but simultaneously subordinate to Japanese literature, the literature of the ethnic Japanese, which does not need to be particularized as seen in Aono's book title. On the other hand, Korean literature registers as something necessary to make Japanese literature complete so that the latter can become the literature of the Japanese empire, which ultimately must be inclusive of Korean literature and Taiwanese literature along with the Japanese literature of the Japanese folk. Thus, Korean literature simultaneously portends the presence of Japanese literature, as in the literature of the Japanese folk, and traces the lack of it, as in the literature of the Japanese empire. In other words, Japanese literature emerges at the moment when Korean literature is placed in juxtaposition to it. This dynamic inevitably establishes a hierarchical relationship between Korean literature and Japanese literature. Japanese literature is thus assumed to be the standard against which the value of Korean literature is judged. Moreover, the hierarchy in discourse mirrors the hierarchical relationship between the colonizer and the colonized in colonial society.

Ch'oe's attempt to frame the particularity of Korean culture as the fence to protect its autonomous space was parasitically dependent on the hierarchical structure of colonial society. The parasitic dependence was clearly revealed at the moment Ch'oe argued that Korean literature advanced the theory of national literature further than its Japanese counterpart because Japanese loyalty to the Japanese state was a given.[88] Japanese ethnicity automatically ensured the allegiance of those identified as the Japanese folk (*minzoku*) to the Japanese state. Needless to say, not only was the end goal for Koreans to become part of the Japanese nation (*kokumin*) temporally placed in the future when Koreans' allegiance to the Japanese state would no longer be questioned, but the model of the Japanese nation for Koreans was also spatially assigned to the Japanese folk (*minzoku*) whose loyalty did not need to be interrogated as rigorously as that of Koreans. Ch'oe's deployment of nation was thus destined to preserve the colonial order that prioritized the Japanese folk over Koreans, despite his intention to neutralize the centrality of Japanese folk by using the term nation, exactly because he never intended to challenge the legitimacy of colonial domination. Instead, he intended to beg for as much autonomy for Korean culture as the Japanese colonial authorities would allow.

Unlike the many other Korean intellectuals who halfheartedly collaborated with the Japanese colonial government when being forced to commit themselves to the Japanese colonial policy of assimilation, Ch'oe tackled the contradictions brought about by the assimilation policy in the late stage of Japanese colonial rule over Korea. Ch'oe's writings centered on two contradictions: that between the autonomy of culture from politics and the supremacy of politics over culture and that between Korea as a cultural community distinct from Japan and Korea as a political community subject to the Japanese state. However, Ch'oe never attempted to overcome the contradictions politically even though they were rooted in the politics of colonization and the ensuing assimilation policy. Instead, he struggled to deal with them aesthetically by calling for the establishment of national literature. Needless to say, the irony was that his endeavors in the realm of aesthetics to establish a new national culture and literature not only ensued from the political demands of the assimilation policy but also colluded with the politics of colonial domination.

4. Translation and Its Postcolonial Discontents

The Postwar Controversy over Tōma Seita's Reading of Kim Soun's Japanese Translations of Korean Poetry

It was a chilling moment in Japanese literary circles in 1956 when the translator Kim Soun attacked an ostensibly sympathetic reading of his own new collection of Korean poetry in Japanese translation, an expansion of a series of colonial-era anthologies dating back to 1940. Kim, the preface to whose earlier collection of Korean folksongs in Japanese translation was by Kitahara Hakushū and was discussed in the introduction, opened his scathing denunciation of commentaries published in 1954 by the renowned Japanese historian Tōma Seita (1913–): "I feel it even more difficult to offer corrections and explanations to wild speculation and dogma held by a historian especially because they do not derive from his ill will but come shrouded in good will for the Korean nation."[1] The language of Kim's response was harsh and judgmental throughout, and even sarcastic at times. Such a hostile response from Kim must have been disconcerting to Tōma, given that his essays held the Korean poetry in high regard. What was it that so incensed Kim, whose translations of Korean folk songs, children's songs, and modern poetry during the colonial period earned him respect and a reputation as the authoritative guide and consummate translator of Korean culture and literature in the Japanese language? The chapter delves into that question, which, as demonstrated below, requires an examination of a series of additional questions concerning history, representation, literature, translation, nationalism, and modernity in the context of Japanese colonialism in Korea.

A prominent Marxist historian specializing in ancient Japanese history, Tōma is best known for his endeavor to raise a national consciousness conducive to a democratic society by proposing during the postwar period a new national history centered on the Japanese people (the *minzoku,* or ethnic nation) rather than the state or ruling elite. He hoped that such a national history would not only refute the right-wing chauvinist history dominant in prewar and wartime Japan but also lead the Japanese masses to rally against what postwar Japanese leftists saw as American imperialist hegemony in East Asia.

In 1954, Tōma ventured outside of his vocational realm and wrote a series of essays titled "Notes on Korean Poetry." In his view, the Korean poems, which were written during the colonial period and subsequently collected in Kim's *Korean Poetry Anthology*, could be read as allegories of the Korean people's plight under Japanese rule. Tōma especially valued the collective national identity expressed by the modern Korean poems and reasoned that modern Korean poetry represented the sentiments of the Korean people because it carried on literary traditions from premodern folksongs that had also shown the Korean people's resilience to oppression by the ruling classes.

Tōma deemed "hometown" (*furusato*) to be a recurring theme running through a number of Korean poems in the anthology and held this emphasis up as proof that Korean intellectuals and poets had not lost contact with their people. Moreover, in Tōma's eyes, in the Koreans' nostalgia for the hometown and laments for the irrevocable changes brought to their native land during the colonial period, the poems told allegorically of the people's suffering under Japanese colonial rule. Tōma found modern Japanese poetry, in contrast with Korean poetry, lacking such a thematic emphasis on hometown, a sign of the breakdown of the symbolic linkages between intellectuals and the masses.

While upholding modern Korean poetry over its Japanese counterpart for thematic emphasis on the hometown, however, Tōma hardly touched on the Korean poems' literary value. When he did, he mentioned rather dismissively that they were rustic and unsophisticated (*soboku*) compared to stylistically better crafted modern Japanese poetry. In response, Kim blamed Tōma for simplistically reducing literature to history. In Kim's view, Tōma's reading violently reduced the lyrical poems into easily understood reflections of Koreans' colonial experience. Indeed, in his essays, Tōma did not give due thought to the stylistic quality of the Korean poems because he was reading them for their references to history, crudely assuming that words and phrases from the poems correspond transparently to historical facts and events outside of the textual realm.

On the other hand, it can also be argued that because the Korean poems listed in the 1953 *Korean Poetry Anthology* were written during the colonial period, the conflicts and contradictions of colonial society could not help but have affected the ways in which these literary works were written, no matter how tenuous that influence might have been. One can further argue that colonial experience should be the ultimate hermeneutical horizon on which literary interpretation of colonial literature is located. Because the oppressive mechanisms of colonial rule permeated every nook of colonized society, including its cultural realm, the history of colonial experience lies latent under the surface of every text. Thus, even if a text does not stand in transparent referential relation to colonial history, its narrative nevertheless tells the reader about colonial reality refracted in it. Kim sweepingly denied the possibility of reading colonial history into the poems, however, calling attention to the persistent problem of the relationship between history and literature.

Tōma's reading was especially egregious in Kim's eyes because what he saw as Tōma's misinterpretations relied exclusively on Kim's own translations into Japanese. Tōma knew no Korean. The problem of translation loomed even larger than Kim insisted and Tōma realized. Kim often took the liberty of rendering poems so far beyond usual limits set on translators that many of his translations would easily make Japanese–Korean bilingual readers raise their eyebrows if they were to compare the originals with his translations.[2] Drawing on conventional Japanese poetic diction, Kim often replaced original expressions with his own, expunged words without providing alternatives, and even added entirely new words to his translations. Kim defended his method, saying that to communicate the spirit of the original poems to Japanese readers he had to sacrifice literalness and alter the sense of the originals because irreducible difference in language and culture between Japan and Korea prevented literal translation from conveying the poetic sentiments of the originals.

Kim's tendency for liberal translation is pertinent to a discussion of Tōma's controversial interpretations especially because the historian's first essay on the 1953 *Korean Poetry Anthology* pivoted on Kim's own expressions, which he inserted in his Japanese translations, critical alterations of the original poems that Tōma did not have the linguistic abilities to detect. Despite his righteous condemnations of what he saw as Tōma's misreadings of the poems, Kim himself did not say a word about his own intentional mistranslations even though it was his alterations that provided Tōma with motifs for reading the Korean poems as the national allegory of Koreans' plight under Japanese rule. Tōma's absolute dependence on translation in appreciating the poems and Kim's troubling silence on his amendments raises the question about what makes translation felicitous in colonial and postcolonial contexts. This question of translation is another focus of discussion in this chapter.

The chapter examines the theoretical implications of the issues raised by the debate between Tōma and Kim through Fredric Jameson's 1986 essay "Third-World Literature in the Era of Multinational Capitalism."[3] Even at a cursory glance, Tōma's reading of modern Korean poetry echoes Jameson's contentious essay in which Jameson suggested that the literature of non–Western, former colonies should be read as national allegory. As shown by Aijaz Ahmad's trenchant criticism, Jameson's essay has been criticized for its problematic demarcation of the so-called Third World, its indiscriminate grouping of vastly diverse bodies of literature under the single rubric of "Third-World literature," and its reductive reading of "Third-World" literature as the allegory of non–Western peoples' collective experience with colonialism.[4]

Jameson himself was well aware that his approach risked positing differences of the other. Invoking Edward Said's *Orientalism*, he conceded that his argument could not help "othering" non–Western literature. In other words, Jameson knew well that his advocacy for Third-World literature as national allegory could not help but commit the epistemological violence of appropriating the radical difference of the other even though it was intended to affirm rather than deny the value of non–Western literature. Jameson suggested there are only two options available to Western intellectuals when encountering Third-World literature: They can either approvingly recognize its difference or unreflectively evaluate it against Western cultural standards. He was willing to take the risk of appropriating the radical difference of Third-World literature through recognition of its value rather than repeating the mistake of evaluating it against conventional standards based in Western liberal and humanistic universalism.

The fundamental issue of representation lies at the core of the problem that pervades Jameson's discussion on Third-World literature, and it is not easily resolved. Nevertheless, the difficulty in tackling the issue should not lead to settling for either the domestication of the other's radical difference or a return to liberal and humanistic universalism. Envisioning an alternative is another thread of this chapter's argument. To look beyond the two modalities to which Jameson confined himself in encountering the other, I interject Emmanuel Levinas, who criticized Western philosophy for violating the radical difference of the other and assimilating it into the same.

It cannot be stressed enough that my intention in this chapter is not to dismiss the sincerity of progressive Japanese intellectuals in their attempt to align the Japanese with other Asian peoples. I rather call attention to a blind spot in their attempt to emulate the nationalism of the formerly colonized and to reconfigure Japanese nationalism for progressive causes. More specifically, I critique the Japanese leftist intellectuals' lack of attention to the difference between Japan and Korea in their alignment with Korean nationalism. In other words, I intend not to demean the Japanese leftist intellectuals' sincere endeavors to establish solidarity with Koreans but to examine their failure to uphold the otherness of Koreans in their endeavors. Furthermore, I emphasize that failure to recognize the alterity of the other is not limited to the particular historical moment of postwar Japanese leftist nationalism. I bring in Fredric Jameson's thesis on Third-World literature to discussion exactly because I want to highlight the persistent difficulty of upholding the alterity of the other when progressive intellectuals positively evaluate the cultures of formerly colonized nations. As briefly mentioned earlier and further discussed later, the problem lies at the center of the issue of representation itself. By invoking Levinasian ethics, which urges reflection on the violence inherent in representation and restraint from violating the alterity of the other, I argue that only the radical insistence on ethicality in one's relationship with the other can serve as a guide out of the pitfalls that beleaguer progressive intellectuals when they attempt to ally themselves with the formerly colonized.

To be sure, as noted in my preface, Levinas was unwilling to identify actual colonized peoples, especially the victims of the Israeli state's violence, as the other. Furthermore, his indifference to cultures outside the West makes one hesitant to invoke him to critique colonial and postcolonial texts and contexts.[5] Nevertheless, his relentless concern for the alterity of the other merits attention partly because it is inspiration to see the ethical issues lying at the center of the epistemological problem of representation. In other words, his concern demands his readers realize that ethics is the first philosophy, preceding epistemology, ontology, and politics. The Levinas I invoke in the chapter is more Levinasian than Levinas himself, because he hesitated to condemn the violence of the Israeli state and refused to identify Palestinian refugees as an other. It is instead a proper name, which exceeds the person to whom the name is attached. It is Levinasian thinking rather than Levinas himself, the thinking that requires opening up to unceasing ethical concern for the other. The theoretical discussion in this chapter is a Levinasian gesture.[6]

THE PREHISTORY OF THE 1953 *KOREAN POETRY ANTHOLOGY*

An examination of the prehistory of Kim's *Korean Poetry Anthology* is necessary to understand the colonial and postcolonial contexts of its publication. The translator Kim Soun first published an anthology of modern Korean poetry in 1940 under the title *Chichi Iro no Kumo* (Milky Clouds). It contained translations of 101 poems by 43 poets, almost all of whom were to become canonical figures in modern Korean literary history. Kim seems to have selected the poems by consulting other anthologies available in Korea in the late 1930s.[7]

Following the outbreak of the Sino-Japanese War in 1937, the importance of Japan's largest colony, Korea, had come into clearer view because of its proximity to China and its large population. Accordingly, Japanese interest in the colony and its culture surged as the war in the Asian continent intensified. The publication of Kim's *Milky Clouds* marked this rising interest in Korean culture. The anthology was very well received by the Japanese literary establishment. The fact that Shimazaki Tōson, one of the most established Japanese writers, wrote the preface demonstrated how much attention its publication attracted in Japanese literary circles. Although graciously commending the anthology, Tōson's preface was, however, no more than a gentle encouragement from a literary luminary.

A substantial response to the publication of the anthology was given by the poet, writer, and critic Satō Haruo, who, in a welcoming remark included in the anthology, praised the "poetic spirit of Asia" he found in the Korean poems. In his view, the Asian poetic spirit the Korean poems gave off was unadulterated by Western literary influence because Korea had escaped Western colonization. Certainly, such a remark can be interpreted as a defense of Japan's preemptive colonization of the country, indicating how Satō's essay clearly showed the political circumstances of the specific historical juncture when Japanese ideology emphasized the solidarity of the Asian race not only to secure the loyalty of its Asian colonies but also to justify its expansion into China and to criticize the increasing pressure from the United States and Britain.

Although this aspect of Satō's essay may lead to it being characterized as a cowardly concession to the Japanese government propaganda, the essay itself was not a mere vindication of the political motivations behind rising interest in Korean culture in the early 1940s. To be fair to Satō, his essay contained criticism of Japanese colonial language policy even though the criticism was muffled in the ambiguity of convoluted rhetoric. Satō asked himself, for example, "whether or not we can be deeply touched by the special case similar to a situation in which poets sing the last songs in their own language which is about to perish."[8]

Satō's introductory essay suggestively revealed the limits of a liberal and conscientious intellectual of the colonizing country, a writer who was critical of colonial oppression but unconscious of the collusion between colonial domination and his own patronizing sympathy toward the colonized. One glaring example was his remark that oppressive rule from the late Koryŏ period throughout the Chosŏn period had turned the Korean people into a nation of scheming incompetents, although—he conceded—they were not so by nature. He followed with praise for Korean poetry, which he found blessed by excellent poets singing about daily life and ordinary people. Satō neatly concluded that the people excelled in the realm of poetry despite failing in politics. In other words, to stress his praise for the excellence of Korean poetry, Satō contrasted it with Korea's loss of self-government, reiterating dominant colonial discourse on the misery of the Korean people under oppressive rule before colonization and reproducing a biased image of scheming, incompetent Koreans. Although, as he brought his essay to an end, Satō reminded the reader that, historically, the influence of civilization from the Asian continent always spread to Japan not only geographically through the Korean peninsula but culturally through the mediation of Korean interpreters, this recognition corresponded primarily to his earlier valuation of the pure Asian poetic spirit in Korean poetry, which served obliquely to justify Japanese colonization of Korea.

Kim himself regarded his anthology as the introduction of Korean poetry to the Japanese literary establishment. In the afterword written in an epistolary form addressed to his friend R, obviously a Japanese with little knowledge about the Korean literary scene, Kim mentioned that he had intended to publish an anthology of modern Korean poetry for more than 10 years because he hoped such an introduction of modern Korean literature would help overcome the marginality of Korean poetry on the Japanese literary scene.[9] Kim did not miss the chance to lament the grim future of the Korean language as it was rapidly disappearing from the public sphere in the colony as the colonial government increasingly encouraged the exclusive use of Japanese. The anticipated doom of the Korean language, however, did not spoil the optimistic mood of the afterword. Kim claimed in an optimistic tone that no matter what happened, Korean literature would survive, although he did not specify how it would survive and what it would turn out to be like. An even more celebratory note from the prominent Korean intellectual Yi Kwangsu also appeared in the anthology. Yi took the publication of the anthology as a promising opportunity for strengthening ties between the Japanese and Koreans. Yi reasoned that because the Japanese (*yamato*) and Korean nations (*minzoku*) are destined to unite in defense of the empire of Japan, the task of literature was to foster such unity by touching the hearts of the two peoples.[10]

At the request of the Japanese publisher Kōfūkan, Kim launched another poetry anthology project soon thereafter, culminating in the publication in 1943 of a two-volume anthology titled *Chōsen Shishū* (Korean Poetry Anthology). A planned third volume was never published. Out of the 101 poems collected in *Milky Clouds*, 90 reappeared in Kim's 1943 *Korean Poetry Anthology*. The new anthology also included 97 newly translated poems. Kim gave a more concrete reason behind his continuing publication projects of Korean poetry anthologies: In the preface, he complained that Korean literature had been placed ambiguously with respect to Japanese literature. Kim concurred with the view that it should not be treated as foreign literature like German and French literature, but, at the same time, he accepted that Korean literature could not be part of (Japanese) national literature (*kokubungaku*) and so ended up awkwardly lumped together with Manchurian and Chinese literature under the rubric of "continental literature" (*tairiku bungaku*). Kim anticipated that under the circumstances of accelerating assimilation policies, the Korean language would be completely replaced by Japanese as the literary language of Korea, but he contended that that process would be completed only in the future and that Korean literature was still "crossing the bridge" from tradition based on the Korean language to a new future premised on Japanese. He further argued that given the importance of this juncture, the Japanese literary establishment needed to extend a helping hand to Korean literature and lead it to becoming an integral part of Japanese culture. He saw his new anthology as an attempt to encourage the Japanese literary establishment to step up such an effort.[11]

The poetry collection that Tōma consulted when writing his essay "Notes on Korean Poetry" was a new one-volume anthology published in 1953 under the same title as the previous edition in the *Korean Poetry Anthology*. Except for eight newly translated poems, all the poems were taken from the previous two anthologies without modification. Kim did not provide any introductory essay this time, but a postscript written by a Yun Chawōn positioned the anthology as a representative record of the Korean mind under colonial rule. Yun reminded the reader that some of the poets included in the anthology disappeared while in exile abroad or lost their lives during the colonial period and claimed that the suffering of the Korean nation intensified their national sentiments and cultivated their affection for their homeland. His postscript went on to argue that the poems recorded the history of Korean mind expressing the emotions about life under foreign rule. Thus, even though this new anthology did not differ much from the previous ones in terms of contents, the way in which it was characterized by Yun's postscript was in marked contrast with the characterizations given to the colonial-era anthologies. As a matter of fact, this valorization of the new anthology as the literary manifestation of the Korean nation's love for their homeland is a key to understanding why Tōma paid attention to the new anthology.

Around the time that the new *Korean Poetry Anthology* came out in 1953, political developments in East Asia and Japan were pushing Japanese leftist intellectuals to imagine a potential Japanese revolution in the framework of nationalism. In the initial phase of the occupation, the Japanese Communist Party took a moderate stance on the U.S. presence and on the appropriate goals and tactics for revolution in Japan. The Party viewed the completion of a bourgeois-democratic revolution as the immediate task and regarded the occupation as a necessary stage of the "progressive" bourgeois-democratic revolution in Japan. As a consequence, the party espoused a peaceful revolution.

As Communist Party influence grew in the Japanese labor movement and communist sentiments mounted in East Asia, U.S. occupation authorities tried to "reverse course." Public employees were prohibited from launching strikes, and the leftist labor movement was suppressed, beginning as early as 1948. A number of leftists were blacklisted and purged from public positions between 1949 and 1950 and later also from the private sector. Authorities also reinstated right-wing wartime leaders who had been purged in the initial phase of the occupation.[12]

Meanwhile, the Chinese communists had driven Chang Kaishek and his army into Taiwan and taken power in mainland China in 1949. The Korean War also broke out in 1950 when communist North Korea launched a full-scale attack against U.S.-backed South Korea. The war was one of the first military conflicts exploding out of the Cold War tension between the communist bloc and the U.S.-led Western world. Meanwhile, the Japanese government began rearmament in 1950, and signed a security treaty with the United States in 1951 over international protests and objections from Japanese dissidents.

The Japanese Communist Party came under severe criticism from the Cominform in Moscow for its conciliatory attitude toward the occupation forces. As a consequence, the party changed its orientation from peaceful democratic revolution to militantly nationalistic anti-imperialism. For example, in his report to the central committee plenum in January 1950, the secretary-general of the Japanese Communist Party, Tokuda Kyūichi, called attention to the revolutionary struggles for national liberation in China and compared Chang Kaishek's Guomindang government to the Yoshida administration in Japan.[13] In the eyes of Japanese leftists, the Communist takeover of China was the victory of Chinese nationalism, and the Korean War was the anti-imperial struggle of the Korean nation. Many intellectuals believed that as the war on the Korean peninsula escalated, the ever-expanding presence of American military forces in Japan had turned the country into a virtual colony of the United States. After Japan signed the San Francisco Treaty in 1951, the archipelago became an invaluable military base for American forces in the region.[14] The Japanese government's willing compliance with the demands of the United States was in sharp contrast to the Chinese Communist Party's victory over the Guomindang government and North Korea's tenacious fight against the U.S.-led United Nations forces.

The leftist intellectuals looked to Asian nationalism as a model for Japanese nationalists to emulate in standing up to American imperialism as well as in remedying the ultranationalism of wartime Japan. Reconfiguring Japanese nationalism, however, required rewriting the historical relationship of Japan to Asia and to the United States. By positing a colonial relationship to the United States, Japanese leftist intellectuals conflated the Japanese people with Asian peoples who had strived for liberation from the shackles of colonialism. Moreover, by casting the Japanese people as subalterns to the Japanese government, the leftist intellectuals also let them escape accountability for Japan's own colonial expansion in the past. Thus, while attempting to differentiate their vision of nationalism from prewar right-wing nationalism, the leftist intellectuals obfuscated the Japanese people's own responsibility for colonial expansion.

Nationalism came to the fore in Japanese literature as well. As the theme for its 1951 conference, the *Nihon Bungaku Kyōryokukai* (Japanese Literature Cooperative Association) discussed "*Minzoku Bungaku*" (ethnic nation literature). The "ethnic nation" or "folk" (*minzoku*) became the most fashionable topic in the Japanese literary establishment. Their vision was of a national literature that would contribute to the Japanese people's struggles against American imperialism and the reactionary Japanese government sycophantically obedient to the United States.

Tōma's attention to the 1953 *Korean Poetry Anthology* can be best understood when read against the background of the surge of interest in nationalism during the postwar period. In his essays on Kim's anthology, Tōma attempted to encourage his readers to see what was absent from modern Japanese poetry, by which he meant the collective identity of intellectuals as the integral part of the nation, who, in his eyes, constitute the base for healthy nationalism. Tōma urged Japanese poets and writers to learn from the ways in which the Korean poems represented the sentiments of the masses. That was a pressing imperative for Tōma because Japan was not a colonizing power any more and was now a virtual colony under U.S. hegemony. The Japanese needed to build up a national consciousness on the basis of the masses to resist both U.S. hegemony as well as the reactionary Japanese government.

The next part of the chapter will examine Tōma's 1954 essay titled *"Furusato: Chōsenshi ni Tsuite no Nōto I"* (Hometown: Notes on Korean Poetry I) and revisit the issues raised above: the relationship between history and literature, the problem of translation, and the appropriation of radial difference in representing the other.

LOST IN TRANSLATION: TŌMA'S INTERPRETATIONS OF KOREAN POETRY AND KIM'S REFUTATION

Over the course of 1954, Tōma published four essays on Korean poetry in the literary journals *Nihon Bungaku* (Japanese Literature) and *Bungaku* (Literature).[15] The essays make up the core chapters of a book published the following year by the Tokyo University Press under the title *Minzoku no Shi* (The Poetry of a People). Here, I am focusing on the first essay titled "Hometown: Notes on Korean Poetry, Part I," because it raises questions about the issues of translation and the relationship between history and literature and took the brunt of Kim's criticisms of Tōma's essays on Korean poetry.

The essay begins with Tōma's reading of two Korean poems written by Yi Hayun and Pak Yongch'ŏl, respectively.[16] For Tōma, the two poems stand out due to their strong nostalgia for one's native place.

GRAVE OF AN UNKNOWN SOUL

A grave of
An unknown soul
Covered with grasses
Along the north gate road.

A wandering
Traveler stops,
To catch his breath
Beside it.

With the building
Of the national road
The grave was flattened,
No trace remaining.

How empty it makes one feel
That the moss and dirt
That covered the grave
Were swallowed up by the road.

A grave of yesterday
Is weeping with a song of the passing years
As heartless people
Trample it underfoot.

Here lies
The unclaimed grave of an unknown soul,
A traveler's
Resting place.

無縁塚

北門の
道の傍(かたへ)に草生える
無縁佛の
塚一つ

さすらひの
旅ゆく人が足とめて
塚のほとりに
憩ひしが、

國道の
拓かれてより　かの塚の
押し潰(くづ)されて
跡もなく、

塚の上(へ)に
蔽(おほ)へる土や苔草の
道に食(は)まれて
はかなしや

こゝろなき
人に踏まれて過ぎし日の
うたに噎(むせ)ぶや
昨(きぞ)の塚

主(あらじ)なき
無縁佛の塚ありて
旅ゆく人の
憩ひしが。[17]

In Kim's translation *"Muenzuka"* (The Grave of an Unknown Soul) of Yi's poem *"Irŏjin Mudŏm"* (A Grave Lost), Tōma interpreted the grave destroyed by the construction of a road as the symbol of the hometown irrevocably transformed by the cultural and economical changes of the colonial period. Tōma associated the grave extradiegetically with a Korean folk custom of burying those who died without leaving descendents to attend to their graves beside the road outside of their villages. These unfortunate souls included those who died too young to marry and those who died with their families as a result of epidemics. Located outside a village, the graves also provided a place for travelers to rest. Travelers felt especially close to those buried in such graves because they themselves were treated as deceased by the families and villages they left behind. Tōma understood that because Korean villages were so isolated from the outside world, anyone who left home was regarded as in another world and no longer among the living. Out of compassion, passing travelers piled small stones on these graves to prevent wild animals from violating the dead bodies as a way of consoling and appeasing the spirits of the dead. Tōma reasoned that such a custom disappeared when the graves were destroyed by the progress the new road symbolizes in the poem.

Tōma acknowledged that the narrative voices in the poems are not identical to the poets themselves, and he recognized that both Yi and Pak came from wealthy families and even studied in Japan and thus would have not suffered as much as the ordinary Korean masses had under Japanese colonial rule. Nevertheless, he conflated the narrative voices of the poems with the poets themselves because, in his view, the poems reveal the poets' consciousness about their nation: They are not alienated from the Korean masses and they share a communal identity with the Korean nation, the majority of which is rural. Put differently, Tōma argued that their poems prove their communal identity because they express empathy with the Korean masses who suffered traumatic changes brought about by colonial rule.

In a similar way, Tōma focused on the image of the village well (*muraido*) in Pak's poem *"Kohyang"* (Hometown) translated by Kim as *"Furusato o Kohite Nanisemu."*

WHAT GOOD IS IT TO LONG FOR MY HOMETOWN?

What good is it to long for my hometown?
When ties with my kin are cut off and our house is lost?
I wonder if a lone evening crow is crying.
I wonder if the village well has been moved.

Leaving the dreams of my childhood
At Mother's grave, I became a wanderer.
Ten years a floating cloud are gone away.
What good is it to long for a hometown?

Shall I try to paint on the sky
A new hope and pleasure?
Wind, blow the scattered blossoms of memory
Over my restless body!

In vain was the dream of my hometown
Trampled underfoot now,
Like the sorrow of the first love
I vowed to a girl
From whom I was kept away.

ふるさとを戀ひて何せむ

ふるさとを戀ひて何せむ
血縁(ちすぢ)絶え　吾家の失せて
夕鴉(ゆふがらす)ひとり啼くらむ
村井戸も遷されたらむ。

をさな夢　母の墓邊に
とどめてぞさすらひ流る
浮雲の十年(ととせ)はるかよ
ふるさとを戀ひて何せむ。

かの空に描(ゑが)きても見む
新らしき希望(のぞみ)、歓び、
想ひ出は散らしく花の
吹けよ風　憩ひなき身に。

はかなしや　ふるさとのゆめ
いまははた踏みしだかれて
契(ちぎ)りつゝ人に堰(せ)かれし
初戀のせつなきに似る。[18]

The village well functions as a motif that allows Tōma to historicize the poem. Because the Korean mountains were denuded of trees, he explained, rain escaped quickly to rivers as soon as it hit the ground and people had a hard time finding enough water to sustain themselves. In the face of such difficulties, villagers cooperated in digging wells, which then served as the center of communal interactions in rural villages. Tōma argued that moving the village well as described in the poem thus suggests a drastic change taking place in the village. At this point, Tōma speculated that such a drastic change must have to do with "development" projects carried out in rural areas by the colonial government.

Tōma's reading hinges figuratively on a chain of metonymies and hermeneutically on the assumed referential connection between the text and the external world. Both "the grave of an unknown soul" and "the village well" symbolize the hometown, which, in turn, ultimately expresses the ethnic nation. Needless to say, the nation refers outside the text to the historical reality of the Korean nation, which suffered under Japanese colonial rule. Furthermore, according to Tōma, the poems reflect the total process of transformation that the Korean nation underwent under Japanese colonial rule.

Reasoning that tradition constitutes a cultural reservoir for the nation, Tōma ascribed the poets' feats to the tradition of folksongs modern Korean poetry allegedly carries on. In Tōma's view, Korean poets struggled with their tradition and did not break free from it. They realized that no matter how much they tried to come up with a new self free from the age-old tradition, they could not help but return to their nation as symbolized by the hometown in their poems. In contrast to modern Korean poetry, modern Japanese poetry lacked such expressions of communal identity.

Tōma contended that because the Japanese middle class had grown rapidly following the Russo-Japanese War, an increasing number of intellectuals came from the middle class and these individuals were instrumental in the development of modern literature. In contrast, Korean intellectuals may have been "baptized" by modern thought but were still under the sway of the dominant feudal norms of society. He further reasoned that Korean intellectuals were so much under the heavy pressure of the traditional norms of society that they must have been envious of their Japanese counterparts because Japanese intellectuals were more free and individualistic, that is, more modern. He went on to conjecture that as a result Kim was moved by Kitahara Hakushū's poetry and asked him to write the preface to his collection of Korean folksongs.

Nevertheless, Tōma argued, although Japanese intellectuals could afford to be apolitical, Korean intellectuals were made politically aware as colonized by colonial realities whether they liked it or not. No matter how much they became like Japanese, they were faced daily with discrimination and prejudice and could not think of themselves apart from their nation. Tōma asserted that however attracted they were to the greater freedom and literary development achieved by Japanese intellectuals, Koreans were kept away from an individualist world view in which the Japanese were entrapped.

Tōma argued that the situation had drastically changed since the end of the war. The confined world of Japanese intellectuals had been shattered when Japanese imperialism was defeated, although its legacy lingered on in the form of racial prejudice against Koreans. Tōma concluded with a call for a united front between the masses and intellectuals under the leadership of the proletariat to lead Japan to genuine modernity.

On the occasion of the re-publication of Tōma's essays two years later as a book titled *Minzoku no Shi* (The Poetry of a People), Kim published his harsh refutation of Tōma's readings in the journal *Literature*.[19] In the beginning of the essay, Kim revealed that Tōma had contacted him before writing the essays. Feeling obliged as the translator of the poems and knowing Tōma was a respected historian, Kim did his best answering Tōma's questions but, when reading Tōma's essays published in the journals *Japanese Literature* and *Literature*, he could not help but feel distraught because Tōma had almost completely ignored his input and offered what Kim saw as distorted interpretations to advance his own agenda. Kim confided in the reader that the reason he was belatedly responding to Tōma's essays two years after the publication of the original essays was that, as translator, he could not tolerate any more of the confusion Tōma's misinterpretation would cause the Japanese readers.

Kim devoted the first half of his essay to debunking Tōma's reading of the two poems by Yi and Pak. Kim's criticism was aimed at exposing how misinformed and misleading Tōma's interpretation of some key words of the poems was. For example, Kim focuses on the word grave in "The Grave of an Unknown Soul" because Tōma had anchored his reading on the word and interpreted the poems as an elegy for a hometown irrevocably changed by colonial development, which the construction of a new road symbolized for Tōma. Kim argued that the grave the poem describes is not the type of graves on which Tōma dwelled. He pointed out that the grave in the poem is covered with grass, not stones and pebbles as Tōma described it. He then asserted that this was not a grave where a lonely traveler might stop to rest. Out of a groundless assumption about the grave, Tōma developed his thesis on the exclusiveness of Korean rural communities and defined colonial development as the antithesis to the hometown. Thus, Kim contended that Tōma's reading relying on a chain of metonymies made no sense at all because it began with a false assumption. Although Tōma explained the poem as an allegory of the violent change an isolated village was subjected to by colonial development, in Kim's view, it was Tōma's reading itself that was violent because he unjustifiably and forcedly read his own agenda into the poem. Kim protested that, in Tōma's hands, the pathos and nostalgia for the hometown evoked by the lyrical poem was turned into a crudely political condemnation of Japanese colonialism.

Kim's criticism of Tōma's reading of "What Good Is It to Long for My Hometown?" similarly centered around the two key words *muraido* (village well) and *hatsukoi* (first love) on which Tōma built his argument. As discussed above, spotlighting the importance of the village well as the center of communal interactions, Tōma reasoned that the moving of the well must symbolize violent change brought about by colonial development. Similarly, first love in the poem was crucial for Tōma to differentiate modern Korean poetry from its Japanese counterpart. Tōma argued that first love is inseparably connected to the hometown in "What Good Is It to Long for My Hometown?" whereas love in Kitahara Hakushū's poetry refers to no more than amorous feelings. Thus, the word first love enables Tōma to highlight modern Japanese poets' disconnection from their hometowns.

Kim curtly responded that villagers moved their wells whenever they deemed it to be necessary and that colonial development did not necessarily have anything to do with it. Kim asked why these Korean poems should be read as allegories of the Korean nation's colonial experience when similar elegies for the hometown are found all over the world.[20] Kim further asserted that although Japanese colonialism could and should be criticized for many reasons, these lyrical poems ought not be reduced to political condemnation of Japanese colonialism.

As mentioned briefly in the beginning of this chapter, Tōma's readings pivoted on Kim's less-than-faithful translations. Tōma was aware that his readings vulnerably depended on translation and questioned why Kim had not included in his anthology more overtly political poems equivalent to Japanese proletarian poems.[21] His question was, however, limited to the range of Kim's selection of poems in terms of their political consciousness. Given the assertiveness of his arguments about the Korean poems, Tōma did not seem suspicious of the faithfulness of Kim's translations. However, the problem of translation was much more crucial than Tōma may have realized. One of the key expressions on which Tōma's reading pivoted was one of Kim's substitutions for the original phrase. Here is my English translation of Pak Yongch'ŏl's poem, which Kim translated into Japanese under the title of *"Furusato o Kohite Nanisemu"* (What good is it to long for my hometown?). As noted above, its original title is *"Kohyang"* (Hometown).

HOMETOWN

For what shall I return to my hometown?
My family is scattered and the house is decayed.
I wonder if autumn grasses make the evening crow cry,
If the brook near the village has changed its course.

Leaving the dream of my childhood behind on top of my dear
Mother's grave,
I went staggering on,
Following drifting clouds for ten-odd years.
For what shall I return to my hometown now?

Shall I draw new happiness on the end of the sky?
Why must I not forget what I left behind?
You, ruthless wind, blow to the full.
Where do scattered petals find their rest?

To give a thought to my hometown
Trampled underfoot by rude feet
—even in a hurried trip in a foggy dream—.
Feels like a bitter memory
About my trusty old love who was stolen away.

고향

고향은 찾어 무얼하리
일가 흩어지고 집흐너진데
저녁 가마귀 가을풀에 울고
마을앞 시내도 넷자리 바뀌었을라.

어린때 꿈 엄마 무덤우에
남겨두고 떠도는 구름 따라
멈추는듯 불려온 지 여나무해
고향은 이제 찾아 무얼 하리.

하날가에 새 기쁨을 그리어보랴
남겨둔 무엇일래 못잊히우랴
모진바람아 마음껏 불어쳐라
흩어진 꽃닢 쉬임어디 찾는다냐.

험한발에 짓밟힌 고향생각
—아득한 꿈엔 달려가는 길이언만—
서로의 굳은뜻을 남게 앗긴
옛사랑의 생각같은 쓰린 심사여라.[22]

A glance at Pak's original reveals that Kim replaced the key phrase in the last line of the first stanza "the brook near the village" (*maŭl ap sinae*) with "village well" (*muraido*) in his translation. Thus, Tōma based his extended argument on Kim's own word choice, which was not found in the original. The original phrase does not quite support Tōma's overall argument because Tōma put so much emphasis on the village well as the center of a rural community and interpreted the dislocation of the well as the result of an irrevocable change to the village caused by colonial development. Any possible correlation between the change of the brook's path and colonial development was much more tenuous than that between the change of the village well's location and colonial development. Nor was "first love" in the last line of the fourth stanza, the other phrase Tōma focused on, an exact translation of the original. Its literal translation should be "past love." The original phrase squared less with Tōma's argument about the hometown because "past love" could be just one of many amorous relationships unlike "first love," which is singular, similar to one's hometown.

Tōma's interpretations of Kim's mistranslations do not, however, entirely invalidate his reading of the poem as an allegory of the Korean national suffering under Japanese rule. Tōma could still read the poem allegorically even though the specific arguments he based on Kim's replacements and mistranslations were less convincing once it is apparent what alterations Kim made to the original poem. More important, that is not the only translation-related problem at issue.

In publishing his first anthology *Milky Clouds* (1940), Kim altered some of the poems he included not for literary reasons but for political ones. To avoid conflict with the colonial authorities, he either altered or expunged original expressions from his translations that would possibly raise red flags with the censors. One example, as noted by the literary critic Yu Chongho, was his problematic translation of Chŏng Chiyong's

"Kap'e P'ŭrangsŭ" (Café France). Because this example illustrates well the central issue of translation with regard to colonial censorship, it merits discussion, although neither Tōma nor Kim mentioned it.[23] Kim rendered one crucial sentence, *"na nŭn narado chipto ŏptanda"* (I have neither country nor home), as *"watashi ni wa ie mo sato mo nai"* (I have neither home nor hometown) in his Japanese translation. As Yu points out, there could not have been any justifiable reason for the change other than Kim's concern about censorship. Put simply, Kim replaced the Korean *"nara"* (country) with the Japanese *"sato"* (home village) because he worried that the original word might lead the censor to interpret the poem as a lamentation about the loss of Korean independence because of Japanese colonization, if the censor had considered the sentence to refer to political reality external to the text. Kim replaced "country" with "hometown" because he must have thought that although the latter was metonymically associated with the former it would be regarded as a less subversive term. It is interesting to note, in other words, that it is not unthinkable, even for Kim, to suppose that "hometown" can fill in for "country" or even nation. That is exactly what Tōma assumed in his reading of the Korean poems, although, in his reading, the metonymic conversion from "hometown" to "nation" is the reverse of Kim's intentional mistranslation.

"Muenzuka" (The Grave of an Unknown Soul) is another instance in which Kim preempted a political interpretation by altering the original text. As seen in my English translation from the original poem *"Irŏjin Mudŏm"* (A Grave Lost), the possessive "the mortal enemy's" (*wŏnsu ŭi*), which modifies "new road" in the first line of the third stanza, clearly shows the narrator's antagonism toward the road that destroyed the grave. In his Japanese translation, however, Kim expurgated the expression and neutralized the poem's clear antagonism toward the change brought to the hometown.

A GRAVE LOST

On a solitary path
Around the mound of the north gate
There was the thick-grass-covered grave
Of an unknown soul.

Whenever a lone vagabond
Passed by,
He would sit and rest
Before the grave.

After the mortal enemy's new road
Was built over it,
No trace of the grave is found
Anywhere.

Dirt and grass
Covering the grave
Turned into a road
Tramped over and over,

Are now singing
A sorrowful old song
Whenever heavy footprints are
Left on them.

Here was
The grave of an unknown soul
Where a drifting passerby
Used to rest nearby.

일허진 무덤

北門턱 외딴길에
풀닙 거츠른
님자일흔 무덤이
하나 잇더니

放浪의손 외로히
지날때 마다
무덤앞에 안저서
쉬고 가더니

원수의 신작로가
생긴이후로
패여간 무덤자최
간곳 업노라

무덤우에 덮엇든
흙과 잔듸는
밟히고 짓밟히는
길이 되여서

묵어둔 발자욱에
눌닐때 마다
애닯흔 옛노래를
읇고 잇노라

님자일흔 무덤이
하나 잇서서
흘러가는 行人이
쉬고 가더니[24]

By calling attention to Kim's surreptitious alteration of the original texts, however, I do not intend to criticize his self-censoring and deference to the Japanese government. What is at issue is Kim's attitude toward translation in general and his refutation of Tōma's political reading in particular. In the afterword of *Milky Clouds*, his 1940 anthology on which the postwar *Korean Poetry Anthology* was based, Kim remarked that although ideally the poetry translator should not take translated poems as his own, he himself had failed to achieve such a state of mind. He even confessed that the anthology amounted to a collection of his own poetry. He nevertheless refused to be apologetic because he reasoned that apologizing for his mistakes implied that he would not do the same thing again, but, he declared, he could not help but do it over and over again as long as he was translating Korean poetry.[25] As noted above, when publishing the postwar anthology, Kim did not revise the translations originally included in *Milky Clouds*. The three poems discussed here were originally translated for the first anthology and were included without revision in the postwar anthology.

In his afterword to the 1943 version of *Korean Poetry Anthology*, Kim revealed that he had abandoned a translation of No Ch'ŏnmyŏng's poem "*Puni*," which depicts a mother's sorrow over Puni, the daughter she has lost, because the poem resisted Kim's efforts to transfer its sentiments into Japanese even though he was very much moved by it and eager to translate it.[26] He seemed to imply that if an original text resists a translator's will to render it appropriately in the target language, the translator should not force it into translation. Although this notion appeared to testify to Kim's respect for the integrity of the original text, what it actually revealed was that the poems Kim translated were those that, in his eyes, surrendered to his will. This attitude of Kim's toward his translations offers a clue to understanding his absolute rejection of Tōma's political reading of them. For him, those poems were as much his own literary works as the poets'. In his mind, he absolutely knew the authorial intentions because the poems translated into Japanese were almost his own literary creations. When he asserted that the anthology was his, the possessive "his" was purely possessive. His assertion did not indicate any willingness to face up to any inevitable injustice he had done to the original. Kim's attitude toward his translations lacks self-reflectivity. Put differently, his view on translation did not recognize the alterity inscribed in the original, which no translator can domesticate.

ENCOUNTERING THE OTHER

However problematic Kim's views on translation were, he did raise important issues relevant to any meaningful discussion on postcolonial encounters between the former colonizers and colonized in the realm of culture. As mentioned earlier, he demanded to know why the Korean poems should be read as allegories of the Koreans' colonial experience when similar elegies for one's hometown are common in other countries, too. He wanted to know why Tōma reduced the universal feeling of nostalgia for one's lost hometown expressed in the poetry to the particularity of Koreans' historical experience. In other words, Kim questioned why the history of colonial experience should be the ultimate hermeneutical horizon on which the interpretation of the Korean poetry is placed.

Another point that deserves our attention is Kim's protest at Tōma's representation of Koreans and Korean culture. In denouncing Tōma's inadequate knowledge about Korean culture and literature, Kim was criticizing the general tendency he found among Japanese intellectuals to represent Korean culture based on superficial observation. Kim offered one example of such violent representation: He reported that he had once read an article in the tanka poetry journal *Shinjin* (Man of Truth) about certain peculiarities of the Korean language. The article informed its readers that Koreans say "feeding a clock" instead of "winding a clock" and they use "saw rice" (*topap*) and "plane rice" (*taep'aepap*) to refer to sawdust and wood shavings. From this observation, the author concluded that the verb expression "to eat" appears in so many idiomatic expressions in the Korean language that it must reflect Koreans' obsession with food. Kim responded sarcastically to such a crude reasoning about the Korean psyche by asking rhetorically whether the Japanese are cannibalistic because they say "that guy is inedible" (*kuenai yatsu*) to mean "he is devious" and say "telling a story of having eaten a man" (*hito o kutta hanashi*) to mean "telling a tall tale."[27] Kim's protest at the Japanese representation of Korean culture bears on his criticism of Tōma's reading of Korean poetry, because one of the main complaints Kim lodged against Tōma was that the latter put forth wild speculations about the poems on the basis of fragmented pieces of information and superficial knowledge about Korean literature and culture.

Tōma responded quickly to Kim's criticism in an essay titled "*Gendai Chōsen Bungaku no Hitotsu no Mikata*" (One Perspective on Modern Korean Literature) published two months later in *Literature,* in August 1956.[28] Tōma argued that once a literary work leaves the hands of its author, the critic should respect the reader's interpretation as long as it is reasonable even if the critic believes it to be contrary to the author's intention. Tōma's response itself, however, is not helpful for duly examining the issues raised by Kim.

To fully comprehend the theoretical implications of the issues, I enlist Jameson's essay on non–Western literature, one of the very few attempts to construct a general theory of non–Western literary texts. It was first and foremost an endeavor to grapple with the unease so-called First-World intellectuals have with the radical difference of the Third World. In Jameson's essay, the "Third World" refers to the formerly colonized and semicolonized nations in Asia and Africa, the conditions of which are in contrast to those of the First World, that is, advanced capitalist countries most of which were former colonial powers.[29] In the very beginning of his essay, Jameson remarked that Third-World intellectuals are obsessed with the collective identity of their nations. He summed up the way in which First-World intellectuals feel perplexed about that difference in the following sentences: "This is not the way American intellectuals have been discussing 'America,' and indeed one might feel that the whole matter is nothing but that old thing called 'nationalism,' long since liquidated here and rightly so."[30]

Jameson traced the origin of Western intellectuals' unease with national identity to the split between the private and the public entrenched in the advanced capitalist society of the West. Western culture is overdetermined by a series of splits between the private and the public, the poetic and the political, and the psychic subject and the social subject. These splits ultimately result from the capitalist mode of production, the development of which inheres in Western countries and Japan, an exceptional non–Western First-World country.[31] In contrast, such splits have not yet pervaded Third-World culture because Third-World countries have encountered capitalism as an encroachment on their societies from outside. Put differently, the trajectory of the Third World's encounter with capitalism is the history of colonialism. Because of the history of colonial experience, Third-World literary texts, even when telling private stories with a strongly libidinal dimension, necessarily allegorize "the embattled situation of the public third-world culture and society."[32]

Jameson gallantly endeavored to offer a sympathetic view of non–

Western literature, looking beyond culture to the structural base that determines the production of literary texts in the last instance and debunking the claustrophobic self-referentiality of texts, the interpretive strategy that, in his judgment, dominates Western literary criticism.[33] Certainly, Jameson offered a much more nuanced argument than a crudely reductive reading of literary texts as the transparent reflection of colonial experience, and it would do a disservice to him if his notion of "national allegory" were lumped with Tōma's reductive reading strategy.

Nevertheless, it is also undeniable that Jameson's essay resonates with Tōma's essays in that, for both Jameson and Tōma, colonial history constitutes the ultimate hermeneutic horizon on which the interpretation of literature produced in former colonies should be carried out. Furthermore, Jameson's essay operates on a desire structurally parallel to that which propels Tōma's essays. As mentioned above, Tōma found a strong connection between intellectuals and the masses in modern Korean poetry and lamented the lack of such awareness of collective identity in modern Japanese literature. In a similar vein, Jameson's essay seeks to locate a bond between politics and poetics as well as between the public and the private in literature identified as other than his own while supposing such a bond, much like the lost innocence of the past, disappeared from Western literature with the advent of modernism, a loss that, needless to say, Jameson regarded as his own.

As Marxists, both Tōma and Jameson were concerned with modern individuals' alienation from human beings' natural sociality. Whereas Tōma privileged the nation as the manifestation of such sociality, Jameson certainly did not have such strong faith in the nation or, for that matter, in a collective identity. Nevertheless, Jameson ultimately recognized the political value of such a collective identity, which he observed many Third-World intellectuals invoke for revolutionary causes.[34] Jameson could not agree more on Tōma's view that the primary role of intellectuals in society is political. Both consider the political to involve envisioning utopian possibilities denied us by the current capitalistic system. Finally, although both Tōma and Jameson depended absolutely on translation for their readings of Korean poetry and Third-World literature, respectively, neither gave much thought to the implications of relying on translation. In his scathing response to Jameson's article, Aijaz Ahmad thus complained that Jameson's argument cannot apply to most Third-World texts, as they are not available in Western languages.[35]

The problem of translation, however, is more than the limited availability of non–Western literary texts in Western languages. Translation presupposes the presence of the other in the first place, whom the self cannot understand on its own and which bring the self's understanding into question. The necessity of translation thus reminds us of that ultimately unbridgeable distance from the other. I suspect the lack of concern about translation in both Tōma and Jameson shows symptomatically their fear of encountering the truly radical difference of the other that resists appropriation.

By keeping the parallels between Tōma and Jameson in focus, it is possible to recognize that one important aspect of the controversies over both Tōma's essays and Jameson's argument is the relationship between the self and the other. The problem of Jameson's essay most relevant to this discussion is that when encountering the radical difference of the other, his essay suggests, there is no choice other than to settle for either the appropriation of radical difference or liberal and humanistic universalism. Jameson acknowledged that his call for reading Third-World literature as national allegory inevitably domesticates the radical difference of the other even though it aims to positively evaluate rather than to devalue non–Western literature. Nevertheless, he accepted fatalistically such epistemological violence as an inevitable course in encountering the other because he does not "know how a first-world intellectual can avoid this operation without falling back into some general liberal and humanistic universalism" other than to resort to some sort of orientalism, in Said's sense, which inevitably reifies difference as a tangible quality.[36]

What Jameson accepted as unavoidable epistemological violence deserves careful examination. The argument can be pushed further, to the point where it intersects with the recurrent problem of representation in the Western philosophical tradition. If the experiencing subject has no direct but merely indirect access to reality through representation alone, then the irreparable gap between reality and its representation always poses the question of epistemological violence because, no matter how faithfully that representation corresponds to reality, the two are not identical, and reality is always presented as other than itself through representation. If that is the case, the problem of representation is never limited to the appropriation of the other's radical difference, but it pertains to perception and the conceptualization of every single object, which is brought to consciousness from outside.

The problem of representation in epistemology has been tackled by numerous philosophers among whom Kant stands out for an enduring legacy still strongly felt in many disciplines within the humanities. Kant introduced the transcendental subject to ensure the possibility of objective knowledge about the external world outside of the subject. According to Kant, we human beings can have objective knowledge about the world because we are equipped with the a priori faculty of understanding, although we still do not have direct access to things in themselves and only know the phenomena, objects as structured by the faculty of understanding. Kant's efforts might not be satisfactory enough to ward off the accusation against Western philosophy of epistemological violence, especially when it is necessary to tackle the issue of encountering the radical difference of the other. Among various possible objections to and reservations about Kant's transcendental philosophy, what is particularly relevant to this discussion is the concern about whether the transcendental subject Kant introduced can constitute a universally objective vantage point or coincide only with the perspective of an 18th-century European male cultural elite. Put differently, one might argue that the transcendental subject cannot be completely insulated from all the conventions and customs, let alone prejudices and ignorance, of the particular time and place in which the empirical subject is placed. For example, the categories, the pure concepts of the faculty of understanding in Kant's epistemology, are derived from Aristotle's 10 classifications of terms originating in ancient Greece, although, within Kant's framework, the categories inhere a priori in humans as rational beings regardless of their particular attributes.

Even if the ways in which we make sense of the world are primarily determined by the conventions of the communities to which we happen to belong, our epistemological dependence on communal norms itself will not deal a detrimental blow to the general validity of representation as long as we interact only with those from our own communities, because how to experience reality, that is, how to represent things outside of the subject, is securely anchored in each community's shared norms. The real problem arises only when the self encounters the other with radical difference: How can the self conceptualize and articulate the difference without assimilating it into something familiar and understandable to the self? The problem goes further. Because the other does not share the same epistemological substratum with the self, the self's representation of radical difference always eludes the other. The other thus calls into question the ways in which the self sees the radical difference between itself and the other. When the other approaches the self and disrupts the self's complacency, it emerges as the other, the other with radical difference.

It goes without saying that no community in reality can impose norms on its members to such an absolute degree that the shared norms exhaustively dictate the ways in which its members perceive and conceive the world. There exists no such completely homogeneous community, and every community is fractured from the beginning regardless of its size. As a consequence, the other, the other with radical difference, does not necessarily come from outside of any given community and might come from within.

To envision an alternative way of encountering the radical difference of the other, I turn to Levinas. Levinas suggests that when encountering the other, the alterity of the other subjects the self to constant reflection on the harm the self does to the other and thus makes the self vulnerable to the call from the other to be ethical. What makes such an encounter possible, according to Levinas, is the self's desire for the other coming in need, that is, the other, whom the self cannot appropriate in the self's own image. This desire, however, does not ensue from the egoistic claim of the self. On the contrary, it comes along with the self's shame, which brings the self's legitimacy into question. As the self's desire for the other, as long as it is a desire, is insatiable, the self's obligation to the other cannot be exhausted. Only through constant ethical vigilance can a person confirm subjectivity. There is no logical and chronological priority granted to the constitution of subjectivity over one's ethical relationship with the other. In Levinasian ethics, the subjectivity emerges to be ethical with the other, not to hypostatize the identity of sameness.[37] Levinasian ethics is helpful for understanding the problem of the other underlying Tōma's reading of Korean poetry as well as at the core of Jameson's reading of Third-World literature.

Certainly, it was laudable that Tōma made an effort to understand the culture of Korea, Japan's former colony, and to build solidarity between the former colonized and the people of the former colonizer in their fight against the structures of colonial domination lingering on in East Asia. However, such solidarity should be premised on the recognition of radical difference between the two, and it is questionable whether Tōma's endeavor measured up to such an exacting demand.

Even though Tōma started his essays with an emphasis on the difference of modern Korean poetry from its Japanese counterpart, which resulted from the history of Koreans' colonial experience, such difference, in the end, proves to be not absolute but rather is appropriable because Tōma placed Japan, which he saw as a virtual colony under postwar American hegemony, on the same footing with Korea, a former colony of Japan. In other words, Tōma initially highlighted the difference of Korean poetry only to emphasize the importance of Japanese collective identity as a nation. Thus, when Tōma urged Japanese intellectuals to emulate their Korean counterparts' allegiance to the collective identity of their own nation, he risked appropriating the difference of Koreans for the affirmation of the Japanese self-sameness and losing sight of their alterity with its origins in historical differences between their experiences of colonialism.

In considering the historical difference between the former colonizers and colonized, what especially pertains to this discussion is Levinas's notion of eschatology because it offers a way of recounting the past alternatively to history, which is seminal to both Tōma's reading of Korean poetry and Jameson's reading of Third-World literature. Levinas is critical of history, which tends to totalize different individuals' singular experiences into "a coherent discourse."[38] According to Levinas, individuals in history are deprived of their own voices and presented only "in the third person." Thus, the judgment of history is a trial in absentia. It is inattentive to the unseen sufferings of individuals. To uphold justice, the individual should be present at that trial not only to give testimony but also to apologize if necessary.

No one can, however, testify indefinitely because every person is subject to the violence of death. The voices of the dead can be approached only through their work, the products of their labor, which is, in turn, vulnerable to the interpretations of those who survive. Thus, the past is appropriated by and consumed for the victors, the survivors in history. An individual can be free from the totalization of history only in the individual's interiority, which separates the individual from the totality. Interiority is what grants the individual subjectivity. As a consequence, Levinas appeared to argue that the ethical relationship with the other takes place outside history.[39]

Nevertheless, I argue that Levinas did not completely rule out the possibility of an ethical way of recounting the past. History is callous to the invisible sorrow and pain of individuals. However, the invisible that is outside of history manifests itself when those from the past are welcomed as the other, as strangers who summon the self to be ethical. When the self stops appropriating, taming, and domesticating the other's alterity for its own benefit, it steps out of history. Then, individuals' fear of death that deprives them of a voice in the judgment of history becomes the concern that that individual might annihilate the alterity of the other.[40] At that moment emerges the possibility of an ethical recounting of the past. This is what Levinas called eschatology. Past events are no longer framed in a certain way so that they can serve to legitimize the present.

In eschatology, each individual is given a chance to speak for him- or herself. The erratic and incoherent stories of individual experience are not sacrificed for the teleological narrative of history. Every sigh and murmur is heard. However, the eschatological judgment does not allow an individual to speak whatever he or she wants. The alterity of the other is paramount over the self's freedom in eschatology. The totality of history breaks down and the difference of an individual stands out in eschatology, revealing that an individual being has an infinity that the totality of history cannot encompass.[41] Eschatology is thus radically different from both Tōma's conventional Marxist history and Jameson's "History as the Real," which is indirectly accessible only through narration but nonetheless determinant in the production of texts.[42] Eschatology does not narrate past events in relation to the present.

One might ask whether it is possible to think of eschatology without acknowledging the presence of God. Is eschatology nothing but a theological view of history? The eschatology in the Levinasian sense does not necessarily presuppose the presence of omnipotent and omnipresent God who tells the good from the bad. However, the concept of eschatology is certainly meaningless without the possibility of redemption. In eschatology, an individual is given a chance to be redeemed from the loss of the past, which is condemned to oblivion in history.[43]

Then how does eschatology materialize as a discourse? Through memory, according to Levinas. It is imperative to remember the sorrow and pain of those of the past. However, such remembrance should not be aimed at ironing out the wrinkles of the past for the benefit of the survivors in the present.[44] Memory is not to interiorize the past within one who remembers in the present. Remembering the past involves patiently lending an ear to the sighs and murmurs of the past even though they may be incoherent and unreasonable to the self and exceed the self's totalizing comprehension of the past. Eschatological remembrance does not constitute a volitional or spontaneous act on the part of the self, which would suggest the self's supremacy as the transcendental ego. If the self was such a transcendental ego, it would suppress the alterity of the past by synthesizing the erratic contours of an individual's lived experience of the past into the coherent narrative of history.[45] The past cannot be brought back to be present or even represented in the consciousness of the ego through the act of remembrance issuing from the ego's freedom. In remembering what concretely happened in the past, the self is rather being haunted by the memory of the past as a trace, the absolute absence, which establishes the self's relationship with the past as the other and thus enables the constitution of the self as the ethical subject. As saying disrupts the said and ethics unsettles politics as discussed in the preceding chapters, eschatology thus interrupts and disjoints history, which, claiming to conjure up the past as presence within the consciousness of the ego, confirms the ego's totalizing cognitive power. Certainly, it is impossible to face all the concrete details of the past. However, it is possible to move closer to the ethical by struggling to remember in response to the call from the other, despite the impossibility of the task.

This insight from Levinas points to the possibility of solidarity between the former colonized and colonizer in protest against colonial domination. Eschatology serves to keep the people of the former colonizer vulnerable and responsive to the ethical call from the former colonized, the victims of colonial violence. Only through responding to the call is it possible to avoid the problem of appropriating the radical difference of the former colonized. The exacting demand on former colonizers to constantly be alert to the alterity of the former colonized might be mistaken for the Manichean world view on which colonial domination itself relies. However the ethical attention to the difference between former colonizers and colonized need not involve any essentialist identification premised on race, ethnicity, culture, language, or nationality as already discussed in Chapter 2. Having originated in colonial domination and its unceasing differentiation between colonized and colonizer as it institutes discrimination against the former in favor of the latter, difference is what constitutes the alterity of the former colonized.

The controversy over Tōma's essays on Korean poetry is indication of just how hard a task respecting the alterity of the other is. Even conscientious people in a former colonizing power need to be constantly alert to the risk that their good will may lead them to appropriate the radical difference of the postcolonial other.

5 Toward a Monolingual Society

South Korean Linguistic Nationalism and Kim Suyŏng's Resistance to Monolingualism

An entry the poet Kim Suyŏng (1921–1968) wrote in his diary 16 years after liberation provides a window into the plight of the generation of Korean intellectuals who were more fluent in Japanese than Korean because of the colonial education they had received.

> 僕ハ僕ニ死ネトダケイヘバ死ヌシ、死ヌナトイヘバ死ナナイコトモ出来ルソウイウ**馬鹿ナ瞬間**[1] ガアル。
>
> ミンナガ夢ダ。
>
> コレガ「疲レ」トイフモノカモ知ラナイシ、コレガ狂気トイフモノカモ知ラナイ。
>
> ボクハ話ニナラナイ低能児ダシ、ボクノ詩ハミンナ芝居デ、嘘ダ。
>
> 革命モ、革命ヲ支持スル僕モミンナ嘘ダ。タダコノ文章ダケガ**イクラカ**[2] 真実味ガアルダケダ。僕ハ「孤獨」カラ離レテ何ト長イ時間生キタンダラウ。今僕ハコノ僕ノ部屋ニ居リナガラ、何処カ遠イトコロヲ旅行シテイルヤウナ気ガスルシ、郷愁トモ死トモ分別ノツカナイモノノナカニイキテヰル。或ハ**日本語**[3] ノナカニ生キテイルノカモ知レナイ。
>
> ソシテ至極正確ダト自分ハ思ッテイルコノ文章モドコカ少シハ不正確ダシ狂ッテイル。
>
> マサニ僕ハ狂ッテイル。ガ　狂ッテイナイト思ッテ生キテイル。
>
> 僕ハシュルリアリズムカラアマリニ長イ間離レテ生キテイル。僕ガコレカラ先(何時カ)　本當ニ狂フトシタラソレハ僕ガ**シュルリアリズム**[4] カラアマリ長ガイ間離レテイタセイダト思ッテ呉レ。妻ヨ、僕ハ遺言状ヲ書イテヰル気分デイマコレヲカイテヰルケレドモ、僕ハ生キルゾ。[5]

> I had *a moment so idiotic* that I would die if I am told to and not if I am told not to.
>
> It was all a dream.
>
> It might be what is called "fatigue" and might be what is called insanity.
>
> I am a hopelessly feebleminded kid and my poetry is all just performance, lies.

> The Revolution and I who support it are all lies.[6] Only this writing has *any* ring of truth. What a long time I've been away from my "isolation"? Here in this room of mine, I feel like I am traveling to some place far away and I am living in a place that is distinguishable from neither nostalgia nor death. Or, perhaps, I live in the *Japanese language*.
>
> However, even this text which I consider extremely accurate is somewhat inaccurate and even insane.
>
> Certainly, I am insane. But, I live believing I am not.
>
> I have been living far away from *surrealism* for too long a time. Believe me, if I really go insane (sometime) from now it is because I have been far away from surrealism for too long.
>
> My dear wife, although I am writing this with the feeling that I am making my will, I will live on.

By the time this diary was written, Korea had experienced the U.S. occupation of the South and the Soviet occupation of the North (1945–1948), the establishment of separate governments in the South and in the North (1948), and a fratricidal civil war (1950–1953) that resulted in at least three to four million casualties, a corrupt dictatorship in the South, and the fortification of the communist regime led by Kim Ilsŏng in the North. In South Korea there was a brief period of exuberance following the popular uprising in April 1960 that overthrew the dictatorship of Yi Sŭngman, its first president.

Through trauma and violence, the North and South had each built a modern nation state. As each side claimed it would continue to force Japanese colonial legacies out of its sovereign territory, what was shared across the virtually impenetrable border that divided the peninsula was anti–Japanese nationalism. The remnants of Japanese culture, Japanese customs, and, above all, the Japanese language were identified as colonial legacies both in the North and the South. As a consequence, the Korean nation was most vividly imagined in opposition to "Japan."

In that context, the most telling detail about Kim's diary is that it was written in Japanese. Furthermore, it was written in *katakana* and in the prewar orthography no longer in use in postwar Japan. In the private space of the diary some 16 years after the end of Japanese colonial rule, Kim confessed to himself that he still lived in Japanese. "What is distinguishable from neither nostalgia nor death" is what is associated with the word "Japanese"; the reader can justifiably conclude that to the author Kim Suyŏng, Japanese was something nostalgic and dying out, or more precisely, it had the whiff of nostalgia because it was disappearing.

Kim left a series of notes on his poetry, and they attest to the lingering presence of colonial bilingualism in postliberation South Korea despite the South Korean state's systematic suppression of it. In the notes, Kim confessed that writing for him entailed continual negotiation between the Korean and Japanese languages. His case calls into question the ideology of the national language that works to obliterate the foreignness of speech and reinforces monolingualism as the normative linguistic condition of a cultural community.

Certainly, the Japanese language spread unevenly through Korea during the colonial period. The colonial government census of 1930 recorded that less than 7 percent of Koreans could understand Japanese. Moreover, where about 16 percent of Korean men were conversant in Japanese, fewer than 2 percent of women were. Only about 22 percent of Koreans were literate even in Korean, and there was a large gap in literacy in general between the urban and rural populations. The capital and also such provincial centers as Taegu and Kunsan had much higher Japanese and Korean literacy rates than rural areas. In short, Korean speakers of Japanese tended to be urban, elite, and male.[7] The experience of the poet and literary critic Kim Pyŏnggŏl reflects these discrepancies. Born in a rural area of the peripheral province of Hamgyŏngnamdo and raised in a nonaffluent family, he went to an uncertified elementary school. Because the school operated outside of the formal education system, Korean was used as the instructional language, although Japanese was also taught. In his autobiography, Kim recalled that when he went to Japan at the age of 18 in 1939 for further education, he could not say a single word in Japanese, whereas those Korean youth who had received formal education at certified elementary schools could speak Japanese. Nor could the Koreans he met delivering newspapers in Tokyo understand his heavy Hamgyŏngdo dialect.[8] As time passed, however, not only did his Japanese improve vastly, but he also began writing poetry in the language. He continued to write poetry in Japanese even after liberation because he felt he could not do so in Korean. Like many of his generation, his primary literary language was Japanese, not Korean.[9]

Certainly, the Japanese and Korean languages were placed on different planes during the colonial period. Whereas one was the language of administration, education, abstract thought, and science, the other was "the mother tongue," associated with feeling and emotion. Korean remained the dominant mode of literary expression throughout the colonial period, but Korean intellectuals and students began to lean toward Japanese literature from the 1930s until the end of Japanese rule. Moreover, by that time, more and more young people were not able to read and write Korean because they had not learned it at school. They became more fluent in Japanese than in Korean and, as a result, certain segments of the population in postcolonial Korea were more fluent in Japanese than Korean.[10]

The number of Koreans who understood Japanese increased rapidly after 1937 as the assimilation policy was accelerated in the last phase of colonial rule. After liberation, the leading authority on the Korean language, Yi Hŭisŭng, argued that the common use of Japanese words in everyday life was the biggest obstacle to cleansing liberated Korea of Japanese colonial legacies. Lamenting the lack of patriotism in people's language use, Yi demanded that Koreans should learn to speak the standard Korean language correctly.[11] His lament was testimony to the mark the Japanese language policies had left on the daily language use of the Korean people.

The suppression of postcolonial bilingualism was an essential part of modern nation state-building in Korea. Immediately after the liberation of Korea from Japanese colonial rule in 1945, Yi offered a definition of national language that succinctly captures the inseparable connection between the national language and the modern nation state. Yi defined national language as both the language in which the majority of the nation communicates and the official language of the state.[12] As Koreans aspired to build a modern nation state, it was not only inevitable but also imperative for them to have one unifying and unified national language.

In the process of building a monolingual society, the Japanese language was forced to disappear from public spaces in South Korea (as well as in the north) through the systematic suppression of the Japanese–Korean bilingualism of the generation of Kim Suyŏng and Kim Pyŏngŏl. Many of the generation that had to learn the Korean writing system (*hangŭl*) as young adults after 1945 familiarized themselves with it through reading Korean literature. Thus Korean literature functioned as the primary institution through which Korean youths were inculcated with the national language.

In this chapter, I tackle the issue of national language in postliberation South Korea by examining the process by which postcolonial bilingualism disappeared from Korea and monolingualism came to dominate. Paying special attention to the role of literature in the dominance of monolingualism in South Korea, I also explore the experience of the generation of Koreans who were more familiar with the Japanese language than with Korean because of their colonial experience and education. Many of them had to learn the Korean writing system after liberation when they were in their teens or early 20s because of the oppressive language policy during the final stage of colonial rule. The process of learning the writing system of their supposed native language was quite traumatic. Intellectuals of this generation felt shame and even guilt because they did not know "their own language," and instead were versed in the colonizer's language. During the colonial period, they did speak Korean at home and in private and, as a consequence, knew the colloquial language. Conversely, after liberation, they continued to speak Japanese with their friends out of school despite scoldings from their teachers. A number of primary sources indicate that they felt more comfortable with the Japanese language, as discussed in detail below.

Finally, by focusing on Kim Suyŏng's notes on his poetry, the chapter highlights Kim as a rare example of a critical intellectual who warned against the repressive nature of monolingualism in postliberation South Korea.

THE LANGUAGE SITUATION IN COLONIAL KOREA

It is often said that the Japanese colonial authorities aimed at eradicating Korean and replacing it with Japanese. However, the language policy of Japanese colonialism was actually more complicated. It was only in the final stage of Japanese colonial rule that the colonial government systematically suppressed the use of the Korean language and promoted Japanese as "the national language" (*kokugo*) in colonial Korea. Earlier, the Japanese colonial government had also aimed to standardize the Korean language, and particularly its orthography, to bring a colony-wide order to the educational system. When the colonial government announced the first colonial education law (*Chōsen Kyoikurei*) in 1911, a combined Korean and classical Chinese (*Chōsengo oyobi Kanbun*) course was designated as mandatory for elementary education.[13] In 1912, the colonial government issued a set of standard rules of orthography for elementary school education (*Futsū Gakkō Genbun Teijihō*). In 1921, the colonial government put out a revised version of the rules, replacing them yet again in 1930 with a new version that reflected the suggestions of Korean scholars of linguistics who participated in the research committee formed by the colonial government.[14]

Korean linguists themselves took pains to standardize Korean orthography independently of the Japanese colonial government. For them, the standardization of orthography was the first step toward a modern Korean language on par with the languages of other civilized nations.

They believed that the modernization of Korean would stimulate the development of modern Korean culture. Thus, the prominent Korean linguist, Yi Kŭngno, calling for the compilation of a Korean lexicon, argued in 1932 that a nation with aspirations to advance its culture must standardize the language that constitutes its cultural foundation.[15]

Despite the common nationalist desire to renovate Korean culture through the standardization of the language, Korean linguists through the 1920s lacked a unified voice concerning the Korean grammar and orthography. Opinion was split between the supporters of the *Chosŏn Ŏhak Yŏnguhoe* (Association for Research in Korean Linguistics), led by Pak Sŭngbin (1880–1943) and those of the *Chosŏnŏ Yŏnguhoe* (Association for Korean Language Research), organized by the disciples of the pioneering Korean grammarian Chu Sigyŏng (1876–1914). The two groups of Korean linguists competed to control the standardization of the Korean language.

Chu's disciples and their *Chosŏnŏ Yŏnguhoe,* however, began to dominate in 1930 when the colonial government's new version of orthography included many of its suggestions. That same year, it changed its name to the *Chosŏnŏ Hakhoe* (Association for Korean Language Studies) and reformulated its organizational structure. When it issued its unified orthography of Korean (*Hangŭl Mach'umpop T'ong-iran*) three years later in 1933, such Korean newspapers as *Tong-a Ilbo* (East Asia Daily) and *Chosŏn Ilbo* (Korea Daily) expressed their support.[16] In 1941, *Chosŏnŏ Hakhoe* issued a set of rules for the transliteration of foreign words. Throughout this period, the association made a tremendous effort to spread its version of orthography by offering workshops for the general public.

The Japanese colonial government sometimes competed and other times allied itself with Korean linguists in the standardization of Korean orthography. Some apologists for Japanese colonialism today even argue that Japanese colonialism helped modernize the Korean writing system (*hangŭl*) and contributed to the development of the Korean language. For example, 55 years after the end of Japanese rule in Korea, Nishio Kanji, a cofounder of the right-wing *Atarashii Rekishi Kyōkasho o Tsukurukai* (Japanese Society for History Textbook Reform), argued that the Korean writing system had been slighted and ignored by the indigenous *yangban* elite who had privileged classical Chinese, and that it was only under Japanese colonial rule that the writing system was integrated into the elementary school curriculum.[17]

However, even though the Japanese colonial government did take part in standardizing Korean and did not begin to systematically suppress the language until 1938, the Korean language did not receive equal treatment in the colonial period. Even before 1938, there were cases of schools discouraging students from speaking Korean not only in class but outside of it as well. For example, the Korean newspaper *Tong-A Ilbo* published a column in 1931 denouncing an elementary school in northern Kyŏngsang province for forbidding students from speaking Korean. According to the column, the faculty of the school forced students to report those who spoke Korean even outside of class and penalized them.[18]

Japanese was the official language of the Japanese empire in Korea. All government documents were issued in Japanese. The colonial civil service exam and bar exam were given in Japanese. Legal cases were tried in Japanese at court. In principle, classes were instructed in Japanese at school. All school textbooks except those for the Korean language and classical Chinese were written in Japanese.[19] Furthermore, Japanese was the primary language through which Korean intellectuals encountered the world. By the 1930s, about 90 percent of all books imported to Korea came from Japan.[20] It is not an exaggeration to say that educated Koreans were bilingual in Korean and Japanese. They learned Japanese at school in Korea and many went to Japan for further education. In contrast to colonial Korea, which was under the suffocating control by the colonial authorities, Japan offered relative freedom to Korean students, at least until the highly regimented mobilization for the war of 1941. In the late 1920s, quite a few Korean nationalist and leftist groups printed pamphlets and leaflets in Japan and shipped them home to Korea to avoid the tight censorship of the colonial government. Throughout the colonial period, Marxist and Communist books easily available and freely circulated in Japan were often arbitrarily confiscated in Korea.[21]

Above all, Korean intellectuals could encounter modern trends in arts and scholarship imported from the West much sooner in Tokyo than in Seoul. Thus, the modernist poet Yi Sang not only wrote poems in Japanese as well as in Korean but also went to Tokyo to experience the modernity offered by the metropole.[22] The diarist at the center of this chapter, Kim Suyŏng, stayed briefly in Japan during the colonial period and was fascinated by such Japanese modernist poets as Nishiwaki Junzaburō, Miyoshi Tatsuji, and Murano Shirō as well as T. S. Eliot, W. H. Auden, and Stephen Spender. To young Korean intellectuals who were attracted to modernism and sensitive to language, Tokyo was the place of modernity, and Japanese was the language of literary creation.

Although Koreans who could speak and understand Japanese remained a minority, their numbers rose rapidly throughout the 1930s. By 1943, the rate of Japanese literacy among Koreans had reached around 22 percent, largely because of the intensification of the promotion of Japanese as the national language after 1938.[23] Nonetheless, literature remained one of the cultural realms in which the Korean language was dominant. A 1929 essay on Korean literature by the critic Yi Kwangsu can be understood as an attempt to maintain the dominance of Korean in literature. Yi wrote in response to the decision made by the Korean Language and Literature department of Keijō Imperial University to use a Confucian text written by Yi I in 1577 called *Kyŏngmongyogyŏl* (Enlightening Those Who Are Ignorant and Recalcitrant) about the morality and manners expected from the Confucian gentleman as a textbook for a Korean literature course. Yi argued that the text should not be considered as part of Korean literature because it was neither creative nor scientific writing and thus was not qualified as a literary work no matter how far the boundaries of the category were stretched. More important, he argued that it did not belong to Korean literature because it had been written in classical Chinese. His criticism turned on the preeminence of language in determining the nationality of a work of literature. He asserted that Korean literature should be written in Korean, as English literature should be in English and Japanese literature should be in Japanese. He was also critical of the decision by the department to assign another fictional narrative written in classical Chinese, the late 17th century *Kuunmong* (The Cloud Dream of the Nine). Yi stressed that even though both texts had been penned by Korean writers, the nationality of the writer was not the determining factor. He argued that the nationality of a piece of literature was based neither on *jus soli* nor on *jus sanguinis*. There was another law: *jus lingua* (*songmun*).[24]

To understand why Yi favored Korean not only over English and Japanese but also over classical Chinese, it is necessary to remember that throughout the Chosŏn period (1392–1897), the Korean phonetic writing system (*hangŭl*) had been treated as inferior to classical Chinese. It was only during the colonial period that *hangŭl* achieved the dominant position in Korean literature, as Hong Kimun, the chief editor of the literature section of *Chosŏn Ilbo*, acknowledged at a roundtable discussion in 1936.[25]

Yi saw an inseparable connection between the Korean language and Korean literature. However, despite the prevalence of the Korean language in literary works, intellectuals and high school and college students began to prefer Japanese literature as they became versed in the Japanese language through colonial education. For example, *Tong-A Ilbo*'s 1931 survey of the reading habits of male high school students mentioned only one Korean writer, none other than Yi himself. By contrast, works by such Japanese writers as Kunikida Doppo and Natusme Sōseki were selected as favorites along with those of Erich Maria Remarque, Alexandre Dumas, and Leo Tolstoy. Another survey by *Tong-A Ilbo* in the same year showed a similar tendency among female high school students in Seoul, although Kikuchi Kan was included instead of Kunikida and Henrik Ibsen instead of Remarque in the list of favorite writers.[26]

A more serious threat to the dominance of Korean as the literary language came after 1937 with the intensified assimilation policy as the Japanese colonial authorities attempted to secure Koreans' support for the war in China. The propagation of the Japanese language was an integral part of the assimilation policy, and it coincided with a policy discouraging speaking Korean in public spaces. In 1938, the Japanese colonial government revised the colonial education law. The revision was supposedly aimed at merging the separate education systems for Japanese speakers and for non–Japanese speakers in Korea. The curricula for non–Japanese speakers were changed to be identical with those for Japanese speakers. Accordingly, it negatively affected Korean language education at school because the Korean-language course had been mandatory in non–Japanese speakers' schools and optional in Japanese speakers' schools. Thus the revision resulted in immediate demotion of the Korean language course. At the same time, the use of Japanese language was enforced with greater authority in school.[27]

In 1940, *Tong-A Ilbo* and *Chosŏn Ilbo*, the two largest Korean-language newspapers that had long provided a venue for Korean-language literature, were forced out of business by the colonial government. The only Korean-language newspaper that remained in print was *Maeil Sinbo* (Daily News), which was published by the Japanese colonial government. Korean-language literary journals were also forced out of print around the same time. The two most prominent Korean-language literary journals, *Munjang* (*Writing*) and *Inmun P'yŏngnon* (*Humanities Review*), for example, ceased publication in 1941, and the latter was succeeded by *Kokumin Bungaku* (National Literature) which, initially published in Korean for four issues a year and in Japanese for the remaining eight, soon became an entirely Japanese-language journal. In addition, as discussed in Chapter 3, Korean writers and poets were pressed to produce literary creations in Japanese.

It was in reaction to this suppression that Korean intellectuals held up the Korean language as the essence of the Korean national spirit. In particular, the 1942 arrest of members of the *Chosŏnŏ Hakhoe* by the colonial authorities helped engrave in the minds of Koreans the ruthless suppression of their language under Japanese rule. The members were suspected of hiding anti–Japanese activities behind the façade of Korean language research. Coupled with the overall suppression of Korean language use around the time, the persecution of the members of the Korean language research group came to symbolize the plight of Korean nationalist resistance to the ruthless suppression of the language by Japanese colonialism.

By the time of liberation, an overall consensus had already been reached among Koreans over the importance of the Korean language in building a new Korean nation state. The dispute between Yi T'aejun and Kim Saryang over Korean writers' literary production in Japanese demonstrated well the ultimate nationalist value bestowed on the Korean language. About a year after liberation, the leftist journal *Inmin Yesul* (*People's Art*) convened a roundtable discussion and invited such prominent writers and literary critics as Kim Namch'ŏn, Yi T'aejun, Han Sŏrya, Yi Kiyŏng, Kim Saryang, Yi Wŏnjo, Han Hyo, and Im Hwa. Except for the writer Yi T'aejun, the panelists had been leftists or leftist sympathizers during the colonial period.[28] They were requested to reflect on their activities as men of letters during the colonial period.

During the discussion, tension began to escalate when Yi T'aejun denounced those who had written in Japanese under Japanese colonial rule. He accused the writers of collaboration because they had succumbed to the pressure from the Japanese colonial authorities while Korean linguists were being persecuted and Korean-language media was being shoved out of print. He unequivocally insisted that Korean had been on the verge of annihilation because of the colonial government's persecution and argued that, under the circumstances, writing in Korean should have been the primary task of all Korean writers. The tone of his argument was self-righteous.[29]

In response to the charge, Yi Wŏnjo, the leftist literary critic, reasoned that not all the writers who had written in Japanese had in fact collaborated with the Japanese. For some of them, he said, writing in Japanese might have been better than writing nothing at all. Yi pointed out that writing in Japanese allowed one to escape censorship more easily. The most vehement refutation of Yi T'aejun's accusations, however, came from Kim Saryang, whose story "Deep Grass" I discussed in the introduction. Kim had made his debut in the Japanese literary establishment with his Japanese-language short story "*Hikari no Naka ni*" (Into the Light), which had been selected one of the finalists for the Akutagawa literary award in 1940. Countering Yi, Kim emphasized that the content of literature should be considered more important than its language. He vigorously maintained that the passive act of retreating into silence was no better than the active move of writing in Japanese. Nonetheless, in newly liberated Korea, his protest sounded feeble. The nationalist imperative was to favor Korean as the sole national language.[30]

NATIONAL CULTURE, NATIONAL LITERATURE, AND NATIONAL LANGUAGE IN POSTCOLONIAL KOREA

Discourse on national culture (*minjok munhwa*), national literature (*minjok munhak*), and national language (*minjokŏ* or *kugŏ*) proliferated in liberated Korea.[31] While leftist intellectuals were calling for a new national literature that would connect with the masses and contribute to social revolution, conservative intellectuals tended to stress the nebulous idea of national spirit. As part of the violent strife between leftists and rightists in the political turmoil of South Korea, leftist intellectuals denounced their rightist counterparts as national chauvinists who, in turn, accused leftists of using literature to instigate class struggle.

Pak Chonghwa, one of the writers in the rightist camp, argued that a nation was based on shared tradition, including myths, language, and a writing system. He praised those Korean writers who had taken pains to preserve Korean by creating literature in the language in opposition to the Japanese colonial language policy.[32] In a similar vein, another intellectual in the rightist camp, the poet Cho Chihun, argued that culture was significant as the site in which national subjectivity would emerge to overcome class, gender, and regional differences within the Korean nation. He analyzed the crisis of Korean culture as resulting from a lack of national subjectivity (*minjokjŏk chuch'e ŭi uigi*). He explained that because the national self (*cha-a*) had not yet been established, the Korean nation could not critically digest foreign ideas nor could it collectively struggle against foreign forces that were attempting to expand their influence on the Korean peninsula.[33]

On the other hand, the leftist intellectual and writer Kim Namch'ŏn stressed the pedagogical function of literature. He urged writers and poets to promote literacy among the masses and to educate them to appreciate literature and to write their own literary works. He especially focused on the need for linguists, writers, and poets to cooperate in promoting Korean because, he declared, literature is the art that relies on language. He also proposed that the purpose of literature is to express correctly and aesthetically the sensations of the everyday life (*saenghwal kamjŏng*) of ordinary Korean people and to discover, clarify, and create beautiful words in the Korean language.[34]

Leftist intellectuals were more cautious about broaching nationalist sentiments in promoting Korean. For example, Yi Wŏnjo warned that the Korean language itself was not the manifestation of an unchanging national spirit.[35] Yi noted that Korean had risen to the epitome of national consciousness during the colonial period in opposition to the suppression of the language by the Japanese colonial authorities. He recounted the ways in which the Korean people had taken pains to preserve Korean culture and language in reaction to the assimilation policy of Japanese colonialism, which aimed at eliminating Korean national consciousness. For this reason, he said, the Korean language had been valorized as the most precious trait of the Korean nation. In other words, he called attention to the moment in which there took place an inversion that the Korean language itself became equated with national consciousness.

Yi, however, reminded his readers that language was the instrument or expression of national consciousness, not national consciousness itself. He said that this error had made people fetishize the Korean language. Despite this fetishism, he pointed out that Korean changes like any other language. Thus, he argued, the means of developing the language should not consist of excavating an ancient Korean from the past or creating lifeless new expressions. In his view, literature had the most important role in the advancement of the language. He explained that the creation of language by literature meant that literature should describe change and development in society and social consciousness through linguistic expressions.[36]

Even among the leftists, different thinkers placed emphasis on divergent aspects of the problem. Nevertheless, both leftists and rightists agreed that ideally a nation constitutes a culturally homogeneous community and that national literature and national language should play a central role in generating such cultural homogeneity. Furthermore, although various political factions in Korean literary circles presented different ideas of national literature, almost all of them brooked no doubts about the language in which the national literature should be written. These intellectuals of vastly different spectrums, in fact, all agreed on the point that there was the inseparable connection between national literature and Korean as the national language.

Although the political status of Korean as the national language was unchallenged, there were obstacles to its becoming the national language that would bridge gaps between classes, genders, localities, and generations. The remnants of Japanese in people's daily language use were viewed as one of the most serious problems. For example, a newspaper article published three years after liberation reported that one could easily hear the influence of the Japanese language and Japanese culture while walking through the streets of Seoul. The author of the article chastised young women he overheard using such Japanese expressions as "*ara, iyada*" (oh dear, no) and "*jissai*" (in truth). The author also denounced those shops that still played records of "*naniwa bushi*" (Japanese storytelling to the tune of samisen music) and castigated the radio station for airing Japan-made "*Jazu*" (jazz).[37]

To the intellectuals, Korean had been polluted by Japanese during the colonial period, and it was urgent to cleanse it of the impurities left by the occupiers. Chang Chiyŏng, linguist and vice chief of the school textbook publication section in the U.S. occupation government, published an article in the journal *Hangŭl* illustrating the intellectuals' concern over the influence of Japanese in the people's daily language use. Chang began by identifying Korean as the linguistic medium for expressing a Korean national spirit. He lamented that it had been contaminated by Japanese words that had infiltrated into Korean during the colonial period and argued that Japanese words used in the present-day Korean language could not be compared to Latin or Greek words in English or French. Although the English and the French had borrowed words from Latin and Greek to enrich their languages, Japan had robbed Koreans of their language and literature and forced them to speak Japanese. He warned that as long as Japanese words remained in Korean, the Japanese spirit would haunt the Korean nation.[38]

Such concern about the pollution of Korean by Japanese led Korean officials in the U.S. military government in South Korea to initiate a Korean language purification campaign. Although the U.S. military government ruled South Korea until 1948, Korean officials in the government held the real power in making education policy. The U.S. military government rubber-stamped proposals from an advisory board of education composed of South Korean elites. In this case, the Ministry of Education instituted a "committee on national language purification." In its "proposal for the restoration of our language," the committee listed 862 Japanese words frequently used in daily conversation and their Korean alternatives. Despite a minority voice against such coercion, the government prohibited the use of the Japanese words and enlisted cooperation from newspapers and the only radio station in South Korea, the

Seoul Central Broadcast Station, to encourage people to use the Korean alternatives.[39]

The lingering influence of Japanese was not the only problem plaguing Korean, however. Despite all the efforts to standardize orthography during the colonial period, a thorough standardization of Korean had yet to be achieved. Yi Hŭisŭng attributed the lack of standardization to the chaotic state of mind of Koreans after liberation.[40] The division of society, Yi argued, went beyond the conflicts between rightists and leftists and between communism and democracy. He recounted a students' political gathering in which Korean students gave patriotic speeches using Japanese words, and he argued that the linguistic chaos testified to the deficiency of Korean national subjectivity. Thus, in his view, the chaotic state of the Korean language was the result not only of Japanese colonialism but also of a lack of a firm national subjectivity. Yi argued that consequently the standardization of national language would contribute to producing a strong national subjectivity that would unify the divided society of postliberation Korea.[41]

Thus, for those who insisted on the inseparable relationship between nation and language, "purifying" and "standardizing" Korean was equated with eradicating Japanese colonial legacies and unifying a divided society into a modern nation state. Virtually no one in liberated Korea, North or South, objected to this nationalist imperative. However, it does not take much to extrapolate the conspicuous internal contradictions in the ideology of national language. The concept of purification presumed the existence of a pristine Korean language before its pollution by Japanese, thus locating the ideal language in the past before colonization by Japan or even before the sinicization of Korean culture. On the other hand, the emphasis on standardization indicated aspirations to a unified Korean language that was not only absent in the present but had also never existed in the past. In other words, the purification policy presupposed an authentic Korean language to which present-day Koreans should return to establish a national language. But the urgent need to standardize Korean revealed that the language had existed only as divergent linguistic practices that had never been systematically unified despite decades of effort. Thus, the institutionalization of a national language involved not a return to a mythical pristine state of natural Korean before colonization or sinicization, but rather the invention of a standardized grammar and orthography to regulate diverse linguistic practices. This entailed reifying the ideology of an internally homogeneous language unit whose boundaries coincided with the boundaries of the community interpellated as the nation.

Japanese colonial rule not only had a drastic but enduring effect on the Korean language, but it also produced bilingual Koreans. To avoid any unnecessary misunderstanding, it is necessary to specify what this bilingualism was. As discussed above, because Japanese was the official language used in such public realms as education, court, government, and the military in colonial Korea, it was the language of learning, legal authority, and state power. Even in the field of literature, although the majority of works were still produced in Korean, an elite Korean readership had grown fond of Japanese literature and Western literature in Japanese translation. However, although Korean became gradually marginalized to the private realm of family, especially after 1938, younger generations still had to speak the language to communicate with older generations. Again, it should be remembered that the bilingual population was concentrated in urban areas, and to the younger generations, the educated elite, and men. Although the bilingual population was unevenly distributed, its numbers rapidly increased because of the intensive promotion of Japanese as the national language in the last stage of Japanese colonial rule. Bilingual Koreans were likely to be more fluent in Japanese in reading and writing even though they spoke Korean in daily conversation with their grandparents and parents.

Pak Wansō, one of the most celebrated writers in South Korea, offered a personal memory about her school days during the colonial period, and it echoes the experience that many in her generation went through to learn Japanese.[42] When she was a young girl, her family lived in the countryside around Kaesŏng, a commercial city northwest of Seoul. Because her family had moved there from Seoul, they spoke the Seoul dialect, marking their social superiority over those who spoke the local dialect. However, when she moved back to Seoul to attend one of the most prestigious elementary schools in colonial Korea, her linguistic ability was meaningless because Korean, even her proud Seoul dialect, was prohibited at school. Her classmates, who came from good families in Seoul, picked on her for not understanding Japanese, the language of instruction.

To make her mother proud, she quickly picked up the language, but, as she became fluent in Japanese, she felt ashamed of her mother who could not understand the language at all and needed an interpreter to talk to her teacher at PTA meetings. As she entered her teenage years, her facility in Japanese made her independent of her mother. She could read whatever she wanted in Japanese, without worrying about her mother finding out and scolding her.

The liberation of Korea came when Pak was 14. Japanese at school was prohibited overnight. Pak could speak Korean, but she did not know how to write and read in the language. Even in speaking, she felt much more comfortable with Japanese. She continued to talk to her friends privately in Japanese, risking punishment from her teachers. Japanese still remained the language through which she encountered the world, as she put it. Used bookstores were filled with Japanese books Japanese residents had left behind when returning to their country. She read Japanese literature and Western literature in Japanese translation. Akutagawa Ryūnosuke's *"Haguruma"* (Cogwheels) fascinated her and her friends because of its description of the split psyche of the main character on the verge of madness. She reminisced about a tense discussion she and her friends had over the story.[43] Her literary sensitivity grew in Japanese.

Even though Pak had pleasant memories of her school days before and after liberation, the experience must have been traumatic. An anecdote introduced in the journal *Puin* (*Woman*) in 1946 testifies to the traumatic experience of the whole generation of Korean youth who were forced to learn Japanese during the colonial period only to be prohibited from using it after liberation. The anecdote concerns Chŏngae, an elementary schoolgirl who is picked on by her classmates because she cannot speak Japanese well and given the nickname "the punishable" (*pŏljaeng'i*). Whenever her teacher, Mr. Kaneyama, finds her using Korean words, the teacher shouted *"Baka!"* ("idiot" in Japanese) at her and slaps her. That is how she received her nickname. After liberation, a girl transfers to Chŏngae's school. Her family has lived in Japan for a long time and she was born and raised there and cannot speak Korean well. She is always alone and other children call her by her Japanese name Kyōko. Chŏngae feels sorry for her and wants to make friends with her. When she speaks to her in Japanese to make her feel comfortable, the same Mr. Kaneyama, who has by now changed back to his Korean surname Kim, hears her and slaps her, angrily shouting "Didn't I tell you not to speak in Japanese?"[44]

This tragic–comic scene demonstrates the validity of Jacques Derrida's provocative point that "All culture is originarily colonial." In *Monolingualism of the Other or the Prosthesis of Origin,* Derrida deliberates on his relationship with the French language from his childhood and youth in colonial Algeria as a Jewish Algerian through his first encounter with the metropole to his later experiences as a prominent French scholar at international conferences. Derrida recounts his school days at a lycée in colonial Algeria and reminds the readers how the colonial system constantly subjected students, including Derrida himself, to "the interdict" to prioritize the colonizers' language over that of the colonized and to view the colonial linguistic hierarchy as natural.

Derrida expands this point by arguing that every culture, colonial or not, establishes and maintains itself by unilaterally enforcing the politics of language. Domination operates, he states, "through the power of naming, of imposing and legitimating appellations."[45] In other words, culture legitimizes domination, especially through language. Even though Derrida's discussion of domination and language tends to stress a more subtle and less physically coercive aspect of cultural legitimization, he is helpful in recognizing the commonalities between Japanese colonial education and that in a liberated Korea. Both worked at the service of legitimizing cultural domination through language.

To Korean intellectuals who aspired to the establishment of a new nation state, the presence of Korean–Japanese bilingualism symbolized an embarrassing colonial legacy that needed to be eradicated as soon as possible. Nevertheless, colonial bilingualism did not die out overnight, as seen in the case of the writer Pak Wansŏ. To those Korean youth in their mid-teens and early 20s at the time of Korea's liberation in 1945, Japanese was the language of abstract thought, artistic creation, and scientific research.[46] Many Korean writers and poets of that generation wrote their literary works in Japanese and translated them into Korean well into the 1950s. What they thought in Japanese had to be translated into what they wrote in Korean. Even as late as 1961, the poet Chŏn Ponggŏn, for example, confessed that Japanese was still his primary mode of literary expression. When liberation came in 1945, he "barely read Korean," and it was only after practicing reading Korean diligently that he was finally able to read it as quickly as he could Japanese. He admitted that even many years after liberation, he still developed poetic images in Japanese in his mind and translated them into Korean.[47] Chŏn's confession reflected the common experience of the writers and poets of his generation. Thus, one could dare to argue that Korean literature by the generation in the 1950s and early 1960s was translated from Japanese.[48]

At the same time, literature was the most important medium through which the generation learned how to read and write Korean. For example, one of the leading writers of the 1950s, Chang Yonghak, did not learn hangŭl until after liberation. In his memoir about Korean literary circles of the 1950s, the poet Ko Ŭn stated that Chang read "*Poktŏkpang*" (A Real Estate Office), one of Yi T'aejun's famous short stories from 1937, for the first time after liberation so he could study Korean. According to Ko,

Chang had to copy a Korean dictionary word by word over the course of a year before he could read the language.[49]

Yi T'aejun's 1940 primer *Munjang Kanghwa* (Lectures on Writing) was very influential in teaching this generation Korean. A writing textbook that drew examples from such prominent writers and poets as Yi Kwangsu, Kim Tongin, Chŏng Chiyong and Yi Sang, *Munjang Kanghwa* was initially serialized in the journal *Munjang* in 1939 and published as a book in 1940, then republished after liberation in 1947.[50] Just as the book is still regarded as one of the most authoritative writing textbooks in South Korea, it stood out among a number of books in the genre of writing textbooks popular from the 1910s through the 1930s because the author tackled the issue of the relationship between writing and speech.[51] From the beginning, Yi insisted on the idea of writing based on spoken language (*ŏnmunilch'i*) by emphasizing that "writing records and expresses language. In other words, writing cannot exist independently of speech (*mal*). Unless letters turn into pictorial images (*hoehwa*), writing will remain the record of language."[52] At the same time, Yi pointed to the difference between the written and spoken language. He stressed that although one could speak without consciously practicing speech, one must practice to write aesthetically and informatively. In other words, writing is not the verbatim record of speech but rather a system of principles one should follow to write effectively. Yi also emphasized the importance of individual style, arguing that one should avoid conventions of writing to be original. Thus, the two seemingly opposed imperatives of normativity and originality alternate in Yi's argument. These two imperatives worked together to establish Korean as a fully functional literary language.

Yi's endeavors to refine Korean-language writing provided him with support when he confronted Kim Saryang for writing fiction in Japanese during the colonial period at the roundtable discussion mentioned above. Yi had taken pains to develop Korean as a fully functional modern language in the face of the dominance of Japanese. Furthermore, *Munjang Kanghwa*, along with Yi's literary works, helped Korean youth to learn how to read and write in Korean after liberation.

AN ELEGY FOR THE DISAPPEARING LANGUAGE

Thanks to such literary contributions as Yi's *Munjang Kanghwa*, Korean grew to maturity as a modern literary language during the colonial period. From its inception, however, the development of Korean as a modern literary language and modern Korean literature itself was also deeply influenced by modern Japanese literature. Kim Suyŏng, the poet who wrote the Japanese-language diary introduced at the beginning of this chapter, was one of the few intellectuals in postliberation South Korea who publicly acknowledged the determining influence of modern Japanese literature over the development of modern literature in Korea. In an essay published in 1964, he observed that many literary works produced after liberation were merely repetitions of works written during the colonial period. This was not because postliberation writers consciously imitated such prominent colonial literary figures as Yi Hyosŏk, Kim Yujŏng, and Sim Hun, but because the determining influence over both the colonial and postcolonial writers came from the same source: modern Japanese literature.[53] What was a problem in Kim's eyes was that the younger generations of writers were ignorant of foreign literature, both Japanese and Western. Unlike their older colleagues, who were very well-read in modern Japanese literature and conscious of its influence over their literary work, the younger generations of writers were ignorant of modern Japanese literature despite its influence over them. Furthermore, they were poorly informed about American literature although they had been under its influence since liberation. To be more exact, Kim continued, just as Korean literature was influenced during the colonial period by Western literature through the mediation of Japanese literature, postliberation Korean literature continued to be influenced by Western literature but later western literary influence was imposed on it through the mediation of American literature.[54]

Certainly, Kim was not the first literary figure to make such a public acknowledgement about the determining influence of foreign literature on the development of Korean literature. During the colonial period, the prominent literary critic, poet, and literary historian Im Hwa wrote a series of controversial essays in which he asserted modern Korean literature developed through the "transplantation" and "imitation" of Western literature, and such transplantation and imitation proceeded through the mediation of modern Japanese literature.[55] Im especially emphasized the importance of Japanese literary influence over the development of modern literature in Korea. He also contended that Meiji literature produced within the Japanese movement to modernize its own writing under the rubric of *genbun itchi* (literally, the unification of speech and writing) was decisively influential in the development of modern Korean literature because modern Korean literary pioneers, inspired by the Japanese vernacular writing, experimented with different styles of vernacular writing and developed the Korean literary vernacularism.[56]

What is especially worthy of attention in Kim's essay, however, is the implication that foreign influence over Korean literature is necessary for its survival and prosperity. Although Kim seems to have made a rather trite remark about the shift in cultural hegemony in South Korea from Japan, the former colonial master, to the United States, the guardian of the anti–Communist regime in the newly independent country, his real aim in the essay was to criticize his fellow Korean writers who pursued literary styles of Western literature but failed to understand its spirit or *raison d'être*. In his view, the spirit of Western literature is the aspiration to absolute freedom, and the task of literature is to continuously invent and innovate modes of expression that bring to life such freedom in language.

By suggesting that Korean literature requires foreign influence to innovate and sustain itself not only in styles but also in spirit, Kim argued not for a slavish pursuit of Western literature or Japanese literature as the necessary mediation of Western literary influence but rather he believed that literature and culture become stale and ultimately perish if they are insulated from interactions with outside. That is why he warned against strong nationalistic sentiments permeating the poetry of nationalist poet Sin Tongyŏp, which he saw as growing into xenophobic chauvinism despite Sin's poetic prowess and progressive and populist political views.[57] In a similar vein, he was concerned that the poetic consciousness of many younger poets who advocated social engagement was couched in crude nationalist sentiments.[58]

Kim's admonition against nationalist chauvinism manifested in post-liberation and post–Korean-war literature carried over into his attitude toward language and culture. In his 1966 essay titled "*Kajang Arŭmdaun Urimal Yŏlkae*" (Our Ten Most Beautiful Words) he claimed that the most beautiful linguistic expressions are those alive in poetry and they are what should constitute the genuine language of Koreans. Kim stressed, however, that those expressions need not necessarily be native Korean words and further argued that nationalism should not dictate culture. Obviously in opposition to linguistic nationalism, he went on to insist that language naturally changes as the daily life of the masses changes, and any forced nationalist attempt to police culture would be futile.[59]

Kim's critical view of cultural and linguistic nationalism shaped his attitude toward the Japanese language. Kim left a series of "notes" on his poetry, mostly fragmentary thoughts on his poems as he was writing them and on poetry in general.[60] In one note, originally composed in 1966, Kim's complicated attitude toward Japanese is revealed not only in its content but in the fact that he wrote it in Japanese. As such it is evidence for the existence of Japanese–Korean bilingualism in 1960s South Korea, despite systematic efforts to eradicate it through education, literature, and mass media. Kim sent the original Japanese-language manuscript to a journal that decided to translate it into Korean, likely for the benefit of readers who did not understand Japanese.[61] However, the poet's intention and the journal's reaction can be fully understood only in the light of the intense anti–Japanese sentiment that had arisen at that time over the reestablishment of diplomatic relations between South Korea and Japan.

In South Korea, a series of fierce protests erupted against the normalization of relations with Japan between 1964 and 1966. Although normalization negotiations between the South Korean and Japanese governments had been held since 1952, progress had been impeded by disagreements over such issues as reparations for Japan's colonization of Korea and maritime border disputes. However, as the military government of Pak Chŏnghŭi in South Korea began to put its economic development plans into practice, South Korea desperately needed economic aid and loans from Japan. The military government understood well that its legitimacy would hinge on the success of its economic development program.[62] The Japanese government saw the reestablishment of diplomatic relations as an opportunity to begin exporting Japanese capital to the rest of Asia.[63] The United States further pushed the two countries to normalize relations, hoping to bolster its anti–Communist sphere of control in East Asia.[64] Because all three countries favored the reestablishment of diplomatic relations, the pace of negotiation hastened. The majority of people in South Korea, however, objected to the normalization of relations because they believed the South Korean government was too willing to give in to the demands of the Japanese government. They regarded the diplomatic normalization as a national humiliation. The opposition of the Korean people to the normalization grew coupled with antimilitary government sentiments. The military government felt compelled to declare martial law.[65]

Kim clearly anticipated that his readers would accuse him of being pro–Japanese for writing in Japanese. He began by pointing out that the Japanese writer Koyama Itoko had been ignored completely by the local media during a trip to South Korea. Clearly, the progovernment media avoided dealing with Japan-related topics because it feared possible negative reactions both from the opposition party and from radicalized university students. On the other hand, he argued, the dissident media harped on Japan-related matters only to sustain anti–Japan sentiments. Thus, he concluded that anti–Japanism in South Korea was inescapable.

Kim ironically claimed that he wrote in Japanese to respect the anti–Japanese principle. He recognized that his writing in Japanese served only to provoke criticism from readers, and thus no writer thereafter would dare to write publicly in Japanese. Kim, however, immediately contradicted himself by adding that he decided to write intentionally in unnatural Japanese to give others a chance to write back in better Japanese. He also admitted that for the first time since the liberation of Korea he was finally publishing what he wrote without "translating" from Japanese. In other words, in his mind, his writing in Korean had, in fact, always been a translation from Japanese.[66]

Kim further raised the question of translation by focusing on the colonial-era experimental poet Yi Sang. He explained that he was currently translating Yi's Japanese-language poem *"Aiya"* (Sad Night).[67] While calling attention to the fact that Yi wrote in both languages during the colonial period, he expressed dissatisfaction that Yi wrote "Korean lyricism in Korean and Japanese lyricism in Japanese." He insisted that Yi should have expressed Korean lyricism in Japanese and Japanese lyricism in Korean.

Although Kim seemed to suggest that Yi's poems were couched in uniquely Korean poetic sentiments, the poetry, known for its experimental abstractness, was not marked with distinctly national sentiments that could be unequivocally associated with either Japanese or Korean lyricism. For example, intentionally avoiding the conventional diction rooted in either tradition, Yi used mathematical symbols and equations in many of his poems, both in Japanese and Korean. Because Kim did not offer any further explication, it was not clear what he thought of the nature of the difference between Japanese and Korean lyricism that he argued was inhered in Yi's poetry.[68] What is certain, however, is that Kim envisioned the possibility of what he called "ultimate irony," the irony that undermines the tenacious nationalist idea about literature that the literary sentiments of a nation can be expressed only by the national language.

Kim argued that the way he used the Japanese language was different from the way Yi had used it 30 years earlier. He enigmatically stated that his own Japanese was not Japanese at all: He implied that it was "a ghost."[69] He then listed reasons why he still used Japanese: sympathy for things people do not use anymore, exasperation with Korean, relative ease in Japanese expression, among other reasons. Moreover, he argued that he could still look up words in his old Japanese–English dictionary.

Through all these experiences, which would not be available to him did he reside only in one language, he reflected on and recognized the transformation of his poetic reality, Kim wrote.

Kim's testament to bilingualism went further than merely noting that some Korean intellectuals still wrote in Japanese or that they felt more comfortable with the former colonizer's language in postliberation South Korea. It also indicated Kim's resistance to the monolingualism that had been foisted on his generation. Kim noted the subversive irony that could be achieved by writing Japanese lyricism in Korean and Korean lyricism in Japanese. What is at issue is not that a poet should be versed in more than one native tongue but that he had to translate his poetry from Japanese to Korean, and it exposed the gulf between the native tongue and the national language. Kim's native tongue was the Korean he had learned from his mother, but that language was different from the national language that he could not wield freely enough to write poems without the help of Japanese. The native tongue was not Kim's own, either. As discussed below, no one possesses language or even a language, although he or she belongs in it.

Not only did Kim's poetry writing involve translation from Japanese to Korean. Kim was also a prolific translator of English. He translated articles and stories from such English-language journals as *The Atlantic Monthly*, *Encounter*, and *Partisan Review* for Korean journals and magazines. As mentioned earlier, he was also influenced by such English modernist poets as Eliot, Auden, and Spender. He even asserted that the secret of his poetry hid in his translations.[70] Kim's poetry written through translation brings into question the ideology behind the naive belief that a poet should master his or her native tongue to express poetic images most effectively. Such an ideology erases the alterity of language and reinforces monolingualism as the normative linguistic situation for a cultural community. In other words, by suppressing the alterity of language, the tenacious ideology of "national language" presumes that one's native tongue is inseparably and naturally connected to the language of a nation in which one belongs.

Again, Derrida's deliberation on his relationship with the French language is helpful for appreciating the alterity of language, which the ideology of a native tongue cannot completely exorcize. Derrida insisted that French, the only language in which he felt at home, was nevertheless not his, not only because he was born into a non–French, Jewish family in colonial Algeria and was temporarily deprived of French citizenship under Vichy rule as an Algerian Jew—even though he was educated and immersed in French—but also because his experience exemplified the alienation inherent in any person's relationship with language. Because of this inescapable alienation, he concluded, every language is a language of the other.[71] No one can possess a language because it is impossible to draw fixed boundaries around a language as an enclosed and autonomous unit because of the fact that no language is in isolation from other languages. If language cannot be assumed to be a clearly demarcated unit of a language, then, can it be possible to possess a language? More fundamentally, however, no one can own a language because it is impossible to have a language at one's complete disposal. Language always exceeds the limits of human freedom. The recognition of the alterity of language led him to realize that even if one can speak only one language, one's monolingual practice is still "absolute translation," albeit an act of translation that does not proceed from a source language, an originary language that originates in the ipseity (selfhood) of the speaker. It only aims to arrive at a target language, a language of the other. According to Derrida, nevertheless, no one is ever free from the desire to restore an originary language. Preceding even the selfhood of the subject, such desire is derived from the endeavor to arrive at a target language that never fully succeeds. He termed the never-existent originary language "a prior-to-the first language." Because such a preoriginary language does not exist, the desire for it becomes instead the desire to invent one. This language that will appear only in the future is the language of the other.[72] For Derrida, the language of the other happens to be an idiom that is called French. What should be kept in mind, however, is that Derrida's French should not be equated with the national language of France, whose unity can be thought of only through the schematization to identify diverse linguistic practices as derivatives of one homogeneous language called French. The language of the other rather suggests the alterity of language, and the alterity of language in turn serves as a reminder of the inevitable alienation from any given language, even one's own native language. A language one can posses as one's own does not exist, not least because ultimately there is no core in any given language that forms myriad instances of linguistic practice into a transparently identifiable and thus countable unit of language as a conventional understanding of language suggests. A language thus always remains as a promise yet to be fulfilled in the future. More important, this promise makes speech possible and enables each person to engage in dialogue with the other. The language of the other bears on language's ethicality because the language of the other constitutes not the language *of* the other but rather the language *for* the other.[73]

As the alterity of language led Derrida into envisioning even monolingual practice as an act of translation, the translation that Kim's poetry writing required must have constantly alerted him to the alterity of language. Even a poet cannot tame, control, and appropriate language completely. Thus, the recognition of language's alterity made him challenge the widely accepted belief that because the poetic mind of a poet can be fully expressed only in that poet's native tongue, poetry is the literary genre that resists translation most completely.[74]

At the same time, Kim's elegiac acceptance of the disappearance of Japanese from South Korea reflected the inevitable dominance of monolingualism based on the ideology of national language.[75] Kim felt attached to Japanese because it was disappearing. To be more precise, the Japanese language use resulting from colonial bilingualism was forced into extinction in South Korea. The majority of the new generations of Kim's readers would not know that his literary roots lay in part in Japanese modernist poets. Colonial bilingualism was disappearing from Korea along with the generation of Kim Suyŏng. But until its, and his, extinction, Japanese continued to haunt Korea like a ghost.

Notes

PREFACE

1. The mission statement of UNESCO about its two literary translation projects provides a good example of such a view. It says, "UNESCO promotes cultural diversity and intercultural understanding through two publishing projects, the Index Translationum, a longstanding publication, and the more recent Clearing House for Literary Translation." UNESCO, "Broader and Easier Access to the World's Variety of Literary Works," http://portal.unesco.org/culture/en/ev.php-URL_ID=12312&URL_DO=DO_TOPIC&URL_SECTION=201.html (accessed March 27, 2013).

2. As I argue below, translation of Korean classical literature into Japanese also played an important role in introducing Korean culture to Japan. Hosoi Hajime, the pioneering Japanese translator who set out to introduce Korean literature to Japan during the colonial period, focused on translating such classical Korean literary works as *Simch'ŏngjŏn* [The Tale of Simchŏng], *Kuunmong* [The Cloud Dream of the Nine], *Hong Kiltongjŏn* [The Tale of Hong Kiltong], and *Ch'unhyangjŏn.* [The Tale of Ch'unhyang].For more information, see Kajii Wataru, "*Chōsen Bungaku Honyaku no Ashiato*" [The Traces of Korean Literature Translation], 12 parts, *Kikan Sanzenri* [Three Thousand Leagues Quarterly] 22 (1980): 203–15; 23 (1980): 230–39; 24 (1980): 175–85; 25 (1981): 198–208; 26 (1981): 204–13; 27 (1981): 204–24; 28 (1981): 225–35; 29 (1982): 196–205; 30 (1982): 162–72; 31 (1982): 216–26; 32 (1982): 217–27; 33 (1983): 200–51.

3. Tejaswini Niranjana, *Siting Translation* (Berkeley and Los Angeles: University of California Press, 1992).

4. Throughout the book, unless it is indicated otherwise, the surnames come first for Chinese, Japanese, and Korean names except for those of writers whose English-language works are referenced. Thus, An Hwak's surname is An.

5. Benedict Anderson, *Imagined Communities: Reflections on the Origin and Spread of Nationalism* (London and New York: Verso, 1991).

6. Nicholas B. Dirks, "Introduction: Colonialism and Culture," in *Colonialism and Culture*, ed. Nicholas B. Dirks (Ann Arbor: University of Michigan Press, 1992).

7. The concrete practices of this policy included barring the use of Korean in public spaces, the coerced changing of names to Japanese-style ones, and forced attendance at Shinto shrines. The enforcement of these practices was intensified after the Sino-Japanese War began in 1937. Japan needed to secure Korean support for the war effort because of Korea's geographical proximity to China and Manchuria, as well as the large size of its population. For more information about the Japanese assimilation policy in its colonies, see Miyata Setsuko, *Chosŏn Minjung kwa 'Hwangminwha' Chŏngch'aek*, [The People of Korea and the Imiperialization Policy], trans. Yi Yŏng-rang (Seoul: Ilchogak, 1997); Oguma Eiji, *"Nihonjin" no Kyōkai* [Boundaries of "the Japanese"] (Tokyo: Sinhyōsha, 1998); Ch'oe Sŏggyŏng, *Ilche ŭi Tonghwa Ideorogi ŭi Ch'angch'ul* [The Construction of the Japanese Assimilation Policy] (Seoul: Sŏgyŏng Munhwasa, 1997); Mark E. Caprio, *Japanese Assimilation Policies in Colonial Korea 1910–1945* (Seattle: University of Washington Press, 2009).

8. The Korean intellectual Hyŏn Yŏngsop, who worked for *Ryokki*, the Japanese-language journal published in colonial Korea, suggested total eradication of the Korean language in public spaces to Governor General Minami Jirō in 1937. Im Chongguk, *Ch'inil Munhangnon* [A Treatise on Pro-Japanese Literature] (Seoul: Pyŏngwha, 1966), 50.

9. Naoki Sakai, *Translation and Subjectivity* (Minneapolis: University of Minnesota Press, 1997), 1–17.

10. I use the term *colonial discourse*, following Edward Said's lead, while acknowledging that Said's use of the term is problematic when judged against Michel Foucault's concept of discourse, as Robert Young and Bart Moore-Gilbert have already pointed out. Nonetheless, I have decided to use it because it is valuable to describe how diverse texts intersect and weave the web of meanings, informing the way colonial relations are perceived and practiced. Inspired by Homi Bhabha's use of the same term, I employ it also to emphasize the ambivalence toward the relationship between the colonizer and the colonized found in the texts and statements. Edward Said, *Orientalism* (New York: Vintage Books, 1979); Robert Young, *White Mythologies* (London and New York: Routledge, 1990); Homi K. Bhabha, *The Location of Culture* (London and New York: Routledge, 1994); Bart Moore-Gilbert, *Postcolonial Theory* (London and New York: Verso, 1997); Robert Young, *Postcolonialism* (Malden and Oxford: Blackwell, 2001).

11. Karl Marx, *Grundrisse* (London: Penguin Books, 1993), 163.

12. George Steiner, *After Babel* (Oxford: Oxford University Press, 1975), 318–19. Tejaswini Niranjana argues, against Steiner, that equal exchange in translation is impossible in the colonial context. Niranjana, *Siting Translation*, 59–61.

13. Lydia H. Liu, "The Question of Meaning-Value in the Politics of Econ-

omy of the Sign," in *Token of Exchange*, ed. Lydia H. Liu (Durham, N.C.: Duke University Press, 1999).

14. Both Homi Bhabha and Robert Young have already paid attention to the possibility of Levinasian ethics as a radical criticism of colonial domination: Bhabha, *Location of Culture*, 15–17; Young, *White Mythologies*, 12–18. For a more recent discussion on Levinas's ethics and its implications for postcolonial thought, see Robert Eagleston, "Postcolonial Thought and Levinas's Double Vision," in *Radicalizing Levinas*, ed. Peter Atterton and Matthew Calarco (Albany: SUNY Press, 2010), 57–68; John Drabinski *Levinas and the Postcolonial* (Edinburgh: Edinburgh University Press, 2011). Drabinski's book treats the difficulties inherent in Levinas's thought when one attempts to criticize colonialism by drawing on his philosophy. In the book, Drabinski also explores the ways in which his insights are crucial to addressing issues concerning the colonial and postcolonial relationships nevertheless by reading such postcolonial thinkers as Frantz Fanon, Gayatri Spivak, and Homi Bhabha through the lens of Levinas's thought. Unfortunately, I came across Drabinski's edifying book too late, only after producing the final draft of my manuscript and regretfully could not benefit from his lucid expositions of Levinas's relevance to postcolonial studies for my own discussion on the subject. In any case, such attention to Levinas within colonial and postcolonial studies has been sparse however. Levinas's influence over postcolonial studies has been limited in comparison with that of Michel Foucault, Jacques Derrida, or Jacques Lacan. The Argentine philosopher Enrique Dussel is a rare exception in that he acknowledges the profound impact of Levinas's thought on his criticism about colonialism and neocolonialism in Latin America. Dussel reads Marx through Levinas to underline the ethicality embedded in Marx's criticism of capitalism. Enrique Dussel, *Philosophy of Liberation* (Maryknoll: Orbis Books, 1985); Enrique Dussel, *The Underside of Modernity: Apel, Ricoeur, Rorty, Taylor, and the Philosophy of Liberation* (Atlantic Highlands: Humanities Books, 1996). However, even Dussel is critical of Levinas's failure to look at Europe and the tradition of Western thought from beyond. Walter D. Mignolo, "Dussel's Philosophy of Liberation," in *Thinking from the Underside of History*, ed. Linda Martin Alcoff and Eduardo Mendieta (Lanham, Md.: Rowman & Littlefield, 2000), 27–50.

15. Emmanuel Levinas, *Totality and Infinity* (Pittsburgh: Duquesne University Press, 1969); Emmanuel Levinas, *Otherwise than Being* (Pittsburgh: Duquesne University Press, 1998).

16. Quoted in George Alexander Lensen, *The Russian Push Toward Japan, 1697–1875* (Princeton: Princeton University Press, 1959), 44–45.

17. Bhabha, *Location of Culture*, 66–84.

18. Levinas, *Totality and Infinity*, 242–43.

19. Salvoj Žižek, *Organs Without Bodies: Deleuze and Consequences* (London and New York: Routledge, 2004), 106. For a more sympathetic explication of Levinas's hesitance in condemning the Israeli state, see Howard Caygill, *Levinas and the Political* (London and New York: Routledge, 2002), 190–94.

20. There have been ample studies done on the implications of Levinas's ethics for politics. One of the most influential studies is Simon Critchley's work. Critchley argues that the potentiality of radical politics embedded in deconstruction can come into view only when deconstruction is placed in dialogue with Levinas's ethics of alterity. Simon Critchley, *The Ethics of Deconstruction: Derrida and Levinas* (West Lefayette: Purdue University Press, 1999).

21. For Levinas's privileging Israel, see Emmanuel Levinas, "Politics After," in *Levinas Reader,* ed. Seán Hand (Oxford and Cambridge: Blackwell, 1989): 277–83.

22. One of the subtly nuanced but crucially critical questions Derrida raised in his response to Levinas's *Totality and Infinity* bears on the issue. Jacques Derrida, "Violence and Metaphysics: An Essay on the Thought of Emmanuel Levinas," *Writing and Difference* (Chicago: University of Chicago Press, 1978), 79–153.

23. Levinas, *Otherwise than Being or Beyond Essence,* 5–8; 37–51.

24. Ibid., 154–55; 162.

25. Levinas, *Totality and Infinity,* 84.

26. Ibid., 174.

27. The Japanese translator and political writer Hosoi Hajime's idea of love, which is discussed in Chapter 1, describes the self's capacity to understand the other well enough.

28. Levinas, *Otherwise than Being or Beyond Essence,* 37–38, 64–67.

29. Emmanuel Levinas, "Dialogue," *Of God Who Comes to Mind* (Stanford, Calif.: Stanford University Press, 1986), 141.

30. Karl Marx, *The Critique of the Gotha Programme* (New York: International, 1966), 10. Nevertheless, scant attention has been paid to the affinity between Marx and Levinas. Dussel's work is a notable exception, as mentioned earlier. Following are previous scholarly endeavors in English to read Marx and Levinas together. James Daly, "Totality and Infinity in Marx," *Irish Philosophical Journal* 4, no. 1 and 2 (1987): 120–44; Robert Gibbs, *Correlations in Rosenzweig and Levinas* (Princeton: Princeton University Press, 1994), 229–54; Asher Horowitz and Gad Horowitz, "An Ethical Orientation for Marxism: Geras and Levinas," *Rethinking Marxism* 5, no. 2 (2003): 181–95.

31. Jacques Derrida, *Monolingualism of the Other: Or, The Prosthesis of Origin* (Stanford, Calif.: Stanford University Press, 1998).

32. Ibid., 39.

INTRODUCTION

1. "*Che Samgukche ŭi Chiryŏng Pada Haengdong Kangnyŏng ŭl Surip*" [Writing a Mission Statement Following an Order from the Third International], *Chosŏnilbo* [Korea Daily], September 12, 1930.

2. For more information, see Yamada Hiroto, "*Nihonjin Keisatsukan ni Taisuru Chōsengo Shōrei Seisaku*" [Japanese Police's Korean Language

Learning Policy], *Chōsenshi Kenkyūkai Ronbunshū* [Collected Articles of the Korean History Research Association] 38 (2004): 123–49.

3. The story was first published in First High School's journal *Kōyūkai Zasshi* [Alumni Magazine] in 1929. In this chapter, I use the story republished in *Nakajima Atsushi Zenshū* [Collected Works of Nakajima Atsushi], ed. Hikami Hidehiro and Nakamura Mitsuo, 3 vols. (Tokyo: Chikuma Shobō, 1976), 2: 50–64. Nakajima (1907–1942) went to Korea at the age of 11 when his father took a teaching position at Ryūzan Middle School in Keijō, present-day Seoul, Korea. Having grown up in Korea until returning to Japan in 1926 to enter First High School (*Dai Ichi Kōtō Gakkō*), he wrote a number of stories set in Korea, including "*Toragari*" [Tiger Hunt] (1934).

4. Yamada, "*Nihonjin Keisatsukan ni Taisuru Chōsengo Shōrei Seisaku.*"

5. Kim Saryang (1914–?) was born into a rich family in Pyŏngyang, Korea. After being expelled from high school for his involvement in an anti-Japanese classroom walkout, he went to Japan to continue his high school education in 1931. He entered Tokyo Imperial University in 1936, majoring in German literature. His story "*Hikari no Nakani*" [In the Light] was selected as one of the finalists for the Akutagawa Award in 1940. While serving in the North Korean Army as a war correspondent during the Korean War, he went missing. Kim published "*Kusa Fukashi*" in the Japanese literary journal *Bungei* [Literature] in July 1940. Here I use the story republished in *Kim Saryang Zenshū* [Collected Works of Kim Saryang], ed. Kim Saryang Zenshū Henshū Iinkai, 4 vols. (Tokyo: Kawade Shobōshinsha, 1973–1974), 1: 147–70.

6. The story appeared in the Japanese journal *Kaizō* [Reconstruction] in September 1922. Here I consult the story republished in *Chosen: "Gaichi" no Nihongo Bungakusen* [Korea: Selected Japanese-language Literary Works from "Overseas"], ed. Kurokawa Sō (Tokyo: Shinjuku Shobō, 1996): 27–73. The author, Nakanishi, after trying his hands at various jobs in Japan became a reporter for *Heijō Nichinichi Sinbun*, the Japanese-language newspaper in Pyŏngyang. He made his literary debut in 1922 with his novel *Akatsuchi ni Megumu Mono* [That Which Sprouts from Red Soil] in which he depicted Japanese settlers who were involved in drug trafficking in Korea.

7. The March First movement refers to a series of demonstrations organized by nationalist activists in Korea starting on March 1, 1919. Korean demonstrators protested against repressive Japanese rule and demanded Korea's independence from Japan. The colonial government reacted violently, deploying a large number of troops and police officers. The violent suppression resulted in mass arrests and heavy casualties among the demonstrators.

8. Arguably the most sympathetic and significant portrayal of a translator in Japanese literature written during the colonial period is found in the 1912 novel *Chōsen* [Korea] by the prominent haiku poet and writer Takahama Kyoshi (1874–1959). Based on Kyoshi's experiences during his travels in Korea in 1911, a year after the annexation by Japan, the novel was serialized in the two newspapers *Ōsaka Mainichi Shinbun* [Osaka Daily Newspaper] and *Tōkyō Nichinichi Shinbun* [Tokyo Daily]. One of the important characters

in the novel, Hong Wŏnsŏn, once a person of high standing, is now working as a translator and interpreter for Japanese visitors. He had lost his status and wealth because he was anti–Japanese at the time of the annexation. Although Kyoshi portrayed some of the pro–Japanese high-ranked Koreans with contempt, he depicted Hong as a man of dignity and culture, an excellent speaker who speaks Japanese fluently in the novel. Takahama Kyoshi, *Chōsen* (Tokyo: Jitsugyō no Nihonsha, 1912).

9. The dearth of Japanese functionaries/translators did, of course, not mean their complete absence. For example, when the journal *Chōsengo* (Korean) elicited from government and military translators responses to a question of whether faithful or liberal translation is more desirable, both Japanese and Koreans sent their responses. *"Chūyaku wa Iyakuka Chokuyakuka"* [Should Translation Be Liberal or Literal?], *Chōsengo* (January 1926): 71–74.

10. Kamisaka Taizō, *"Honshi no Chōsengo Kenkyūran Setchi"* [Our Newspaper's Implementation of a Korean Language Study Section], *Chōsen Keisatsu Shinbun* [Korean Police Newspaper], June 15, 1929.

11. Roman Jakobson, "On Linguistic Aspects of Translation," in *Theories of Translation*, ed. Rainer Schulte and John Biguenet (Chicago: University of Chicago Press, 1992): 144–51.

12. Jacques Derrida, *Speech and Phenomena and Other Essays on Husserl's Theory of Signs* (Evanston: Northwestern University Press, 1973), 89.

13. Ibid., 77.

14. Kitahara Hakushū, "Jo" [Preface] to *Chōsen Minyōshū*, ed. and trans. Kim Soun (Tokyo: Taibunkan, 1929), 2–6.

15. The Tokugawas shogunate enforced the "alternate attendance" (*sankin kōtai*) policy, which required local lords to move periodically between their domains and Edo. Local lords were also required to alternate residence in their own domains and Edo, where their wives and heirs were ordered to remain. The main purpose of the policy was to check local lords' financial and political power and ensure their loyalty to the shogunate. The frequent travel of local lords and their retainers contributed to the development of trade routes and the increase of economic and cultural exchange within Japan.

16. Two representative works that trace the emergence of modern Japanese national consciousness through the state apparatus are Carol Gluck, *Japan's Modern Myths* (New York: Columbia University Press, 1985) and T. Fujitani, *Splendid Monarchy* (Berkeley: University of California Press, 1998).

17. Kojin Karatani, *Origins of Modern Japanese Literature* (Durham: Duke University Press, 1993), 11–44. Seiji Lippit offers a lucid explication on this point in *Topographies of Japanese Modernism* (New York: Columbia University Press, 2002), 9–12.

CHAPTER ONE

1. Hosoi Hajime, *Chōsen Bungaku Kessakushū* [Collection of Korean Literary Masterpieces] (Tokyo: Hōkōkai, 1924), 4.

2. Nevertheless, it is arguable whether all the writings Hosoi introduced can be indisputably categorized as Korean literature. For example, at least two works included in *Chōsen Bungaku Kessakushū* (ibid.), *Unyŏngjŏn* [The Story of Unyŏng] and *Suk'hyangjŏn* [The Story of Suk'hyang], were originally written in classical Chinese. They would not belong to Korean literature according to the prominent Korean intellectual Yi Kwangsu's definition of Korean literature. In his essays originally serialized in the Korean-language newspaper *Maeil Sinbo* [Daily News] from November 10 through 23, 1916, Yi refused to regard writings in classical Chinese as Korean literature even though they had been written by the ancestors of present-day Koreans. See Yi Kwangsu, *"Muhak iran Hao"* [What Is Literature?], in *Hagun Hyōndae Munhak Pip'yŏngsa* [History of Modern Korean Literary Criticism] (Seoul: Hanguk Haksul Chŏngbo, 2004), 1: 48–64. This does not mean that Yi's definition corresponds with the officially accepted category of Korean literature in contemporary South Korea. In the South Korean education system, the majority of the literary works Hosoi either translated by himself or had others translate are taught as premodern Korean literature, even though they were written in classical Chinese. Like any other national literatures, the boundaries of Korean literature are not only amorphous but also impossible to draw indisputably.

3. Raymond Williams, *Keywords* (New York: Oxford University Press, 1985), 185.

4. Mikami Sanji and Takatsu Kuwasaburō, *Nihon Bungakushi* [History of Japanese Literature], 2 vols. (Tokyo: Kinkōdō, 1890) 1:25. It is interesting to note that both *Nihon Bungakushi* and Hosoi's 1911 *Chōsen Bunkashiron* [Treatise on the History of Korean Culture] shared the same mistaken view about Korean script, mistaking *idu* for *hangŭl*. Although *idu* may refer to such writing systems as *hyangch'al* and *kugyŏl*, which use Chinese letters to transcribe Korean phonetically, in a narrower sense *idu* refers to the writing system mainly used by scribes for writing administrative documents. The script also borrowed Chinese letters but added certain characters specifically to represent grammatical markers and the endings of Korean verbs. *Hangŭl* is a script that was invented in the 15th century and is not dependent on Chinese letters.

5. Louis Althusser, *Lenin and Philosophy* (New York: Monthly Review, 1971): 127–86.

6. For more information on Hosoi, see Maseki Toshio, *"Taishōki ni Okeru Chōsenkan no Ittenkei"* [The Epitome of a Typical View on Korea During the Taishō Period], *Nihon Kindashi Kenkyū* [Modern Japanese History Research], 8 (1965): 28–38; Takasaki Sōji, *"Aru 'Chōsentsū' no Ikita Michi"* [The Life of a Korea Afficionado], *Kikan Sanzenri* [Quarterly Sanzenri], no. 30 (1982): 104–15; Aono Masaaki, *"Hosoi Hajime no Chōsenkan"* [Hosoi Hajime's View of Korea], *Kan* [Korea], no. 110 (1988): 221–58.

7. It should be noted that all the works Hosoi translated himself had been originally written in classical Chinese. When Hosoi published translations of

works written in vernacular Korean he had others translate them into Japanese. It raises a question about his level of fluency in vernacular Korean. For example, in *Chōsen Bungaku Kessakushū,* the only work Hosoi translated by himself is the early 17th-century *Unyŏngjŏn* [Story of Unyŏng], the original text of which had been written in classical Chinese.

8. Hosoi Hajime, *Chōsen Bunka Shiron* [Treatise on the History of Korean Culture] (Keijō: Chōsen Kenkyūkai, 1911), xix.

9. Ibid., xx.

10. Maseki, "*Taishōki ni Okeru Chōsenkan no Ittenkei,*" 29.

11. Hosoi, *Chōsen Bunka Shiron,* xvi. It can be said that by positioning Koreans as the children of the emperor, Hosoi extended the so-called family-state ideology of prewar Japan to the newly colonized people. In the family-state ideology, the whole nation was imagined as a family, with the emperor as its head. The extension of the family-state ideology to Korea might bear on several occasions of Hosoi's representation of Japan as Korea's big brother, its patriarchal guardian. It is noteworthy that Hosoi resorted to the imperial authority to persuade Japanese to embrace Koreans as part of Japan rather than to force Koreans to accept colonization. As a matter of fact, throughout his texts, Hosoi invoked the family-state ideology only when entreating the Japanese to treat Koreans more benevolently. He underlined what he perceived as the backwardness of Korean culture and society and their national character instead when justifying the inevitability of colonization on the other hand.

12. Hosoi, *Chōsen Bunka Shiron,* xvii.

13. Ibid., 4.

14. Ibid., xvii. During the 1920s, Hosoi came to reevaluate the supposed toadyism of Koreans, if understood correctly, as an advantage the Japanese could tap into to win them over.

15. Hosoi's diatribes against the ruling *yangban* may not only derive from his desire to justify Japanese colonialism but also reflect the lingering influence of the socialism Hosoi had once dabbled in. Even after he had renounced socialism, Hosoi took a dim view of the Japanese ruling elite. In such books as *Seisō to Tōhei* [Political Struggle and Party Evils] (Tokyo: Yakushinkai, 1914) and *Hanzoku Zaiakushi* [History of the Sins of the Clique] (Tokyo: Daitōkaku, 1919), Hosoi subjected the Japanese ruling elite to scathing indictments of political corruptions in Japan.

16. Hosoi, *Chōsen Bunka Shiron,* xvii.

17. Ibid.

18. Ibid., 6–7.

19. Ibid., 1.

20. Hosoi Hajime, "*Kosho Kobun o Tsujite Mitaru Chōsenjin no Shinsei*" [Korean Mind Seen Through Its History and Literature], *Chōsen* [Korea] (Dec. 1921): 54–77.

21. Ibid., 55.

22. For a succinct account of the influence of racial theories and Social

Darwinism in prewar Japan, see Oguma Eiji, *"Nihonjin" no Kyōkai* [Boundaries of "the Japanese"] (Tokyo: Sinhyōsha, 1998), 168–94. For information about the influence of racial theories and Social Darwinism in colonial Korea, see Pak Sŏngjin, *Sahoejinhwaron gwa Singminj Sahoesasang* [Social Evolutionism and Colonial Social Theories] (Seoul: Sŏin, 2003); Jin-Kyung Lee, "Sovereign Aesthetics, Disciplining Emotion, and Racial Rehabilitation in Colonial Korea, 1910–1922," *Acta Koreana* 8, no. 1 (2005): 77–107.

23. Pyŏngjailgi [The Records of the Namhan Castle in 1636] was written by Na Mangap (1592–1642), a government official during the reign of the Chosŏn King Injong (1544–1545); Na Mangap, *Pyōngja Namhan Ilgi* [The Records of the Namhan Castle in 1636] (Seoul: Sŏmundang, 1977). *The Records of the Namhan Castle in 1636* records social chaos and political and military failures during the Manchu Invasion of Korea in 1636. It is usually called *Pyōngjarok* or *Pyōngja Namhan Ilgi*. The book should not be mistaken for the diary written in vernacular Korean from 1636–1640 by Lady Cho, the wife of the high ranking government official Nam Iung (1575–1648); Lady Cho, *Pyŏngja Ilgi* [The Records of 1635] (Seoul: Yejŏnsa, 1991). *Mongminsimsŏ* [Admonitions on Governing the People] was written by Chōng Yagyong (1762–1836) during his exile for his religious faith in Roman Catholicism, which was banned by the Chosŏn government. Chōng Yagyong, *Mongminsimsŏ* [Admonitions on Governing the People] (Seoul: Ch'nagjak kwa Pip'yŏngsa, 2005). Chōng completed the book in 1818 when he returned from exile. In the book, Chōng described rampant corruption in local administration and proposed reforms.

24. The best known version of kabuki play based on the life of the Tokugawa-period folk hero Banzuiin Chōbei (1622–1657) was *Kiwametsuki Banzhui Chōbei* [Banzui Chōbei, authorized version] written by Kawatake Mokuami (1816–1893); Kawatake Mokuami, *Mokuami Meisakusen Dai Go Kan* [Great Works of Mokuami, vol. 5] (Tokyo: Sōgensha, 1953), 173–224.

25. Hong Kildong Chŏn [Story of Hong Kildong] was written in vernacular Korean by Hŏ Kyun (1569–1618); Hŏ Kyun, *Hong Kildong Chŏn* [Story of Hong Kildong] (Seoul: Yŏnsei Taehakkyo Munkwa Taehak Kugŏ Kungmunhak Yŏn'gusil Panggakpon Ch'ongsŏ Kanhaenghoe, 1971). The fiction was inspired by the real-life thief during the reign of Yŏnsangun (1494–1506). Nezumikozō (1797–1832) was a famous thief in the late Tokugawa period who inspired many stories and plays. He is said to have stolen only from corrupt samurai and merchant families.

26. Hosoi Hajime, *Chōsen Tōchi Shinri no Konponteki Henkō ni Kansuru Ikensho* [A Statement Concerning Fundamental Changes in the Mentality of Ruling Korea] (publisher unknown, 1924), 42–44. This was Hosoi's policy suggestion to the Japanese colonial government in Korea. Its preface states it was written before the great Kantō earthquake but published afterward, in 1924. The publisher and publication place are not given in the document.

27. Hosoi, Hajime, *Senman no Keiei: Chōsen Mondai no Konpon Kaiketsu* [Administrating Korea and Manchuria: The Fundamental Solution to the Korean Problem] (Tokyo: Jiyūtōkyūsha, 1921), 8.

28. Hosoi, *Chōsen Tōchi Shinri no Konponteki Henkō ni Kansuru Ikensho,* 20.

29. An Hwak, "*Chosŏn ŭi Munhak*" [The Literature of Korea], in *Hanguk Hyŏndae Munhak Pip'yŏngsa* [History of Modern Korean Literary Criticism], ed. Kwŏn Yŏngmin, 8 vols. (Seoul: Hagun Haksul Chŏngbo, 2004), 1: 34–47. The essay was originally published in the July issue of the Korean journal *Hakchigwang* [Light of Knowledge] in 1915.

30. Ibid., 34. In "*Munhak iran Hao*" [What Is Literature?], in *Haguk Hyōndae Munhak Pip'yŏngsa,* ed. Kwŏng Yŏngmin, 8 vols. (Seoul: Hanguk Haksul Chŏngbo, 2004), 1: 48–64, the better known treatise on literature, which came out in 1916, Yi Kwangsu also defines literature as creative and imaginative writing expressive of aesthetic sentiments, favoring feeling over intellect. In that sense, both An's and Yi's views on literature were romanticist. As Terry Eagleton points out, delimiting the category of literature to "creative" and "imaginative" writing and emphasizing "imaginative vision" in writing, the modern concept of literature is Romanticist, having emerged only after the rise of Romanticism in the early 19th century Europe. Terry Eagleton, *Literary Theory: An Introduction* (Minneapolis: University of Minnesota Press, 1983), 17–22.

31. An, "*Chosŏn ŭi Munhak,*" 39. It is not clear in the text what An meant by the trend of pessimism in 19th-century European literature. It might refer to the rise of pessimism in literature influenced by Arthur Schopenhauer.

32. An was not alone in blaming Chinese influence for the decline of the Korean nation. Even before the annexation of Korea by Japan, Korean nationalist intellectuals, in favor of the modernization of Korea modeled after Western nations, disparaged China as a backward country and denounced the Chinese cultural influence over their country in the past as the cause of its backwardness in the present. Andre Schmid, *Korea Between Empires 1895–1919* (New York: Columbia University Press, 2002).

33. An, "*Chosŏn ŭi Munhak,*" 44

34. Ibid., 45.

35. Ibid., 46.

36. Ibid., 47.

37. Ibid., 47.

38. In *Senman no Kei* , however, Hosoi maintained that Koreans were not competent enough to be independent of Japan and held that their incompetence was derived from their national character. Besides, he argued that Koreans' discontent with Japanese colonial rule resulted primarily from their misunderstanding of Japan's benevolent intentions toward the colony. Hosoi, 231–56.

39. Ibid., 109–35.

40. After the earthquake and ensuing fires had devastated the Kantō area in 1923, there circulated a rumor that Korean immigrants in the region plotted to launch sabotage activities and revolt against the Japanese government. Japanese vigilante groups organized to hunt down Koreans in reaction to the

rumor. It is still subject to dispute how many Koreans were killed by vigilante groups. The number of Korean victims of the massacre ranged from a couple of hundreds to more than six thousand, depending on the source. For more information, see Kang Tŏksang, *Kantō Daishinsai* [The Great Kantō Earthquake] (Tokyo: Chūōkōronsha, 1975).

41. Another noteworthy issue concerning Hosoi's idea of love is whether it was influenced by Christianity. Hosoi's concept of absolute love parallels Christian love because it differs from sensual desire while bringing the subject and the object into unity. Hosoi's socialist background might explain the similarity between his concept of love and Christian love since the early socialist movement in Meiji, Japan, was heavily influenced by Christian socialism. However, any textual evidence to connect Hosoi to Christianity has yet to be found.

42. Hosoi Hajime, "*Naisenjin Ketsugō no Kitan*" [Beginning of Union Between the Japanese and Koreans], in *Kantō no Shinsai to Chōsenjin* [The Great Kantō Earthquake and Koreans], ed. Zaigai Chōsenjin Jijō Kenkyūkai (Keijō: Zaigai Chōsenjin Jijokenkai, 1923), 10–19

43. Hosoi Hajime, *Chōsen Mondai no Kisū* [The Destiny of the Korean Problem] (Tokyo: Asea Bunka Renmei, 1925), 25.

44. A similar point was already made by Aono Masaaki. Aono does not necessarily disagree that the identity of the Japanese nation had existed before such colonial discourse as Hosoi's, however. Aono, "*Hosoi Hajime no Chōsenkan*," 237.

45. Hosoi, "*Naisenjin Ketsugō no Kitan*," 18–19.

46. Hosoi Hajime, "*Gojosōai no Taigi to Chōsen Mondai*" [The Great Significance of Mutual Support and Love, and the Korean Problem], *Chōsen Shakaijigyō* [Korean Social Work] 4, no. 1 (1926): 1–47.

47. Hosoi Hajime, *Nihonjin no Ketsui* [The Determination of the Japanese] (Tokyo: Dai Nihon Yūbenkai Kōdansha, 1932), 186.

48. Hosoi, "*Gojosōai no Taigi to Chōsen Mondai*," 9.

49. Ibid., 41.

50. Ibid., 13.

51. Ibid., 23.

52. Ibid., 14–15.

53. Ibid., 42.

54. Hosoi, "*Gojosōai no Taigi to Chōsen Mondai*," 34.

55. G. W. F. Hegel. "The Spirit of Christianity," *Early Theological Writings* (Philadelphia: University of Pennsylvania Press, 1971), 182–301.

56. Ibid., 236.

57. Ibid., 279.

58. G. W. F. Hegel, *Elements of the Philosophy of Right* (Cambridge: Cambridge University Press, 1991), 199.

59. Hegel, *Elements of the Philosophy of Right*, 272.

60. Ibid., 209.

61. Ibid., 207.

62. Jean Hyppolite, *Genesis and Structure of Hegel's Phenomenology of Spirit* (Evanston: Northwestern University Press, 1974), 344.

63. Immanuel Kant, *The Philosophy of Law* (Edinburgh: T. & T. Clark, 1887), 109–113.

64. Hegel, *Elements of the Philosophy of Right*, 206.

65. Ibid., 212–14.

66. Kongbosil, *Wollam Yi Sangjae Sŏnsaeng Yakchŏn* [Abridged Biography of Wŏllam Yi Sangjae] (Seoul: Kongbosil, 1956), 131–33.

67. Hegel, *Elements of the Philosophy of Right*, 202.

68. In *Senman no Keiei*, Hosoi deplored the Korean family and society in which women were denied freedom and were treated like slaves. In Hosoi's view the low status of women testified once again to the backwardness of Korea. On the other hand, Hosoi demeaned and eroticized Korean women by arguing that Korean wives allegedly tended to cheat on their husbands as revenge for the oppressive treatment they faced at the hands of their husbands. Hosoi, *Senman no Keiei*, 185.

69. Hosoi himself once invoked the marriage of the Korean Prince Yi Un and the Japanese Princess Nashimoto no Miya Masako (who changed her name to Yi Pangja after the liberation of Korea in 1945) to underline unity between Korea and Japan. Hosoi, *"Gojosōai no Taigi to Chōsen Mondai,"* 10.

70. As already discussed above, however, Hosoi's own texts revealed that Japan was an already fractured community.

71. In response to the official colonial policy in the early 1940s of encouraging Japan–Korea unity (naisen ittai), quite a few Korean writers wrote stories about romance and marriage between Japanese and Koreans. This phenomenon has caught the attention of scholars because many of the stories reverse the conventional gender relationship between the colonizer and the colonized by featuring a Korean male and Japanese female. The scholars have also noted that many of the stories portray irreducible differences between Koreans and the Japanese in customs and traditions and insurmountable opposition from the Korean man's family. With such notable exceptions as Yi Kwangsu's Japanese-language story *"Kokoro Aifurete Koso"* [Touching Your Heart], *Ryokki* [Green Flag], 3 (1940): 74–93; 4 (1940): 88–107; 5 (1940): 112–32; 6 (1940): 89–105; 7 (1940): 105–17, the majority of the stories stop short of letting romance bloom into marriage. For more information, see Yi Sanggyŏng, *"Ilche Malgi Sosŏl e Nat'anan 'Naesŏn Kyŏrhon ŭi Ch'ŭngui"* [The Layers of "Japanese-Korean Marriage" Portrayed in Late Colonial Period Novels] in *Ch'inil Munhak ŭi Naechok Nolli* [The Internal Logic of Pro-Japanese Literature], ed. Kim Chaeyong et al. (Seoul: Yŏllak, 2003).

72. Hosoi, *"Naisenjin Ketsugō no Kitan,"* 18–19.

73. Hosoi, *"Gojosōai no Taigi to Chōsen Mondai,"* 43.

74. One of the criticisms Levinas made against Hegel is relevant here. Levinas criticizes Hegel for considering the family primarily in relation to the state. Levinas, *Totality and Infinity* (Pittsburgh: Duquesne University Press, 1969), 306.

CHAPTER TWO

1. Kim Chinyŏng, Kim Hyŏnju, and Kim Hŭich'an, eds., *Ch'unhyangjŏn Chŏnjip* [Collected Works of Ch'unhyangjŏn], 17 vols. (Seoul: Pakijŏng, 1997–2004).

2. The politics I argue for in this chapter is the engagement in conscious activities that constitute resistance to the structure of domination inimical to the ethical relationship. Even though my argument for the ethical relationship is indebted to Emmanuel Levinas, what I mean by politics is more specific than what many believe to be Levinas's definition of politics. As discussed in the preface, in Levinas's thought, politics is the necessary complement to ethics to ensure justice. The self's ethical responsibility for the other can be in conflict with its ethical responsibility for an other because the world is inhabited by multiple others. Often the self has to prioritize the other over an other in its ethical obligation to uphold justice. This effort for justice calls for politics.

3. Noaki Sakai, *Translation and Subjectivity* (Minneapolis: University of Minnesota, 1997), 1–17.

4. My choice of a local version of the Zoque language as an example is not arbitrary. It was inspired by a BBC report that the last two native speakers of a local version of the Zoque language in Ayapan, Tabasco, Mexico have stopped talking to each other since an argument they had, and as a consequence, the language is in danger of disappearance. BBC NEWS, "Split Imperils Mexican Language," http://news.bbc.co.uk/2/hi/also_in_the_news/7097647.stm (accessed March 27, 2013). Even though it might be an exaggeration to ascribe the extinction of a language to personality conflicts, this fascinating story nevertheless concretely illustrates Levinas's view of language that maintains to speak language is, first of all, to approach the other and the essence of language is thus ethical.

5. George Steiner, *After Babel* (Oxford: Oxford University Press, 1975), 318–19.

6. Tejaswini Niranjana, *Siting Translation* (Berkeley and Los Angeles: University of California Press, 1992), 59–61.

7. Homi Bhabha, *The Location of Culture* (London and New York: Routledge, 1994), 85–92.

8. Oguma Eiji, *Tan'ichi Minzoku no Shinwa no Kigen* [Origins of the Myth of a Homogeneous Ethnic Nation] (Tokyo: Shinyōsha, 1995); Oguma Eiji, *"Nihonjin" no Kyōkai* [Boundaries of "the Japanese"] (Tokyo: Sinhyōsha, 1998).

9. Kwŏn T'aeŏk, *"Tonghwa Chŏngch'aeknon"* [Assimilation Policy], *Yŏksa Hakpo* [The Journal of Historiography], no. 172 (2001): 335–65.

10. Takasaki Sōji, *Kenshō Nikkan Kaidan* [The Investigation of Japan–Korea Talks] (Tokyo: Iwanami Shoten, 1996), 51–52.

11. "The subjects in exchange exist for one another only through these equivalents, as of equal worth, and prove themselves to be such through the exchange of the objectivity in which the one exists for the other." Karl Marx, *Grundrisse* (London: Penguin Books, 1973), 242.

12. It is also true, however, that on other occasions, Marx seems to have accepted equal exchange premised on symmetrical reciprocity between colonization and historical progress. For example, in his article for the *New York Daily Tribune* titled "The British Rule in India," Marx recognized British colonialism in India as "the unconscious tool of history in bringing about the revolution" that was necessary to break down ancient social relations and pave the way for progress. See Karl Marx, "The British Rule in India" in *Karl Marx on Colonialism and Modernization*, ed. Shlomo Avineri (Garden City: Doubleday Anchor Book, 1969), 88–95.

13. "Therefore, when the economic form, exchange, posits the all-sided equality of its subjects, then the content, the individual as well as the objective material which derives towards the exchange, is freedom. Equality and freedom are thus not only respected in exchange based on exchange values, but, also, the exchange of exchange values is the productive, real basis of all equality and freedom." Marx, *Grundrisse*, 245.

14. Marx, *Grundrisse*, 249.

15. Ibid., 239–250.

16. Karl Marx, *The Critique of the Gotha Programme* (New York: International, 1966), 10.

17. Emmanuel Levinas, *Ethics and Infinity: Conversations with Philippe Nemo* (Pittsburgh: Duquesne University Press, 1985), 98.

18. Emmanuel Levinas, *Totality and Infinity* (Pittsburgh: Duquesne University Press, 1969); Emmanuel Levinas, *Otherwise than Being* (Pittsburgh: Duquesne University Press, 1998).

19. Levinas, *Totality and Infinity*, 101.

20. "Language qua said can then be conceived as a system of nouns identifying entities, and then as a system of signs doubling up the beings, designating substances, events and relations by substantives or other parts of speech derived from substantives, designating identities—in sum, designating." Levinas, *Otherwise Than Being or Beyond Essence*, 40.

21. It is not the discovery that "it speaks" or that "language speaks" that does justice to this passivity. One must show in saying, qua approach, the very de-posing or de-situating of the subject, which nonetheless remains as irreplaceable uniqueness, and is thus the subjectivity of the subject. This passivity is more passive still than any receptivity, in which for philosophers the supreme model of the passivity of the subject resides.

> To say is to approach a neighbor, "dealing him signifyingness." This is not exhausted in "ascription of meaning," which are inscribed, as tales, in the said. Saying taken strictly is a "signifyingness dealt the other," prior to all objectification; it does not consist in giving signs.

(Levinas, *Otherwise Than Being or Beyond Essence*, 47–48.)

22. Ibid., 120.

23. Chŏng Hayŏng, "*Ch'unhyangjŏn Hanmunbon Haeje*" [Annotation of Classical Chinese Versions of Ch'unhyangjŏn], *Haguk Kojŏn Yŏngu* [Study of Korean Classical Literature] 2 (1996): 347–50.

24. Yi Haejo's *Okjunghwa* published in 1911 was the most popular written text of *Ch'unhyangjŏn* in the early 20th century. Yi based it on a *p'ansori* singer, Pak Kihong's, version of *Ch'unhyangjŏn* in turn. Yi was a writer of *sinsosŏl* (New Novel), which was a literary genre that flourished during the late 19th and early 20th centuries by absorbing influences of Western novels through the mediation of Chinese and Japanese literature. Consequently, Yi employed the *sinsosŏl* style in writing his version, and revised the opening scene and the departing scene. This indirect influence of western and Japanese literature on *Ch'unhyangjŏn* complicates further the hybrid nature of the story already influenced by classical Chinese literary tradition.

25. For more information, see Shirakawa Yutaka, *Shokuminchi Chōsen no Sakka to Nihon* [Writers in Colonial Korea and Japan] (Okayama: Daigakukyōikushuppan, 1995): 191–92.

26. Murayama Tomoyoshi, *"Ch'unhyangjŏn no Tsukiji Jōen ni Tsuite"* [About the Staging of *Ch'unhyangjŏn at* Tsukiji")], *Chōsen oyobi Manshū* (March 1938): 59–60.

27. There is also a long history of the story's translation into Japanese. For example, Nakarai Tōsui's translation was serialized in *Ōsaka Asahi Shinbun* in 1882 even before the annexation of Korea into the Japanese empire. Nakarai Tōsui, *"Keirin Jōwa Ch'unhyangjŏn"* [The Kyerim Love Story, *Ch'unhyangjŏn*], *Ōsaka Asahi Shinbun* [Osaka Asahi Newspaper] (June 25–July 23, 1882).

28. For more information, see Ōzasa Yoshio, *Nihon Gendai Engekishi: Shōwa* [A History of Modern Japanese Theater: The Shōwa Period] , 3 vols. (Tokyo: Hakusuisha, 1993–1995), 2: 304–496.

29. Murayama Tomoyoshi. *"Ch'unhyangjŏn no Tsukiji Jōen ni Tsuite"* [About the Staging of *Ch'unhyangjŏn at* Tsukiji], *Chōsen oyobi Manshū* [Korea and Manchuria] 3 (1938): 59–60.

30. However, it should be kept in mind that *Ch'unhyangjŏn* is filled with allusions to and quotes from the classical Chinese literary tradition such as *San Guo Yan Yi* [The Romance of the Three Kingdoms], *Shijing* [The Book of Songs], and poetry by Li Bai. For more information, see Kim Tonguk, *Jŭngbo Ch'unhyangjŏn Yŏngu* [A Study on *Ch'unhyangjŏn,* Expanded Edition] (Seoul: Yŏnsedaehakkyo Ch'ulpanbu, 1976), 327–30, 335. For more information in English about the influence of classical Chinese literature on Ch'unhyangjŏn, see *Virtuous Women: Three Classic Korean Novels,* trans. Richard Rutt and Kim Chongun (Seoul: Royal Asiatic Society Korea Branch, 1974), 244–47.

31. Chang was born in 1905 in Kyŏngsangbukto, Korea. After graduating from Taegu High Normal School, he became a teacher in a mountainous region of the province. He moved to Japan in 1936. He married a Japanese woman and changed his name to a Japanese one, Noguchi Minoru.

32. Chang Hyŏkchu, *"Ch'unhyangjŏn ni Tsuite"* [About *Ch'unhyangjŏn*] *Bungei Shuto* [Literary Capital] 6, no. 3 (1938): 108–09.

33. Shirakawa Yutaka, *Shokuminchi Chōsen no Sakka to Nihon,* 180.

34. Ch'anggŭk is a genre of stage art that evolved from *p'ansori.* Whereas *p'ansori* is performed by one singer outdoors without stage props or set,

ch'anggŭk has different actors or singers play roles of different characters, as in Western opera. The genre was very popular during the colonial period.

35. Chang, *"Ch'unhyangjŏn ni Tsuite."*

36. Chang Hyŏkchu, *"Ch'unhyangjŏn" Shinchō* [New Tide] 3 (1938): 2–68. In the script, Chang did not provide phonetic readings for the names of the characters in the story except for Pangja, the male servant of the hero Yi Mongnyong, and for the office title of the corrupt and cruel new magistrate. This poses an interesting question about how to read the name of the heroine, Ch'unhyang, in the Japanese text. The name can be read as Shunkō following the convention of the Chinese-derived reading of Chinese characters in Japanese (*onyomi*). However, it also can be read as Haruka following the Japanese reading of Chinese characters (*kunyomi*). The Japanese text offers no clues and, without any preparatory knowledge of the tale of Ch'unhyang, the reader cannot be sure whether the name belongs to Korean or Japanese or even Chinese. I have decided to use the Korean pronunciation even in Japanese text not only to avoid possible confusion but also to emphasize that like any other languages, Japanese is neither self-sufficient nor closed to the outside. As Jacques Derrida demonstrates the simultaneous translatability and untranslatability of a proper name in *"Des Tours de Babel,"* Ch'unhyang as a proper name simultaneously demands and forbids translation. Jacques Derrida, *"Des Tours de Babel,"* in *Difference in Translation*, ed. Joseph F. Graham. (Ithaca: Cornell University Press, 1985), 165–207.

37. The original script Chang published in *Shinchō* in March 1938 was composed of six acts and 15 scenes, but he reduced it to 12 scenes for the publication in a book titled *Ch'unhyangjŏn*. Murayama's revision further reduced the play to 11 scenes. For more information, see Shirakawa, *Shokuminchi Chōsen no Sakka to Nihon*, 194–201. One critic who read the original script and saw the play agreed with Murayama that there were too few dramatic peaks in Chang's original because it was too explanatory. He acknowledged that Murayama's revision made the play's structure more compact by slimming down the original script. Koike Kōshi, *"Chōsen no Kotengei Ch'unhyangjŏn ni Tsuite"* [About the Korean Traditional Performance *Ch'unhyangjŏn*], *Engei Gahō* [Illustrated Magazine of Theatrical Arts] 32, no. 5 (1938): 56–57. For more information, see Shirakawa, 194–201. It is also noteworthy that Chang's *Ch'unhyangjŏn* was not the first Japanese-language play of the story published. In 1922, Asō Isoji had already published a Japanese-language stage play script of *Ch'unhyangjŏn* for *Chōsen* [Korea], a magazine run by the government general of Korea. Asō Isoji, *"Gikyoku Ch'unhyangjŏn"* [Drama *Ch'unhyangjŏn*], *Chōsen* 89 (1922): 2–57.

38. Murayama sought help from the staff of Zenshinza, a progressive *kabuki* company to teach his actors *kabuki*-style acting. Murayama Tomoyoshi, *"Ch'unhyangjŏn Yodan"* [An Idle Talk on *Ch'unhyangjŏn*], *Keijō Nippō* [Seoul Daily], May 31, 1938. However, Chang is said to have been less than enthusiastic about the revision. Shirakawa, *Shokuminchi Chōsen no Sakka to Nihon*, 201–02.

39. Murayama gave up cross-gender casting when staging the play in Korea later in 1938. He cast Takizawa Osamu, a veteran actor, to replace Akagi in the role of the hero Mongnyong. She in turn took the part of the heroine Ch'unhyang, replacing Ichikawa.

40. *"Eigaka Sareru Ch'unhyangjŏn Zadankai Jō"* [Roundtable Discussion on the Movie Version of *Ch'unhyangjŏn*, part 1], *Keijō Nippō* [Seoul Daily], June 9, 1938.

41. Koike, *"Chōsen no Kotengeki Ch'unhyangjŏn ni Tsuite;"* Tsurumi Makoto, *"Ch'unhyangjŏn—Kabukifū no Taishūka e no Tenkō to Shite"* [*Ch'unhyangjŏn*: Transformation to Kabuki-Style as the Conversion to Popularization], *Teikoku Daigaku Shinbun* [Imperial University Newspaper], March 31, 1938.

42. Hirata Isao, *"Ch'unhyangjŏn' Kangeki Shokan"* [Review of *Ch'unhyangjŏn*], *Teatoro* [Theater] 5, no. 5 (1938): 28–29; *Shisō no Kagaku Kenkyū-kai*, ed. *Kyōdō Kenkyū Tenkō* [Collaborative Research Ideological Conversion], 3 vols. (Tokyo: Heibonsha, 1965), 2:159.

43. Fuse Tatsuji, *"Ch'unhyangjŏn' o Mite"* [Viewing *Ch'unhyangjŏn*], *Teatoro* [Theater] 5, no 5 (1938): 25–28.

44. Tsurumi, *"Ch'unhyangjŏn—Kabukifū no Taishūka e no Tenkō to Shite."*

45. *"Ch'unhyangjŏn Hihan Zadankai"* [Critical Roundtable Discussion on *Ch'unhyangjŏn*], *Teatoro* [Theater] 5 no. 12 (1938): 66–81.

46. Murayama Tomoyoshi, *"Chōsen to no Kōryū"* [Interactions with Korea], *Asahi Shinbun* [Asahi Newspaper], September 15, 1938.

47. Akita Ujaku, *"Furusato e Kaeru 'Ch'unhyangjŏn' Yūgōshita Futatsu no Bunka no Kōryū"* [*Ch'unhyangjŏn* Returning to Its Hometown: Cultural Interaction Between Two Harmonized Cultures], *Keijō Nippō*, October 9, 1938.

48. Sin T'aehyŏn, *"Ch'unhyangjŏn Jōen o Mite"* [Viewing the Performance of *Ch'unhyangjŏn*], *Chōsen* 283 (1938): 47–61.

49. Yi Wŏnjo, *"Sinhyŏp Kŭktan Kongyŏn ŭi Ch'unhyangjŏn Kwangŭk-p'yŏng, ha"* [The Review of the Play *Ch'unhyangjŏn* Performed by the Shinkyō Theatrical Company, part 2], *Chosŏn Ilbo*, November 5, 1938.

50. Chang, *"Ch'unhyangjŏn ni Tsuite."*

51. About a hundred versions of the story survive in manuscript, woodblock, and movable print. It has also appeared in diverse genres of literature and performance art including prose, verse, drama, dance, musical, and cinema. Sŏl Sŏnggyŏng, *Ch'unhyangjŏn ŭi T'ongsijŏk Yŏngu* [A Diachronic Study of *Ch'unhyangjŏn*] (Seoul: Yŏnsedaehakkyo Chulpanbu, 2000), 177.

52. Chang Hyŏkchu, *"Chōsen to Ch'unhyangjŏn"* [Korea and *Ch'unhyangjŏn*], *Keijō Nippō* [Seoul Daily], October 4, 1938.

53. A transcript of the roundtable discussion appeared in Japan in the January 1939 issue of the prominent literary journal *Bungakukai* [The Literary World] under the title *"Chōsen Bunka no Shōrai"* [The Future of Korean Culture] 6, no. 1 (1939): 271–79. It had first been serialized in eight parts in *Keijō Nippō* between November 29 and December 8, 1938, under the title of *"Chōsen Bunka no Shōrai to Genzai"* [The Future and the Present of Korean Culture]. In this chapter, I use the transcript published in *Bungakukai*.

Although the transcript in *Keijō Nippō* was published about a month earlier, there is no convincing reason to privilege it over the *Bungakukai* transcript as the source from which a more authentic voice of the Korean intellectuals can be excavated. *Keijō Nippō* was the Japanese colonial government newspaper published in Japanese and tighter censorship was exercised in colonial Korea than in Japan.

54. Ibid., 275.

55. Ibid., 276–77.

56. Marx, *Grundrisse*, 241–45.

57. "The philosophers have only interpreted the world in various ways; the point is to change it." Karl Marx, "Theses on Feuerbach," in Karl Marx and Fredrich Engels, *The German Ideology* (New York: Amherst, 1998), 571.

58. *"Chosŏn Kojŏnmunhak ŭi Kŏmt'o"* [An Examination of Korean Classical Literature], *Chosŏn Ilbo*, January 1–13, 1935; *"Chosŏnmunhaksang ŭi Pokkosasang Kŏmt'o"* [An Examination of the Ideas of Restoration in Korean Literature] *Chosŏn Ilbo*, January 22–31, 1935. For more information, see Hwang Chongyŏn, "1930 *nyŏndae Kojŏn Puhŭng Undong ŭi Munhakjōk Ŭiŭi"* [The Literary Significance of the Renaissance of Classics in the 1930s], *Hanguk Munhak Yŏngu* [Studies in Korean Literature], no. 11 (1988): 217–60. For a general overview of the surge of interest in Korean cultural tradition in colonial Korea in the 1930s, see Yi Chiwŏn, "1930 *nyŏndae Chŏnban Minjokjuŭi Munhwaundongnon ŭi Sŏngkyŏk"* [The Nature of the Nationalist Culture Movement in the first half of the 1930s], *Kuksagwan Nonch'ong* [National History Institute Collected Papers] 51 (1994): 161–84. As she evaluates the attempt to rejuvenate Korean tradition as a Korean bourgeois nationalist movement in the face of the increasing political repression by the Japanese colonial authorities, Yi points out that the cultural movement of the Korean bourgeois was aimed at criticizing the class struggle advocated by Korean leftists. Yi concludes that the cultural nationalism of the movement ended up colluding with Japanese colonialism because it degenerated into totalitarian national chauvinism, which was easily co-opted by the Japanese colonial regime in opposition to the West.

59. *"Kŏnsŏlgi ŭi Minjokmunhak"* [National Literature under Construction], *Tong-a Ilbo*, January 3–6, March 6–23, 1935.

60. Kwŏn Yŏngmin, *Hanguk Minjok Munhangnon Yŏngu* [A Study on the Discourse of Korean National Literature] (Seoul: Minūmsa, 1988), 129–43.

61. Paek Ch'ŏl, *Sinmunhak Sajosa* [History of New Literary Ideas] (Seoul: Singumunhwasa, 1982), 359–64.

62. Pak Hŏnho, *Yi T'aejun gwa Hanguk Kŭndae Munhak ŭi Sŏngkyŏk* [Yi T'aejun and the Nature of Modern Korean Literature] (Seoul: Somyŏng Ch'ulpan, 1999), 102–15.

63. Chi Sugŏl, "1930 *nyŏndae Ch'oban ŭi Chosŏn Minjokjuŭi wa Marŭkŭsŭ Reninjuŭi"* [Korean Nationalism and Marxism-Leninism in the First Half of the 1930s], *Inmun'gwahak Yŏngu* [Humanities Research], no. 1 (March, 1995): 143–70.

64. Carter J. Eckert, *Offspring of Empire* (Seattle: University of Washington Press, 1991), 162–64.

65. The management report of the company in March 1938 ascribed the rapid increase in profit to the Sino-Japanese War. For more information, see Chŏng An-gi, *"Chŏnsigi Chosŏn Pangjik ŭi Taemanju T'uja wa Yŏnggu Pangjik"* [*Chosŏn* Spinning and Weaving Company's Investment in Manchuria and Yŏnggu Spinning and Weaving Company During the Wartime], *Yŏksa wa Kyŏngye* [History and Boundaries], 48 (September 2003): 123–55.

66. Pak, *Yi T'aejun gwa Hanguk Kŭndae Munhak ŭi Sŏngkyŏk*, 94.

67. All the essays were included in Yi's book *Musŏrok*, published in 1941. The essays were reprinted in Yi T'aejun, *Yi T'aejun Chŏnjip* [The Collected Works of Yi T'aejun], 18 vols. (Seoul: Sŏŭm Ch'ulp'ansa, 1988), 15: 229–31, 243–45; 17: 324–27.

68. Hwang Chongyŏn, *"Chŏng Chiyong ŭi Sanmun gwa Chŏntong eŭi Chihyang"* [Chŏng Chiyong's Prose and His Aspiration to Tradition], *Hanguk Muhank Yŏnggu* [Studies in Korean Literature] 10 (1987): 237–57.

69. Kang Samhŭi, *"Sŏgu Kyoyangjuŭi esŏ Tongyangjok Sekero"* [From Western Culturalism to an Orientalist World], *Oeguk Munhak* [Foreign Literature] (Winter 1994): 304–20.

70. Yasuda Yojūrō, *"Kokumin Bungaku ni Tsuite"* [Concerning National Literature], in *Yasuda Yojūrō Zenshū* [Collected Works of Yasuda Yojūrō], 46 vols. (Tokyo: Kōdansha, 1985–89), 11: 38–43. The essay was originally published in 1940.

71. Ibid., 11: 40.

72. Im Insik, *"Chosŏn Munhak ŭi Sinjŏngse wa Hyŏndae Chesang 6-9"* [The New State of Korean Literature and the Diversity of Modernity], *Chosŏn Chungangilbo* [Korea Central Daily] (February 2–5, 1936).

73. Ch'oe Chaesŏ, *"Munhwa Kiyŏjarosŏ"* [As a Contributor to Culture], *Chosŏn Ilbo* (June 9, 1937); Ch'oe Chaesŏ, *"Munhak, Chakka, Chisŏng 1–3"* [Literature, Writer, and Intellect], *Tong-a Ilbo* (August 20–23, 1938). Republished in *Ch'oe Chaesŏ P'yŏngnonjip* [Collected Critical Essays by Ch'oe Chaesŏ] (Seoul: Ch'ŏngun Ch'ulpansa, 1961): 304–11.

74. For example, by comparing *Munjang* with another journal of its day, *Inmun P'yongnon* [Humanities Review], Yi Myŏnghŭi argues that traditionalism and antimodernism manifested in *Munjang* emerged from the critical reflection on modernity that colonialism had brought into Korea. Yi contends that Yi T'aejun's traditionalism was not a call to return to the past but an attempt to rejuvenate Korean tradition in the modern world. Similarly, Kwŏn Sŏngu sympathetically reads traditionalism in Yi T'aejun's essays. Kwŏn argues that it is too simplistic to read only antimodernism into Yi T'aejun's preference for Korean tradition. Kwŏn rather calls attention to the tension between Yi's affection for tradition and continuous interest in modernity. Pak Hŏnho, while being critical of the rise of Korean traditionalism in the 1930s, also differentiates it from the traditionalism of Yi T'aejun and highly evaluates the latter as a form of resistance to the oppressive reality of colonial society that denied the colonized any chance to achieve genuine modernity.

Yi Myŏnghŭi, *"Munjang yi Poyŏjun 'Chŏnt'ong ŭi Ŭimi wa Ŭiŭi"* [The Meaning and Significance of Tradition Manifested in *Munjang*] in *1930 nyŏndae Huban ŭi Kŭndaesŏng gwa Chagi Sŏngch'al* [Modernity and Self-Reflection in the Late 1930s], ed. *Sanghŏ Munhakhoe* (Seoul: Kip'ŭnsaem, 1998), 383–406; Kwŏn Sŏngu, *"Yi T'aejun ŭi Sup'il Yŏngu"* [A Study on the Essays of Yi T'aejun], *Hanguk Munhak Iron gwa Pip'yŏng* [Korean Literature Theory and Critique], no. 22 (2004): 11–33; Pak Hŏnho, *Yi T'aejun gwa Hanguk Kŭndae Munhak ŭi Sŏngkyŏk*, 115.

75. *"Chōsen Bunka no Shōrai; Zadankai,"* 279; *"Chōsen Bunka no Shōrai to Genzai," Keijō Nippō*, December 8, 1938.

76. I do not mean that the Korean intellectuals regarded Koreans as equal to Japanese people in colonial reality politically, legally, and so on. But I believe that they saw that Korean culture and Japanese culture were on the same plane and at the same time demarcated easily and clearly from each other. In that sense, I think that they assumed the symmetrical relationship between Korean culture and Japanese culture and that assumption obscured the utter asymmetry between the colonized and the colonizers.

77. It goes without saying that even in an atmosphere of multiculturalism, specific ethnic groups associated by origin with enemy countries are not safe from both institutional and noninstitutional discrimination.

78. Frantz Fanon, *The Wretched of the Earth* (New York: Grove Press, 1963), 235.

79. Levinas, *Totality and Infinity*, 73.

80. For Levinas, the Western philosophical tradition has been dominated by ontology. In ontology, the other is denied its alterity and is absorbed into the same. Even in Heidegger, who went beyond intellectualism as found in Husserl's phenomenology, his question as to the meaning of being presupposes that it should be comprehended even though it can be only incompletely and partially. As such, being is brought to consciousness and its otherness is incorporated into the same. Emmanuel Levinas, "Is Ontology Fundamental?" In *Basic Philosophical Writings*, eds. Adriaan T. Peperzak, Simon Critchley, and Robert Bernasconi (Bloomington: Indiana University Press, 1996), 1-10; Levinas, *Totality and Infinity*, 42–48.

81. Levinas distinguishes the ego (*le moi*) from the self (*le soi*). Although the former defines oneself in ontological opposition to the other, the latter suggests the subjectivity, which already opens up to the other whose alterity brings the legitimacy of the self into question. Robert Bernasconi, "What Is the Question to Which 'Substitution' Is the Answer?" in *Cambridge Companion to Levinas*, eds. Simon Critchley and Robert Bernasconi (Cambridge: Cambridge University Press, 2002), 234–51.

82. Thus, Levinas emphasizes, "The ego involved in responsibility is me and no one else, me with whom one would have liked to pair up a sister soul, from whom one would require substitution and sacrifice. But to say that the other has to sacrifice himself to the others would be to preach human sacrifice!" Levinas, *Otherwise Than Being or Beyond Essence*, 126.

CHAPTER THREE

1. Ch'oe Chaesŏ, *Insang gwa Sasaek* [Impression and Introspection] (Seoul: Yŏnse Taehak Ch'ulpanbu, 1977), 69–71. It is noteworthy that Ch'oe translated Hawthorne's novel into Korean in the 1950s. Ch'oe is still regarded as one of the best Korean translators of English literature and, in 2005, his 1954 translation of *Hamlet* was selected as the best Korean translation of Shakespeare to date by the Academic Association of English Language and Literature in South Korea. Prior to 1945, Ch'oe was also a seasoned translator of English literature into Japanese. For example, Ch'oe translated Irving Babbitt's trenchant denunciation of romanticism, *Rousseau and Romanticism,* Irving Babbit, *Rosseau and Romanticism* (Boston and New York: Houghton Mifflin, 1919), into Japanese in two volumes that were published by the prominent Japanese publishing house Kaizōsha in 1939 and 1940. Ch'oe Chaesŏ, *Rūsō to Romanshugi,* 2 vols. (Tokyo: Kaizōsha, 1939 and 1940);

2. Ch'oe Chaesŏ, *Insang gwa Sasaek,* 70.

3. Yu Chino, *Yanghogi* [The Records of Raising Tigers] (Seoul: Koryŏ Taehak Ch'ulpanbu, 1977), 102–03.

4. Ch'oe's collaboration with Japanese colonialism was not limited to producing academic discourse to justify Japanese colonial rule in Korea. He was deeply involved in the Japanese colonial propaganda machine. He was one of the founding members of the Korea Association of Men of Letters (*Chosŏn Mun'in Hyŏphoe*), which was established in 1939 by the government general to mobilize Korean intellectuals for the war effort. For more information, see Sŏng Yunja, *"Ch'oe Chaesŏ ŭi Ch'inil Munhak Yŏngu"* [Study on Ch'oe Chaesŏ's Pro-Japanese Literature] (master's thesis, Seoul National University, 2000). Ch'oe's most conspicuous collaborationist activities revolved around the journal *Kokumin Bungaku* (National Literature), in which he hosted numerous roundtable discussions on such issues as a national literature and culture of the Japanese empire, intellectuals' cooperation with the war effort, Japanese-language literary creations by Korean writers, and so on.

5. Ch'oe Chae-sŏ, *Tenkanki no Chōsen Bungaku* [Korean Literature in a Time of Transition] (Seoul: Inmunsa, 1943).

6. Homi Bhabha, *The Location of Culture* (London and New York: Routledge, 1994).

7. Miki Kiyoshi's "philosophy of world history" has received less attention than that of Kōsaka Masaaki and Kōyama Iwao. Compared to those involved in the later movement for a "philosophy of world history," especially that of Kōyama, who ended up justifying Japanese colonialism without problematizing the leadership role of Japan in the construction of the Greater East Asian Co-prosperity Sphere, Miki never recanted his intention of "overcoming imperialism" including that of Japan while himself advocating unity in East Asia. It was Miki's "philosophy of world history" that influenced the Korean intellectual Sŏ Insik in the late 1930s and early 1940s in colonial Korea. Miki Kiyoshi, *"Tōa Shisō no Konkyo"* [The Foundation of

East Asian Thought], *Kaizō* 12 (1938): 8–20. For information about Miki's position on the philosophy of world history, see Yonetani Masafumi, "*Miki Kiyoshi no 'Sekaishi no Testugaku'*" [Miki Kiyoshi's "Philosophy of World History"], *Hihyō Kūkan* [Critical Space] 19 (1998): 40–67. For information about Sŏ and about Miki's influence on Sŏ, see Ch'a Sŭnggi, "*Kŭndae ŭi Uigi wa Sigan-Konggan ŭi Chŏngch'ihak*" [The Crisis of Modernity and the Politics of Temporal-Spatiality"], *Hanguk Kŭndae Munhak Yŏngu* [Study of Modern Korean Literature] 8 (2003): 239–65; Cho Kwanja, "*Sŏ Insik no Rekishi Tetsugaku*" [Sŏ Insik's Philosophy of History], *Shisō* [Thought] 957 (2004): 29–54.

8. Jacques Derrida, *Of Grammatology* (Baltimore: Johns Hopkins University Press, 1976).

9. Jacques Derrida, "Force of Law," *Cardozo Law Review* 11 (1989–90): 965.

10. Ch'oe , *Tenkanki no Chōsen Bungaku*, 171.

11. Ibid., 174–75.

12. Ch'oe, *Insang gwa Sasaek*, 52–54.

13. There were two classes, A and B, in the faculty of letters at the preparatory school. Graduates of class A entered the Faculty of Law at Keijō Imperial University and those of class B went to the Faculty of Letters.

14. Yi Ch'ungu, *Kyŏngsŏng Chegukdaehak* [Keijō Imperial University] (Seoul: Tarakwŏn, 1980), 122.

15. Hyŏn Yŏngsŏp, *Chōsenjin no Susumubeki Michi* [The Path Koreans Should Take] (Seoul: Rokki Renmei, 1938), 188–89; Yi, *Kyŏngsŏng Chegukdaehak*, 122–23.

16. Takagi Ichinosuke, *Kokubungaku Gojūnen* [Fifty Years of Studying National Literature] (Tokyo: Iwanami, 1967), 140.

17. Cho Yongman, *Sansipnyŏndae Munhwa Yesulindul* [Men of Culture and Artists of the 1930s] (Seoul: Pŏmyangsa, 1978); Yi, *Kyŏngsŏng Chegukdaehak*, 122.

18. Ch'oe Chaesŏ, "*Chyoisŭ 'Chŏlmŭn Yesulga ŭi Ch'osang'-Yesul ŭi T'ansaeng*" [Joyce's *Portrait of the Artist as a Young Man*: The Birth of Art], *Inmun Pyŏngnon* [Humanities Review] (January 1940): 120–34.

19. James Joyce, *A Portrait of the Artist as a Young Man* (Oxford: Oxford University Press, 2000), 169.

20. In a similar vein, Kim Yunsik observed that Korean writers, who wrote in Japanese during the colonial period, failed to consciously dismantle the supposed homogeneity of Japanese as Joyce did that of English in *Finnegans Wake* by infusing and confusing English with foreign languages. Kim Yunsik, *Ilche Malgi Hanguk Chakka ŭi Ilbonŏ Kulssŭgi* [Korean Writers' Japanese Language Writing in the Later Colonial Period] (Seoul: Sŏul Taehak Ch'ulpanbu, 2003), 95.

21. In the preface of his first book, *Munhak kwa Chisŏng*, Ch'oe mentioned that he always wanted to remain in academia. Ch'oe Chaesŏ, *Munhak kwa Chisŏng* [Literature and Intellect] (Seoul: Inmunsa, 1938), 6.

22. Kim Yunsik, *Ilchemalgi Hangukjakka ŭi Ilbonŏ Kulssugiron*, 398.

23. According to Yu Chino, who also taught at Keijō Imperial University, the faculty decided that Koreans would not be employed as a professor in charge of regular courses. See Yu, *Yanghogi*, 5–10.

24. Kim Yunsik, *Hanguk Kŭndae Munhak Sasang Yŏngu 1* [Study on Thought in Modern Korean Literature] (Seoul: Ilchisa, 1984), 387.

25. Ch'oe did not slavishly transmit the literary criticism of English-language writers, but rather eclectically highlighted certain aspects of their work that dovetailed with his own thinking on intellect, morality, and the value of literary criticism and literature. He criticized Korean scholars who imported foreign literature without digesting it and establishing their own scholarly system. See Ch'oe Chaesŏ, *"Hojŏkŏmnun Oeguk Munhak Yŏnguga"* [Illegitimate Studies of Foreign Literature, *Chosŏn Ilbo* (April 26, 28, 1936).

26. Ch'oe's interest in the significance of intellect in literary criticism seems to have been inspired by the Japanese literary critic and novelist Abe Tomoji, who had argued since 1929 for intellectualism in literary criticism. For more information, see Kim Hŭnggyu, *Munhak kwa Yŏksajŏk Ingan* [Literature and Man as a Historical Being] (Seoul: Ch'angjak kwa Pip'yŏngsa, 1980), 279–80.

27. Sŏng Yunja, *"Ch'oe Chaesŏ ui Ch'inil Munhak Yŏnguk,"* 24.

28. Hyŏn, *Chōsenjin no Susumubeki Michi*, 188–89.

29. Ch'oe Chaesŏ, *"Pip'yong gwa Moral ŭi Munje"* [Criticism and Moral Problems], originally published in Japanese in the 1938 August issue of *Kaizō*. Translated into Korean and reprinted in Ch'oe Chaesŏ, *Ch'oe Chaesŏ P'yŏngnonjip* [Collected Critical Essays by Ch'oe Chaesŏ] (Seoul: Ch'ŏngun Ch'ulpansa, 1961), 17.

30. Hwang Chongyŏn, "1930 *nyŏndae Kojŏn Puhŭng Undong ŭi Munhakjŏk Ŭiŭi"* [The Literary Significance of the Renaissance of Classics in the 1930s], *Hanguk Munhak Yŏngu* [Studies in Korean Literature], no. 11 (1988): 217–60.

31. Ch'oe Chaesŏ, *"Munhwa Kiyŏjarosŏ"* [As a Contributor to Culture], *Chosŏn Ilbo* (June 9, 1937).

32. Ch'oe Chaesŏ, *"Munhak, Chakka, Chisŏng 1–3"* [Literature, Writer, and Intellect 1–3], *Tong-a Ilbo* (August 20, 21, 23, 1938). Republished in *Ch'oe Chae-sŏ P'yŏngnonjip*, 304–11.

33. Cho Yŏnhyŏn argued that the reason Ch'oe ceased all public activities for 10 years following the liberation of Korea was Ch'oe's sincere repentance about his collaboration. Cho Yŏnhyŏn, *"Ko Ch'oe Chaesŏ ŭi Ingan gwa Munhak"* [Late Ch'oe Chaesŏ: Man and Literature], *Hyŏndae Munhak* [Modern Literature] (January 1960): 18–19.

34. Ch'oe, *Tenkanki no Chōsen Bungaku*, 56.

35. Ibid. 120.

36. Ibid., 125.

37. Ibid., 130.

38. Ibid., 96.

39. Ibid., 97.

40. Ibid., 131–32.

41. Ibid., 14–16.
42. Ibid., 107–11.
43. Ibid., 36–42.
44. For a critical review of world history proposed by Miki, Kōsaka, and Kōyama, see Hiromatsu Wataru, *Kindai no Chōkokron* [On Overcoming Modernity] (Tokyo: Kōdansha, 1989); Tetsuo Najita and H. D. Harootunian, "Japan's Revolt Against the West," in *Modern Japanese Thought,* ed. Bob Wakabayashi (Cambridge: Cambridge University Press, 1998), 232–40.; Takahashi Tetsuya, *Kioku no Echika* [Ethics of Remembering] (Tokyo: Iwanami Shoten, 1995), 175–236; Naoki Sakai, *Translation and Subjectivity* (Minneapolis: University of Minnesota Press, 1997), 163–76.
45. For more information about critics of philosophy of history in Korea during the 1930s and the 1940s, see Son Chŏngsu, *Kaenyŏnsarosŏŭi Hanguk Kŭndae Pip'yŏngsa* [History of Modern Korean Literary Criticism as a History of Ideas] (Seoul: Yŏkrak, 2002), 179–242; Ch'a, *"Kŭndae ŭi Uigi hwa Sigan-Konggan ŭi Chŏngch'ihak"*; Kim Yerim, "1930*nyŏndae Huban Mollak/Chaesaeng ŭi Sŏsa hwa Yŏksa Kihoek Yŏngu*" [Discourse on Decline and Creation, and the Studies of the Philosophy of History in the late 1930s], *Hanguk Kŭndae Munhak Yŏngu* 6 (2003): 195–220.
46. Ch'oe, *Tenkanki no Chōsen Bungaku,* 54–57.
47. Ibid., 24.
48. Nishizaki Kyōko also briefly mentions the tendency to denigrate the abstract nature of theory and privileging the concreteness of the everyday in Shimaki's novel. Nishizaki Kyōko, *"Aru Nōmin Bungakusha"* [A Writer of Peasant Literature], *Kyōdō Kenkyū Tenkō* [Collective Research Ideological Conversion] 3 vols. (Tokyo: Heibonsha, 1965), 1: 218–37.
49. Yoshimoto Takaaki, *"Tenkōron"* [Treatise on Ideological Conversion], in *Yoshimoto Takaaki Zenchosakushū* [Collected Works of Yoshimoto Takaaki], 15 vols. (Tokyo: Keisō Shobō, 1968), 13: 5–27.
50. Kobayashi Hideo, however, put forth a somber reminder in his 1936 essay *"Bungakusha no Shisō to Jitsuseikatsu"* (Ideas and Actual Daily Life of a Man of Letters) that not only are ideas inevitably out of joint with actual life but also the distance between ideas and actual life is necessary. Kobayashi argues that even though ideas should be grounded in actual life, ideas always require the sacrifice of actual life. He soberly points out that ideas can be used to analyze or define actual life exactly because of the abstractness of ideas that keeps the distance between ideas and actual life. The article was originally published in *Bungei Shunjū* [Literary Chronicle] in April 1936 and is reprinted in *Gendai Nihon Bungaku Ronsōshi* [History of Literary Debates in Modern Japanese Literature], ed. Hirano Ken, Odagiri Hideo, and Yamamoto Kenkichi, 3 vols. (Tokyo: Miraisha, 1956), 3: 126–30.
51. Sin Tonguk, *"Kim Namch'ŏn ŭi Sosŏl e Nat'anan Chisigin ŭi Chaa Hwangnip kwa Chŏnhyangja ŭi Chŏgungmunje"* [The Identity of Intellectuals and the Adaptation of Political Converts Described in Kim Namch'ŏn's Work], *Tongyanghak* [Asian Studies] 21 (1991): 207–40. On the other hand, Kim Oegon gives high marks to Kim Namch'ŏn's investigation into every-

day life as a new way to critique modernity, which he aligns with Japanese colonialism. Kim Oegon, "*Chŏnhyang Munhak kwa Kŭndae ŭi Kŭkpok*" [Conversion Literature and Overcoming Modernity], *Oeguk Munhak* [Foreign Literature] (Spring 1995): 330–50.

52. Kim Namch'ŏn, "*Tŭngpul*" [Lantern], *Kokumin Bungaku* [National Literature] (March 1942): 106–25. It was published in Korean. The journal *Kokumin Bungaku* initially planned to publish four issues per year in Japanese and the rest in Korean, but after 1942 it was published only in Japanese.

53. Ch'oe, *Tenkanki no Chōsen Bungaku*, 237–38.

54. The prioritization of everyday life can be seen as an inversion of the intellectual trend since the Enlightenment of regarding reason as the highest human faculty and everyday life as the trivial space where people are preoccupied with mundane concerns. However, such a reevaluation does not dictate support for the status quo of society. For example, Marx already paid attention to everyday life as a site of contestation between the dominant power of capitalism and the struggle against it. Marx implied that human alienation and commodity fetishism are enacted in everyday life.

> Exchange-value thus appears to be a social determination of use-values, a determination which is proper to them as things and in consequence of which they are able in definite proportions to take one another's place in the exchange process, i.e., they are equivalents, just as simple chemical elements combined in certain proportions form chemical equivalents. Only the conventions of our everyday life make it appear commonplace and ordinary that social relations of production should assume the shape of things, so that the relations into which people enter in the course of their work appear as the relation of things to one another and of things to people.

Karl Marx, *A Contribution to the Critique of Political Economy* (New York: International, 1970), 34. However, Marx also pointed out that human beings will be liberated only when the contradiction between the ideal and the actual human being is dialectically overcome and the ideal is realized in everyday life.

> Political emancipation is the reproduction of man to a member of civil society, to an egoistic independent individual, on the one hand and to a citizen, a moral person on the other. Only when actual, individual man has taken back into himself the abstract citizen and has become a species-being in his everyday life, in his individual work and his individual circumstances, only when he has recognized and organized his own powers as social powers so that social power is no longer separated from him as political power, only then is human emancipation complete."

Karl Marx, "On the Jewish Question," in *The Portable Karl Marx*, ed. Eugene Kamenka (New York: Penguin Books, 1983), 114. Henri Lefebvre criticized Western philosophy for trivializing everyday life and disregarding concrete social practices while privileging a set of abstract ideas. Lefebvre, however, was no supporter of the status quo. Following Marx, he argued that everyday life in modern society is the site where human beings are alienated and commodities are fetishized, i.e., domination is reproduced through production and consumption. To overcome the commodity fetishism and human alienation, Lefebvre suggested that it is necessary to maintain a critical distance from the bustle of quotidian living but at the same time ground struggles against domination in everyday life. Henri Lefebvre, *Critique of Everyday Life,* 3 vols. (London: Verso, 1992), 1: 176–200. Thus, everyday life is not only a space in which domination is produced and reproduced but also a space in which domination should be challenged.

55. Ch'oe, *Tenkanki no Chōsen Bungaku,* 60–61.

56. Ibid., 83.

57. Ibid., 86.

58. Ch'oe's endeavors to subsume Koreans as an ethnic group under the Japanese state parallel what Naoki Sakai finds surreptitiously operating in Tanabe Hajime's theorization of the relationship between the individual, the species, and the genus. See Naoki Sakai, "Subject and Substratum: On Japanese Imperial Nationalism," *Cultural Studies,* 14, no. 3 (2000): 462–530.

59. Tanaka Hidemitsu (1914–1949) was a Japanese writer who resided in Korea and worked at the branch office of Yokohama Rubber Company. He made his literary debut with a novella, *"Orimpusu no Kajitsu"* [The Fruit of Olympus], published in *Bungakukai* [Literary World] in 1940.

60. Ch'oe, *Tenkanki no Chōsen Bungaku,* 239.

61. Bhabha, *The Location of Culture,* 89.

62. Ch'oe, *Tenkanki no Chōsen Bungaku,* 97.

63. Ibid., 88.

64. Ibid.

65. Aono Suekichi, *Tenkanki no Bungaku* [Literature in a Time of Transition] (Tokyo: Shunshūsha, 1927).

66. Nevertheless, there are significant parallels between Ch'oe's and Aono's deliberations on literature and society. For example, Aono denounced individualism as fervently as Ch'oe. Aono's censure of capitalism as the underlying principle of economic and political life in modern society concurred with Ch'oe critical view of it. More important, despite their arguments for the establishment of literature ultimately at the service of politics, both held on to the view that values of literary works could not be completely reduced to their political values.

67. Ch'oe wrote a number of stories in Japanese and published them in *Kokumin Bungaku*: *"Hōdōhan Renshū"* [War Correspondent Squad Training] (January 1943); *"Suiseki"* [Flint] (January 1944); and *"Minzoku no Kekkon"* [Marriage of Nations] (February 1945).

68. Kim Yunsik, *Ilche Malgi Hagun Chakka ŭi Ilbonŏ Kunssŭgi,* 77–78.

69. In response to the suggestion made by Hyŏn Yŏngsŏp, Ch'oe's only Korean friend at college and the notorious pro-Japanese collaborator, that Korean should be completely prohibited in favor of Japanese, Governor General Minami Jirō asserted that Korean would not be banned even though the promotion of Japanese in colonial Korea should be touted. *"Kugŏ Pogŭp ŭn Chohŭna Chosŏnŏ Paech'ŏk ŭn Pulga"* [Although the Promotion of the National Language Is Desirable, the Persecution of Korean Should Not Be

Allowed], *Maeil Sinbo* [Daily News] (July 9, 1938). The prominent pro-Japanese intellectual Yi Kwangsu also acknowledged that because Korean life and sentiments could not be fully expressed other than in Korean and only a small portion of the Korean populace could understand Japanese at the time, Korean language literature would remain alive until older generations, who were not conversant in Japanese, passed away. Yi Kwangsu, *"Sin Ch'eje wa Chosŏn Munhwa ŭi Chillo"* [The New Order and the Path of Korean Culture], *Maeil Sinbo* (September 10, 1940).

70. Ch'oe Chaesŏ, *Kokumin Bungaku* (May and June 1942), 44–45.

71. Ch'oe translated Pak Hwasŏng's *"Hangui"* [Thirsty Ghosts] and Yi T'aejun's *"Kkotnamu nŭn Simŏnokko"* [Having Planted a Tree] into Japanese and published them in the journal *Kaizō* in October 1936. Both stories depict the privation of Korean peasants.

72. Ch'oe Chaesŏ, *"Chŏnhyŏnggi ŭi Munhwa Iron"* (Cultural Theory in a Time of Change), *Inmun P'yŏngnon* (February 1941): 18–23.

73. Ch'oe Chaesŏ, *"Munhak Chŏngsin ŭi Chŏnhwan"* (Shift in Literary Spirit), *Inmun P'yŏngnon* (March 1941): 5–10.

74. The cultural nationalism of Japanese intellectuals during the 1930s and 1940s has been studied by quite a few scholars in the United States. One notable example is Harry Harootunian. In his book, *Overcome by Modernity*, Harootunian shows that Japanese intellectual's anxiety about the ever-changing social values triggered by modernity was hardly unique to Japan. He argues that Japanese intellectuals' various responses to the anxiety paralleled similar feelings of unease found among intellectuals in other countries. Only the most advanced countries, such as Great Britain and the United States, escaped the dilemma, he argues. To support his argument that modernity was "coeval" between the West and Japan, Harootunian discusses parallels between the thought of such German intellectuals as Siegfried Kracauer and Walter Benjamin and those of such Japanese intellectuals as Kon Wajirō, Gonda Yasunosuke, and Tosaka Jun. Instead of following Harootunian by treating Japan's anxiety over modernity as a common phenomenon also found in Western societies, however, I bring into question the self-evidence of such concepts as tradition and national culture by discussing parallels between Ch'oe's essays and the contemporary Japanese intellectual discourse on modernity and Japanese culture. Harry Harootunian, *Overcome by Modernity* (Princeton: Princeton University Press, 2000). See also Harootunian, *History's Disquiet* (New York: Columbia University Press, 2000).

75. For more information about the rise of cosmopolitanism and its connection to commercialism in interwar Japanese popular culture, see Jordan Sand, *House and Home in Modern Japan* (Cambridge: Harvard University Asia Center, 2003), 203–27.

76. Hirano Ken, *"Taiheiyōsensōka no Kokumin Bungakuron"* [The National Literature Debate during the Pacific War], *Bungaku* [Literature] 2 (1955), 102.

77. Yun Kŏnch'a, *Minzoku Gensō no Satetsu* [Miscarriage of National Fantasy] (Tokyo: Iwanami Shoten, 1994), 31–38.

78. Kyōgoku Okikazu, *Kindai Nihongo no Kenkyū* [Study on Modern Japanese] (Tokyo: Tōensha, 1998), 262–95.

79. The following articles appeared in the April 1937 issue of *Shisō*: Usui Jishō, *"Minzoku Bunka Kyōdōtai"* [The Community of an Ethnic National Culture]: 13–36; Yanaihara Tadao, *"Minzoku to Dentō"* [Ethnic Nation and Tradition]: 1–12; Imai Tōshiki, *"Minzoku to Toshi no Keitai"* [Ethnic Nation and the Mode of Urbanity]: 38–53.

80. Takata Yasuma, *Minzokuron* [The Theory of Ethnic Nation] (Tokyo: Iwanami Shoten, 1942).

81. For information about the influence of Japanese modernist poetry on Yi Sang, see Kawamura Minato, *"Tōkyō de Shinda Otoko"* [A Man Who Died in Tokyo], *Gendaishi Techō* [Modern Poetry Notebook] (October and November, 1989): 122–30.

82. Ch'oe, *"Chŏnhyŏnggi ŭi Munhwa Iron,"* 23.

83. Hagiwara poetically expressed the emptiness shared by many Japanese intellectuals in the 1930s about Japanese modern culture and the nostalgia for tradition of Japan in *"Nihon e no Kaiki"* in Hagiwara Sakutarō, *Hagiwara Sakutarō Zenshū* [Collected Works of Hagiwara Sakutarō], 15 vols. (Tokyo: Chikuma Shobō, 1975–1978), 10: 485–89. He wrote,

> When inscribing once "the diagram (zu) of the West" in our hearts and dreaming of a mirage of a utopia over the sea, our hearts were full of hope, overflowing with youthful passions. However, having now become disillusioned with the mirage after searching around every corner of the world, we realize that our real home where we should live is no place other than our fatherland, Japan. Nevertheless, in the very home of ours, the diagram of the West is what makes the trains and trolleys run and vulgar buildings built everywhere as poor copies of the West.

Ibid., 487 (translation by author).

84. Ch'oe, *"Chŏnhyŏnggi ŭi Munhwa Iron,"* 18–19 (emphasis added).

85. Emphasis added.

86. Ch'oe, *Tenkanki no Chōsen Bungaku*, 176, 195–198.

87. Jacques Derrida, *Speech and Phenomena and Other Essays on Husserl's Theory of Signs* (Evanston, Ill.: Northwestern University Press, 1973), esp. 88–104; Jacques Derrida, *Of Grammatology* (Baltimore: Johns Hopkins University Press, 1976), esp. 141–64.

88. Ch'oe, *Tenkanki no Chōsen Bungaku*, 119.

CHAPTER FOUR

1. Kim Soun, *"Okusoku to Dokudan no Meiro"* [The Labyrinth of Speculation and Dogma], *Bungaku* [Literature] (June 1956): 86–101. Kim (1908–1981) was a well-known journalist, essayist, poet, and translator of Korean poetry into Japanese. While in Japan, he rose to fame after publishing his translations of Korean folksongs titled *Chōsen Minyōshu* [Anthology of Korean Folk Songs] (Tokyo: Taibunkan, 1929). Kim made acquaintance with a number

of prominent Japanese literary figures, including Kitahara Hakushū, who wrote the preface to *Chōsen Minyoshū*. Kim went on to translate and publish traditional Korean children's songs in 1933. His career as a translator culminated in the publication of his Korean poetry anthology, *Chichi Iro no Kumo* [Milky Clouds] (Tokyo: Kawade Shobō, 1940). As mentioned in more detail later, *Chōsen Shishū* [Korean Poetry Anthology] (Tokyo: Sōgensha, 1953) was based on the earlier anthology.

2. Kim's problematically liberal translations of Korean poems have been pointed out by quite a few scholars. For more information, see Kajii Wataru, *"Kim Soun Tōma Seita no Chōsenshi Ronsō"* [Debates Between Kim Soun and Tōma Seita on Korean Poetry], *Chōsen Bungaku* [Korean Literature] (February 1971): 38–50; Kim Yunsik, *"Hanguk Kŭndaeshi Pŏnyŏk ŭi Munjechŏm"* [Problems of Translating Modern Korean Poetry], *Hyŏndae Munhak* [Contemporary Literature], no.337 (1983): 132–147; Yu Chongho, *"'Chosŏn Sijip' Ilkki"* [Reading *Korean Poetry Collection*], *Munhak ŭi Chŭlgŏum* [Pleasure of Literature] (Seoul: Minŭmsa, 1993): 414–40; Saegusa Toshikatsu, *"Kim Soun ŭn Muŏsŭl Haenŭga?"* [What Did Kim Soun Do?], *Hanguk Kŭnade Munhank kwa Ilbon* [Modern Korean Literature and Japan] (Seoul: Somyŏng Chulp'ansa, 2003): 288–347.

3. Fredric Jameson, "Third-World Literature in the Era of Multinational Capitalism," *Social Text*, no. 15 (Autumn 1986): 65–88.

4. Aijaz Ahmad, "Jameson's Rhetoric of Otherness and the 'National Allegory,'" *Social Text*, no. 17 (Autumn 1987): 3–25.

5. One notorious example of Levinas's indifference to cultures other than Western ones is found in his 1991 interview in which he states, "I often say, although it is a dangerous thing to say publicly, that humanity consists of the Bible and Greeks. All the rest can be translated: all the rest—all the exotic—is dance." Raoul Mortley, *French Philosophers in Conversation* (London: Routledge, 1991), 18. For a succinct but informative discussion on the subject, see Robert Bernasconi, "One-Way Traffic: The Ontology of Decolonization and Its Ethics," in *Ontology and Alterity in Merleau-Ponty*, eds. Galen A. Johnson and Michael B. Smith (Evanston: Northwestern University Press, 1990): 66–80.

6. For a brief but brilliant exposition of the relationship between the proper name of an author and his or her text, see Kojin Karatani, *Transcritique* (Cambridge: MIT Press, 2003), 111–12.

7. Saegusa, *"Kim Soun ŭn Muŏsŭl Haenŭga?"* 301.

8. Satō Haruo, *"Chōsen no Shijinra o Naichi no Shidan ni Mukahen to Suru no Ji"* [Words of Welcoming Korean Poets to Japanese Poetry Circles], in Kim Soun, *Chichi Iron no Kumo* (Tokyo: Kawade Shobō, 1940), 6.

9. Kim, *Chichi Iro no Kumo*, 304.

10. Yi Kwangsu, *"Yakushishū ni Yosete"* [On the Occasion of the Publication of the Poetry Translation Anthology], ibid., 10–11.

11. Kim Soun, *Chosen Shishū* [Korean Poetry Collection], 2 vols. (Tokyo: Kōfūkan, 1943), 1: 1–10.

12. John Dower, *Embracing Defeat* (New York: W. W. Norton, 1999), 254–73.

13. Tokuda Kyūichi, *"Atarashii Jōsei to Kore ni Taiōsuru Waga Tō no Seisaku"* [A New Situation and Our Party's Policy in Response to It], in *Nihon Kyōsantō Gojūnen Mondai Shiryōshū* [Collected Documents of the Fifty Years of the Japanese Communist Party], ed. Mondai Bunken Henshū Iinkai, 3 vols. (Tokyo: Shin Nihon Shuppan, 1994), 1: 11–17.

14. The San Francisco Treaty was signed by Japan and the United States and other allied nations, except for Soviet Russia, India, Burma, and Yugoslavia, in 1952 to conclude the Occupation of Japan and World War II in the Pacific. Under the terms of the treaty, Japan officially relinquished territorial claims to its former colonies.

15. Tōma Seita, *"Furusato-Chōsen no Shi ni Tsuite no Nōto I,"* [Hometown: Notes on Korean Poetry I], *Nihon Bungaku* [Japanese Literature] 3, no. 3 (1954): 39–51; *"Aru Shijin no Shōgai, Jō-Chōsen no Shi ni Tsuite no Nōto II"* [A Poet's Life Part One—Notes on Korean Poetry II], *Nihon Bungaku* 3, no. 6 (1954): 25–34; *"Aru Shijin no Shōgai, Ge-Chōsen no Shi ni Tsuite no Nōto II"* [A Poet's Life Part Two—Notes on Korean Poetry II], *Nihon Bungaku* 3, no. 7 (1954): 20–26; *"Shi to Minyō"* [Poetry and Folksongs], *Bungaku* [Literature] (July 1954): 61–77.

16. Yi Hahyun (1906–1974) was a poet and scholar of English literature. He was better known as a translator of French and American as well as English literature. Pak Yongch'ŏl (1904–1938) was one among the few poets in the early 1930s who advocated pure literature in opposition to both the proletarian and modernist movements. He also translated the works of German poets, including Friedrich von Schiller and Heinrich Heine.

17. Kim Soun, *Chōsen Shishū* (Tokyo: Sōgensha, 1953), 24–26. English translation is mine. The poem's original Korean title can best be translated as "A Grave Lost."

18. Kim, *Chōsen Shishū*, 232–33.

19. Kim, *"Okusoku to Dokudan no Meiro."*

20. Ibid., 91

21. Tōma, *"Furusato-Chōsen no Shi ni Tsuite no Nōto I,"* 50.

22. Kim Yunsik, *"Hanguk Kŭndaeshi Pŏnyŏk ŭi Munjechŏm,"* 135–36.

23. The poem is listed on pages 172 to 174 in *Chosen Shishū* (1953).

24. Kim Yunsik, *"Hanguk Kŭndaeshi Pŏnyŏk ŭi Munjechŏm,"* 134.

25. Kim, *Chichi Iro no Kumo*, 291–92.

26. Kim, *Chōsen Shishū* (1943) 2:335–36. No Ch'ŏnmyŏng (1912–1957) was one of the most prominent female poets in modern Korean literature.

27. Kim Soun, *"Okusoku to Dokudan no Meiro,"* 98–99.

28. Tōma Seita, *"Gendai Chōsen Bungaku no Hitotsu no Mikata"* [One Perspective on Modern Korean Literature], *Bungaku* (August 1956): 99–104.

29. Jameson, "Third-World Literature in the Era of Multinational Capitalism."

30. Ibid., 65.

31. Drawing on Perry Anderson, Jameson notes that capitalism innately developed in Japan and thus implies that Japan is not a Third-World but a First-World country, even though it is an Asian nation. Ibid., 68.

32. Jameson, "Third-World Literature in the Era of Multinational Capitalism," 69.

33. Ibid., 78.

34. Ibid.

35. Ahmad, "Jameson's Rhetoric of Otherness and the 'National Allegory,'" 23.

36. Jameson, "Third-World Literature in the Era of Multinational Capitalism," 77.

37. This insight of Levinas is helpful for seeing the fundamentally ethical problem in what the influential Japanese intellectual Katō Norihiro has suggested concerning Japan's war responsibility. Katō argues in his controversial essay "*Haisengoron*" [Post-Defeat Discourse] that to extend a genuine apology to Asian nations for what Japan did during the war, first, the Japanese should form a national subjectivity through the course of mourning for the three million Japanese killed during the war. Only the Japanese collective identity thus formed can be the subject of a genuine apology to Asian victims of the Japanese aggression and the Japanese dead, who were also the victims of the war, Katō suggests. In Katō's argument, the formation of a national subjectivity precedes reconciliation with Asian nations. Furthermore, in his construction, both the war criminals executed after the Tokyo tribunal and the helpless children killed by the atomic bombs in Hiroshima and Nagasaki belong to the collective Japanese nation. Katō Norihiro, "*Haisengoron*," *Gunzō* [Group] 50, no.1 (1995): 252–94.

38. Emmanuel Levinas, *Totality and Infinity* (Pittsburgh: Duquesne University Press, 1969), 242–43.

39. Ibid., 52, 55–58, 242, 227–28.

40. Ibid., 244.

41. Ibid., 22–23.

42. Fredric Jameson, *The Political Unconscious* (Ithaca: Cornell University Press, 1981), 35.

43. Walter Benjamin also offers revealing insight into the relationship between the eschatological narrative of the past and redemption. He wrote, "To be sure, only a redeemed mankind receives the fullness of its past—which to say, only for a redeemed mankind has its past become citable in all its moments. Each moment it has lived becomes a *citation à l'ordre du jour*—and the day is Judgment Day." Walter Benjamin, "Theses on the Philosophy of History," in *Illuminations*, ed. Hannah Arendt (New York: Schocken Books, 1968), 254.

44. Levinas, *Totality and Infinity*, 56.

45. For information on the distinction Levinas made between the ego and the self, see footnote 81 of Chapter 2.

CHAPTER FIVE

1. In the second line of the original text, an emphasizing dot is put on each of the five letters, 馬鹿ナ瞬間 instead.

2. In the sixth line of the original text, an emphasizing dot is put on each of the four letters, イクラカ instead.

3. In the ninth line of the original text, an emphasizing dot is put on each of the three letters, 日本語 instead.

4. In the 15th line of the original text, an emphasizing dot is put on each of the eight letters, シュルリアリズム instead.

5. Kim Suyŏng, "*Ilgich'o* (II)" [Diary (II)], in *Kim Suyŏng Chŏnjip* [Collected Works of Kim Suyŏng], ed. Kim Suhong, 2 vols. (Seoul: Minumsa, 2005), 2: 508–09.

6. Because the diary was written in February 1961, the revolution referenced here is the April 19th Revolution of 1960 that toppled the corrupt government of Yi Sŭngman (Syngman Rhee) in South Korea. Kim had written a series of poems that celebrated the civil revolution to rout the dictatorship. However, as the revolution wore on and the new government became stymied in its own reform efforts, Kim became increasingly disillusioned with the revolution. However, it was the military coup led by General Pak Chŏnghŭi (Park Chung-hee) in 1961 that took away the last breath of the revolutionary spirit from South Korean society.

7. Wonmo Dong, "Assimilation and Social Mobilization in Korea," in *Korea under Japanese Colonial Rule*, ed. Andrew C. Nahm (Kalamazoo: Center for Korean Studies Western Michigan University, 1973), 146–82; Yi Pyŏnghyŏk, "*Ilcheha ŭi Ŏnŏ Saenghwal*" [Everyday Language Use under Japanese Rule], in *Ilcheha ŭi Singmin Chibae wa Saenghwalsang* [Everyday Life under Japanese Colonial Rule] (Seoul: Hanguk Chŏngsin Munhwawŏn, 1990), 27–80.

8. Kim Pyŏnggŏl, *Silp'aehan Insaeng, Silp'aehan Munhak* [Failed Life, Failed Literature] (Seoul: Ch'angjak kwa Pip'yŏngsa, 1994), 48–57.

9. Ibid., 111.

10. According to a survey conducted by a Korean newspaper in 1931 about reading trends among higher common school students, male students chose twice as many Japanese-language books as Korean-language books. Ch'ŏn Chŏnghwan, *Kŭndae ŭi Ch'aekilki* [Modern Book Reading] (Seoul: P'urŭn Yŏksa, 2003), 362.

11. Yi Hŭisŭng, "*Ilsang Yongŏ e Issŏsŏ ŭi Ilbonjŏk Janjae*" [Japanese Legacies in Daily Language Use], *Sinch'ŏnji* [New World] 2, no. 5 (1947): 60–67.

12. Yi Hŭisŭng, "*Kuggŏran Muŏssinga?*" [What Is National Language?], *Sinch'ŏnji* [New World] 1, no. 3 (1946): 141–46.

13. The revision of the colonial education law (*Dai Niji Chōsen Kyoikurei*) promulgated in 1922 split the Korean language and classical Chinese course into two courses. Although the Korean language course remained mandatory, the classical Chinese course became optional.

14. Mitsui Takashi, *"Singminjiha Chosŏn esŏŭi Ŏnŏjibae"* [Language Policy in Colonial Korea], *Han'il Minjok Munje Yŏn'gu* [Korea–Japan Studies] 4 (2003): 203–28.

15. Yi Kŭngno, *"Chosŏnŏ Sajŏn P'yŏnch'an e Taehaya"* [About Making a Korean Dictionary], *Hangŭl* (May 1932): 12–14.

16. Mitsui, *"Singminjiha Chosŏn esŏŭi Ŏnŏjibae,"* 220.

17. Mitsui calls attention to the argument made by apologists of Japanese colonial rule over Korea in his article. Ibid. See also Nishio Kanji, *Kokumin no Rekishi* [History of the Nation] (Tokyo: Sankei Shinbun, 1999), 709.

18. The column ended with a call for the restoration of Korean as the instructional language at elementary school. *"Ch'odŭng Kyoyuk kwa Yong-ŏ Munje"* [Elementary School Education and the Problem of Language], *Tong-a Ilbo* (December 3, 1931).

19. Kim Hyejŏng, *"Kŭndae Ihu Kugŏgwa Kyojae Kaebal e Taehan Sajŏk Kŏmt'o"* [Historical Overview of the Development of Modern Korean Language Texts], *Kugŏ Kyoyuk Yŏngu* [National Language Education Research] 13 (2004): 404–37.

20. Ch'ŏn, *Kŭndae ŭi Ch'aekilki,* 228.

21. Yi Chungyŏn, *Ch'aek ŭi Unmyŏng* [Fate of Books] (Seoul: Hyean, 2001), 419, 463.

22. Kawamura Minato, *"Yoidorebune" no Seishun* [Youth of "the Drunken Boat"] (Tokyo: Inpakuto Shuppankai, 2000), 147–86.

23. No Yŏngt'aek, *"Ilchesigi ŭi Munmaengyul Ch'ui"* [Change in the Literacy Rate During the Colonial Period], *Kuksagwan Nonch'ong* [Kusagwan Collected Articles] 51 (1994): 109–59.

24. Yi Kwangsu, "Chosŏn Munhak ŭi Kaenyŏm" [The Concept of Korean Literature], *Yi Kwangsu Chŏnnjip* [Collected Works of Yi Kwangsu], 30 vols. (Seoul: Samjungdang, 1968) 16:175–176. The essay is certainly overshadowed by Yi Kwangsu's well known antitraditionalism. Yi's antitraditionalism already conspicuously appeared in his 1922 essay *"Minjok Kaejoron"* [Theory of National Renovation], in which he ascribed the degeneration of the Korean nation to its tradition. Yi Kwangsu, *"Minjok Kaejoron," Kaebyŏk* [Beginning of the World] 23 (1922): 18–72.

25. *"Sam Chŏnmunhakkyo Sa Kyosu Sam Sinmunsa Haggyebujang Munyejŏngch'aek Hoeŭi"* [Conference on Cultural Policies Attended by Four Professors from three Colleges and Three Newspaper Columnists of the Culture Section], *Samch'olli* [Three Thousand Leagues] 8, no. 6 (1936): 226–40.

26. Ch'ŏn, *Kŭndae ŭi Ch'aekilki,* 348–51, 362–64.

27. Yi Myŏnghwa, *"Chosŏn Ch'ongdokbu ŭi Ŏnŏ Tonghwa Chŏngch'aek"* [Language Assimilation Policy by the Government General in Korea], *Hanguk Tongnip Undongsa Yŏngu* [Study on Korean Liberation Movements], 9 (1995): 277–94.

28. During the colonial period, Yi T'aejun distanced himself from political activities in contrast to leftist writers who had been involved in the Korean Artist Proletariat Federation (KAPF, the acronym of Korea Artista Proletaria

Federatio in Esperanto), the leftist literary organization founded in 1925. However, after liberation, Yi was actively engaged in leftist literary activities. He became the central committee chair of the Center for the Construction of Korean Literature, the leftist literary organization that was founded on August 16, 1945, a day after the defeat of Japan in World War II. Yi departed for North Korea in 1946.

29. Despite the righteous tone, Yi had also published a short story in Japanese titled *"Dai Ichigō Sen no Sōga"* [An Episode of Boat No. 1] in *Kindai Chōsen bungaku Nihongo Sakuhinshū* [Anthology of Modern Korean Literature Written in Japanese], ed. Ōmura Masuo and Hotei Toshihiro, 5 vols. (Tokyo: Rokuin Shobō, 2001), 5: 463–68. The short story was originally published in 1945. For more information, see Hotei Toshihiro, *"Ilche Malgi Ilbonŏ Sosŏl Yŏgu"* [Study of Japanese-Language Stories During the Late Colonial Period] (master's thesis, Seoul National University, 1996), 102–09.

30. *"Munhakja ŭi Chagi Pip'an"* [Self-Criticism of Writers], in *Haebang Konggan ŭi Pip'yŏng Munhak* [Literary Criticism During the Post-Liberation Period], eds., Song Kihan and Kim Oegon, 3 vols. (Seoul: T'aehaksa, 1991), 2: 164–72.

31. Minjok is the Korean pronunciation of a compound composed of two Chinese characters read *minzoku* in Japanese. As discussed in Chapter 3 in more detail, even though both *minjok* and *kungmin* (*kokumin* in Japanese) can be translated as nation, more weight is given to the ethnic aspect of nation in minjok and to the people's relationship with the state (*kukka* in Korean; *kokka* in Japanese) in *kungmin.* Since the Korean peninsula was divided and ruled by the Soviet and the American occupation forces until 1948 and two different governments were set up in North and South after that, *minjok* has been regarded as a more appropriate term to refer to the Korean people, bridging North and South.

32. Pak Chonghwa, *"Minjok Munhak ŭi Wŏlli"* [Principle of National Literature], *Kyŏnghyangsinmun* [Kyunghyang Daily], December 5, 1946.

33. Cho Chihun, *"Minjok Munhwa ŭi Tangnyŏn Munje"* [Urgent Problem Concerning National Culture], *Munhwa* [Culture] (April 1947): 6–23.

34. Kim Namchŏn, *"Munhak ŭi Kyoyukjŏk Immu"* [Educational Task of Literature], in *Haebang Konggan ŭi Pip'yŏng Munhak,* 1: 36–42. It was originally published in November 1945.

35. Yi Wōnjo, *"Munhak kwa Ŏnŏ Ch'angjo"* [Creation of Language and Literature], in *Haebang Konggan ŭi Pip'yŏng Munhak* 1: 61–65.

36. Ibid.

37. *"Oesaek ŭi Chanjae nŭn Ajikto Namaitta"* [Japanese Legacies Still Remain], *Chosŏn Ilbo* (August, 15, 1948).

38. Chang Chiyŏng, *"Narat Mal ŭl Kkaekkŭch'i Haja"* [Let U.S. Clean National Language], *Hangŭl* 98 (1946): 22–27.

39. Yi Ŭngho, *Mi Kunjŏnggi ŭi Hangŭl Ŭndongsa* [The Hangŭl Movement under the U.S. Military Government] (Seoul: Sŏngch'ŏngsa, 1974), 78, 80–87, 91, 261–62. At the same time, the "language science general committee" comprising Korean scholars was formed under the Ministry of Education

to invent Korean academic and scientific terminology to replace Japanese in April 1946.

40. Yi Hŭisŭng, *"Kugŏ Kyoyuk ŭi Tangmyŏn Kwaje"* [Urgent Task of National Language Education], *Chosŏn Kyoyuk* [Korea Education] 1, no.1 (1947): 33–42.

41. In fact, in 1946 the Chosŏnŏ Hakhoe pronounced a revision of the proposal of orthography they made during the colonial period. The U.S. military government approved it as the official orthography and enforced it for the publication of school texts and government documents in 1947.

42. Pak Wansŏ, *"Nae an e Ŏnŏ Sadaejuŭi Yŏppogi"* [Linguistic Toadyism Within Myself], reprinted in *Tubu* [Tofu] (Seoul: Ch'angjak kwa Pip'yŏngsa, 2002): 172–98.

43. Ibid., 189.

44. Pak Hongmin, *"Pŏljaeng-i"* [Punishable"], *Puin* [Woman] 3 (1946): 44–46.

45. Jacques Derrida, *Monolingualism of the Other or the Prosthesis of Origin* (Stanford, Calif.: Stanford University Press, 1996). 39.

46. A Korean newspaper reported in 1947 that some Korean middle schools still used Japanese language science textbooks because of the dearth of Korean-language science textbooks. *"Chungdŭnghakyo e Ajikto Ilŏ rŭl Sayong"* [Japanese Still Spoken at Middle Schools], *Urisinmun* [Our Newspaper], November, 22, 1947.

47. Chŏn Ponggŏn, *"Sijak Notŭ"* [Notes on Poetry Writing], in *Hanguk Chŏnhu Munje Sijip* [Collection of Important Postwar Poems], ed. Paek Ch'ŏl (Seoul: Sin'gu Munhwasa, 1961), 403–05.

48. In his discussion on the two leading writers after the Korean War (1950–1953), Son Ch'angsŏp and Chang Yonghak, Kim Yunsik pointed out that their writing had been indebted to the tradition of modern Japanese literature. On another occasion, Kim and Chŏng Houng criticized Korean literature of the 1950s as replete with awkward sentences, which they ascribed to the fact that the generation of writers active then generally had difficulty speaking Korean as an everyday life language. Kim Yunsik, *Kim Yunsik Sŏnjip* [Selected Works of Kim Yunsik], 2 vols. (Seoul: Sol, 1996), 2: 376; Kim Yunsik and Chŏng Houng, *Hangkuk Sosŏlsa* [History of Korean Fiction] (Seoul: Munhak Tongne, 2000), 349.

49. Ko Ŭn, *1950nyŏndae* [The 1950s] (Seoul: Minŭnsa, 1973), 301–05.

50. Yi T'aejun, *"Munjang Kanghwa," Munjang* [Writing], 1, no. 1: 180–87; no. 2: 187–97; no. 3: 189–99; no. 4: 189–201; no. 5: 199–201; no. 6: 202–05; no. 7: 196–205; no. 8: 203–10; no. 9: 278–89. Nine parts from February through October 1939.

51. Ch'ŏn Chŏnghwan relates the popularity of writing books to the emergence of the modern self among Koreans who aspired to express themselves and communicate with others during the colonial period. He also calls attention to the fact that Japanese writing textbooks came to dominate the market from the 1920s. Ch'ŏn, *Kŭndae ŭi Ch'aekilki*, 146–47.

52. Yi T'aejun, *"Munjang Kanghwa," Munjang* 1, no. 1, 180.

53. Kim Suyŏng, *"Hipŭresŭ Munhangnon"* [A Theory of Hipless Literature], *Kim Suyŏng Chŏnjip* 2: 278–86. Kim could not include Yi T'aejun in the pantheon of prominent writers of the colonial period because Yi went to North Korea before the Korean War. In South Korea, it was illegal until the 1980s to publicly mention or discuss the works of "defectors" to North Korea without governmental permission. As a matter of fact, Kim once observed that educated readers in South Korea had believed real writers all went to the North and only charlatans remained in the South. All the three writers he mentioned in the essay died during the colonial period before liberation and the division of the Korean peninsula and thus escaped the ordeal of choosing between North and South Koreas. Kim idiosyncratically used the adjective "hipless" to mean "uprooted and displaced." Yi Yŏngjun, *"Grand Affirmation: Kim Suyŏng's Poetic Vision"* (PhD diss., Harvard University, 2006), 133–34.

54. Kim Suyŏng, *"Hipŭresŭ Munhangnon."*

55. According to Kim's biographer, Ch'oe Harim, Kim respected Im and drew inspiration from the latter's writings. Im was an active member of the leftist organization of writers and poets, KAPF during the colonial period. He went to the North in 1947 after liberation, but was accused of spying for the United States and executed in 1953. Ch'oe Harim, *Kim Suyŏng P'yŏngjŏn* [Kim Suyŏng Biography] (Seoul: Silch'ŏn Munhaksa, 2001).

56. Im Hwa, *"Chosŏn Munhak Yŏngu ŭi Ilgwaje"* [An Issue of Korean Literary Research], 6 installments, *Tong-a Ilbo* (January 13, 14, 16, 18, 19, and 20, 1940). Im, however, did not necessarily dismiss the importance of Korean literary tradition in the development of modern literature in Korea. He argued that tradition should interact with foreign influence to sublate itself dialectically and advance to a new culture.

57. Kim Suyŏng, *"Chamyŏsi ŭi Chŏngni"* [An Overview of Engagement Poetry], reprinted in *Kim Suyŏng Chŏnjip* 2: 386–96.

58. Kim Suyŏng, *"Pyŏnhangŏt kwa Pyŏnhajianŭngot"* [What Has Changed and What Has Not], reprinted in *Kim Suyŏng Chŏnjip* 2: 370.

59. Kim Suyŏng, *"Kajang Arŭmdaun Urimal Yŏlkae"* [Our Ten Most Beautiful Words], *Kim Suyŏng Chŏnjip* 2: 373–78.

60. Kim Suyŏng, *"Sijak Notŭ* 6" [Notes on Poetry Writing 6], *Kim Suyŏng Chŏnjip* 2: 446–53.

61. The Collected Works of Kim Suyŏng lists the Korean translation and explains that it was translated into Korean and published by a journal, but does not disclose what journal published it.

62. Chŏng Haegu, *"Hanil Hoedam gwa Pak Chŏnghŭi"* [Korea–Japan Negotiations and Pak Chŏnghŭi], *Kŭnhyŏndaesa Kangjwa* [Lectures on Modern History] 6 (1995): 187–96.

63. Yi Wŏndŏk, *"Hanil Hoedam gwa Ilbon ŭi Chŏnhu Ch'ŏri Oegyo"* [Korea–Japan Negotiations and Postwar Japanese Diplomacy], *Hanguk kwa Kukche Chŏngch'i* [Korea and International Politics] 1(1996): 35–76.

64. Hong Insuk, *"Hanil Hoedam e Daehan Miil ŭi Kudo wa Taeŭng"* [American and Japanese Plan in Response to Korea–Japan Negotiations], *Yŏksa Pip'yŏng* [History and Criticism] (Spring 1995): 23–37.

65. Kim Suyŏng himself signed the petition against the normalization treaty with Japan initiated by poets Cho Chihun and Pak Tujin. Ch'oe Harim, *Kim Suyŏng P'yŏngjŏn*. (Seoul: Silch'ŏn Munhaksa, 2001), 312.

66. Kim Suyŏng confessed in a previous article in the same series that because he was clumsy with Korean and paranoid, he had to consult a Korean dictionary at least three or four times to write one page in Korean. Kim Suyŏng, *"Sijak Notŭ 4," Kim Suyŏng Chŏnjip* 2: 437–41.

67. *"Aiya"* is categorized as an essay by the majority of Yi Sang scholars. The poetic essay narrates the narrator's visit to a prostitute and ends with his wish to return to his homeland.

68. If carefully examining Kim's essay "Our Ten Most Beautiful Words" in comparison with Yi's short piece written under a similar title, "Beautiful Korean," we might be able to glimpse what Kim thought of Yi's Korean lyricism expressed only in the Korean language. In "Our Ten Most Beautiful Words," Kim listed a number of words, which had been used less and less and were becoming obsolete. While expressing his affection for words he often heard when he was a child, as discussed earlier, however, he asserted beautiful words are not those old words that evoke a strong feeling of nostalgia. Beautiful words are instead those that are alive in poetry, he argued. Furthermore, he emphasized that culture should not be swayed by nationalism. On the other hand, in "Beautiful Korean," Yi eulogized the beautiful musicality of the Sŏdo dialect, which is spoken in the northwestern part of the Korean peninsula. It is interesting to note that the dialect synecdochically stands for the Korean language in Yi's essay as seen in its title. Yi's essay was originally published in 1936. Yi Sang, *"Arŭmdaun Chosŏnmal"* [Beautiful Korean], *Yi Sang Munhak Chŏnjip* [Complete Literary Works of Yi Sang] 3 vols. (Seoul: Somyŏng Ch'ulpansa, 2009) 3:230–31; Kim Suyŏng, "Our Ten Most Beautiful Words."

69. Kim Suyŏng, *"Sijak Notŭ 6,"* 451–52. Kim wrote, "I am not using Japanese but *mangnyŏng* (妄靈)." Although the word *mangnyŏng* usually refers to dotage or senility, I argue that *mangnyŏng* should be interpreted as *mangnyŏng* (亡靈) (apparition or spirit of the dead person) to be closer to Kim's intention. There are two reasons for my argument. First, the Japanese word corresponding to dotage or senility is mōroku (耄碌). Taking into account that the text was originally written in Japanese, Kim Suyŏng should have used mōroku rather than *mangnyŏng* if he intended to say senility. Second, in classical Chinese texts, there are cases in which the two characters read *mang* (妄 and 亡) are used interchangeably. By metaphorizing his postcolonial use of Japanese as an apparition, Kim emphasized that like an apparition, his Japanese was destined to disappear but, nevertheless, was haunting him. For more information about the interchangeability between the two characters, see Tongyanghak Yŏnguso, *Hanhan Taesajŏng* (Classical Chinese-Korean Dictionary) vol. 3 (Seoul: Tanguk Taehakkyo, 2000), 1105.

70. Kim Suyŏng, *"Sijak Notŭ 6,"* 450.

71. Derrida, *Monolingualism of the Other or the Prosthesis of Origin*, 63.

72. Ibid., 61–65. The language of the other will never be entirely separated from existent languages. It should be "written" within a given language. For Derrida himself, French is such a given language. What we should bear in mind, however, is that although Derrida uses such an expression as "a given language," he does not suggest that such existent idioms as French and English exist homogeneously and autonomously.

73. Ibid., 68.

74. Poetry's innate resistance to translation was expressed by Samuel Johnson in an exemplary way. According to his biographer, James Boswell, Johnson said,

> You may translate books of science exactly. You may also translate history, in so far as it is not embellished with oratory, which is poetical. Poetry, indeed, cannot be translated; and, therefore, it is the poets that preserve languages; for we would not be at the trouble to learn a language, if we could have all that is written in it just as well as in a translation. But as the beauties of poetry cannot be preserved in any language except that in which it was originally written, we learn the language.

James Boswell, *The Life of Samuel Johnson* (New York: Modern Library, 1931), 633.

75. The suppression of the Japanese language use was much more extensively carried out in North Korea. Government pressure drove Japanese books out of the market entirely. Even Marxist–Leninist books were seized by the government if they were in Japanese. As a consequence, when Kim Ilsŏng University was founded in 1946, the school library had to buy Japanese-language books on Marxism from Manchuria, China. Yi Chungyŏn, *Ch'aek, Sasŭl esŏ P'ullida* [Books Released from Shackles] (Seoul: Hyean, 2005), 252–53.

Bibliography

Ahmad, Aijaz. "Jameson's Rhetoric of Otherness and the 'National Allegory.'" *Social Text* 17 (Autumn 1987): 3–25.

Akita Ujaku. *"Furusato e Kaeru 'Ch'unhyangjŏn' Yūgōshita Futatsu no Bunka no Kōryū." Keijō Nippō*, October 9, 1938.

Althusser, Louis. *Lenin and Philosophy*. New York: Monthly Review, 1971.

An Hwak. *"Chosŏn ŭi Munhak."* In *Hanguk Hyŏndae Munhak Pip'yŏngsa Charyo*, edited by Kwŏn Yŏngmin ed. Seoul: Hagun Haksul Chŏngbo, 2004, 34–47.

Anderson, Benedict. *Imagined Communities*. London and New York: Verso, 1991.

Aono Masaaki. *"Hosoi Hajime no Chōsenkan." Kan*, no. 110 (1988): 221–58.

Aono Suekichi. *Tenkanki no Bungaku*. Tokyo: Shunshūsha, 1927.

Asō Isoji. "Gikyoku *Ch'unhyangjŏn*." *Chōsen*, no. 89 (1922): 2–57.

BBC NEWS. "Split Imperils Mexican Langauge," http://news.bbc.co.uk/2/hi/also_in_the_news/7097647.stm (accessed March 21, 2013).

Bhabha, Homi. *The Location of Culture*. London and New York: Routledge, 1994.

Benjamin, Walter. "Theses on the Philosophy of History." In *Illuminations*, edited by Hannah Arendt. New York: Schocken Books, 1968.

Bernasconi, Robert. "One-Way Traffic: The Ontology of Decolonization and Its Ethics." In *Ontology and Alterity in Merleau-Ponty*, edited by Galen A. Johnson and Michael B. Smith, 66–80. Evanston, Ill.: Northwestern University Press, 1990.

——. "What Is the Question to Which 'Substitution' is the Answer?" In *Cambridge Companion to Levinas*, edited by Simon Critchley and Robert Bernasconi, 234–51. Cambridge: Cambridge University Press, 2002.

Boswell, James. *The Life of Samuel Johnson*. New York: Modern Library, 1931.

Caprio, Mark E. *Japanese Assimilation Policies in Colonial Korea 1910–1945*. Seattle: University of Washington Press, 2009.

Caygill, Howard. *Levinas and the Political*. London and New York: Routledge, 2002.

Ch'a Sŭnggi. *"Kŭndae ŭi Uigi hwa Sigan-Konggan ŭi Chŏngch'ihak." Hanguk Kŭndae Munhak Yŏngu* 8 (2003): 239–65.

Chang Chiyŏng. *"Narat Mal ŭl Kkaekkŭch'i Haja." Hangŭl* 98 (1946): 22–27.

Chang Hyŏkchu. *"Chōsen to Ch'unhyangjŏn." Keijō Nippō,* October 4, 1938.

——. *"Ch'unhyangjŏn." Shinchō* 5, no. 3 (1938): 2–68.

——. *"Ch'unhyangjŏn ni Tsuite." Bungei Shuto* 6, no. 3 (1938): 108–09.

"Che Samgukche ŭi Chiryŏng Pada Haengdong Kangnyŏng ŭl Surip." Chosŏn Ilbo, September 12, 1930.

Chi Sugŏl. *"1930 nyŏndae Ch'oban ŭi Chosŏn Minjokjuŭi wa Marŭkŭsŭ Reninjuŭi." Inmun'gwahak Yŏngu,* no.1 (March 1995): 143–70.

Cho Chihun. *"Minjok Munhwa ŭi Tangnyŏn Munje." Munhwa* (April 1947): 6–23.

Cho Kwanja. *"Sŏ Insik no Rekishi Tetsugaku." Shisō* 957 (2004): 29–54.

Cho Yongman. *Sansipnyŏndae Munhwa Yesulindul.* Seoul: Pŏmyangsa, 1978.

Cho Yŏnhyŏn. *"Ko Ch'oe Chaesŏ ŭi Ingan gwa Munhak." Hyŏndae Munhak* (January 1960): 18–19.

"Ch'odŭng Kyoyuk kwa Yong-ŏ Munje." Tong-a Ilbo, December 3, 1931.

Ch'oe Chaesŏ. *Ch'oe Chaesŏ P'yŏngnonjip.* Seoul: Ch'ŏngun Ch'ulpansa, 1961.

——.*"Chŏnhyŏnggi ŭi Munhwa Iron," Inmun P'yŏngnon* (February 1941): 18–23.

——. *"Chyoisŭ "Chŏlmŭn Yesulga ŭi Ch'osang"-Yesul ŭi T'ansaeng." Inmun Pyŏngnon* (January 1940): 120–34.

——.*"Hojŏkŏmnun Oeguk Munhak Yŏnguga." Chosŏn Ilbo,* April 26, 28, 1936.

——. *Insang gwa Sasaek.* Seoul: Yŏnse Taehak Ch'ulpanbu, 1977.

——. *"Munhak, Chakka, Chisŏng 1–3." Tong-a Ilbo,* August 20, 21, 23, 1938.

——. *"Munhak Chŏngsin ŭi Chŏnhwan." Inmun P'yŏngnon* (March 1941): 5–10.

——. *Munhak kwa Chisŏng.* Seoul: Inmunsa, 1938.

——. *"Munhwa Kiyŏjarosŏ." Chosŏn Ilbo,* June 9, 1937.

——. *Tenkanki no Chōsen Bungaku.* Seoul: Inmunsa, 1943.

Ch'oe Harim. *Kim Suyŏng P'yŏngjŏn.* Seoul: Silch'ŏn Munhaksa, 2001.

Ch'oe Sŏggyŏng. *Ilche ŭi Tonghwa Ideorogi ŭi Ch'angch'ul.* Seoul: Sŏgyŏng Munhwasa, 1997.

Ch'ŏn Chŏnghwan. *Kŭndae ŭi Ch'aekilki.* Seoul: P'urŭn Yŏksa, 2003.

Chŏn Ponggŏn. *"Sijak Notŭ."* In *Hanguk Chŏnhu Munje Sijip,* edited by Paek Ch'ŏl, 403–05. Seoul: Sin'gu Munhwasa, 1961.

Chŏng An-gi. *"Chŏnsigi Chosŏn Pangjik ŭi Taemanju T'uja wa Yŏng-gu Pangjik." Yŏksa wa Kyŏngye* 48 (September, 2003): 123–55.

Chŏng Haegu. *"Hanil Hoedam gwa Pak Chŏnghŭi." Kŭnhyŏndaesa Kangjwa* 6 (1995): 187–96.

Chŏng Hayŏng. *"Ch'unhyangjŏn Hanmunbon Haeje." Haguk Kojŏn Yŏngu* 2 (1996): 347–50.

"Chōsen Bunka no Shōrai." Bungakukai 6, no. 1 (1939): 271–79.

"Chōsen Bunka no Shōrai to Genzai." Keijō Nippō, 8 parts from November 29 through December 8, 1938.

Chōsen Sōtokufu. *Chōsen ni Okeru Kokumin Seishin Sōdōin Ūndo.* Seoul: Chōsen Sōtokufu, 1940.

"*Chosŏn Kojŏnmunhak ŭi Kŏmt'o.*" *Chosŏn Ilbo*, January 1–13, 1935.

"*Chosŏnmunhaksang ŭi Pokkosasang Kŏmt'o.*" *Chosŏn Ilbo*, January 22–31, 1935.

"*Chungdŭnghakyo e Ajikto Ilŏ rŭl Sayong.*" *Urisinmun*, November, 22, 1947.

"*Ch'unhyangjŏn Hihan Zadankai.*" *Teatoro* 5, no.12 (1938): 66–81.

"*Chūyaku wa Iyakuka Chokuyakuka.*" *Chōsengo* (January 1926): 71–74.

Critchley, Simon. *The Ethics of Deconstruction: Derrida and Levinas.* West Lefayette: Purdue University Press, 1999.

Daly, James. "Totality and Infinity in Marx," *Irish Philosophical Journal* 4, nos. 1–2 (1987): 120–44.

Derrida, Jacques. "*Des Tours de Babel.*" In *Difference in Translation*, edited by Joseph F. Graham, 165–207. Ithaca: Cornell University Press, 1985.

——. "Force of Law." *Cardozo Law Review* 11 (1989–1990): 920–1045.

——. *Monolingualism of the Other or the Prosthesis of Origin.* Stanford, Calif.: Stanford University Press, 1996.

——. *Of Grammatology.* Baltimore: Johns Hopkins University Press, 1976.

——. *Speech and Phenomena and Other Essays on Husserl's Theory of Signs.* Evanston, Ill.: Northwestern University Press, 1973.

——. "Violence and Metaphysics: An Essay on the Thought of Emmanuel Levinas." In *Writing and Difference*, 79–153. Chicago: University of Chicago Press, 1978.

Dirks, Nicholas B. "Introduction: Colonialism and Culture." In *Colonialism and Culture*, edited by Nicholas B. Dirks. Ann Arbor: University of Michigan Press, 1992.

Dong Wonmo. "Assimilation and Social Mobilization in Korea." In *Korea under Japanese Colonial Rule*, edited by Andrew C. Nahm. Kalamazoo: Center for Korean Studies Western Michigan University, 1973.

Dower, John. *Embracing Defeat.* New York: W. W. Norton, 1999.

Drabinski, John. *Levinas and the Postcolonial: Race, Nation, and Other.* Edinburgh: Edinburgh University Press, 2011.

Dussel, Enrique. *Philosophy of Liberation.* Maryknoll, N.Y.: Orbis Books, 1985.

——. *The Underside of Modernity: Apel, Ricoeur, Rorty, Taylor, and the Philosophy of Liberation.* Atlantic Highlands, N.J.: Humanities Books, 1996.

Eagleston, Robert. "Postcolonial Thought and Levinas's Double Vision." In *Radicalizing Levinas*, edited by Peter Atterton and Matthew Calarco, 57–68. Albany: SUNY Press, 2010.

Eagleton, Terry. *Literary Theory: An Introduction.* Minneapolis: University of Minnesota Press, 1983.

Eckert, Carter J. *Offspring of Empire.* Seattle: University of Washington Press, 1991.

"*Eigaka Sareru Ch'unhyangjŏn Zadankai Jō.*" *Keijō Nippō*, June 9, 1938, evening edition.

Fanon, Frantz. *The Wretched of the Earth*. New York: Grove Press, 1963.

Fujitani, T. *Splendid Monarchy*. Berkeley: University of California Press, 1998.

Fuse Tatsuji. "'*Ch'unhyangjŏn' o Mite*." *Teatoro* 5, no. 5 (1938): 25–28.

Gibbs, Robert. *Correlations in Rosenzweig and Levinas*. Princeton, N.J.: Princeton University Press, 1994.

Gluck, Carol. *Japan's Modern Myths*. New York: Columbia University Press, 1985.

Hagiwara Sakutarō. *Hagiwara Sakutarō Zenshū*. 15 vols. Tokyo: Chikuma Shobō, 1975–1978.

Harootunian, Harry. *History's Disquiet*. New York: Columbia University Press, 2000.

——. *Overcome by Modernity*. Princeton, N.J.: Princeton University Press, 2000.

Hegel, G. W. F. *Elements of the Philosophy of Right*. Cambridge: Cambridge University Press, 1991.

——. "The Spirit of Christianity." In *Early Theological Writings*. Philadelphia: University of Pennsylvania Press, 1971.

Hirano, Ken. "*Taiheiyōsensōka no Kokumin Bungakuron., Bungaku* 2 (1955): 99–105.

Hirata Isao. "'*Ch'unhyangjŏn' Kangeki Shokan*." *Teatoro* 5, no. 5 (1938): 28–29.

Hiromatsu, Wataru. *Kindai no Chōkokron*. Tokyo: Kōdansha, 1989.

Hong Insuk. "*Hanil Hoedam e Daehan Miil ŭi Kudo wa Taeŭng*." *Yŏksa Pip'yŏng* (Spring 1995): 23–37.

Hosoi Hajime. *Chōsen Bungaku Kessakushū*. Tokyo: Hōkōkai, 1924.

——. *Chōsen Bunka Shiron*. Keijō: Chōsen Kenkyūkai, 1911.

——. *Chōsen Mondai no Kisū*. Tokyo: Asea Bunka Renmei, 1925.

——. *Chōsen Tōchi Shinri no Konponteki Henkō ni Kansuru Ikensho*, 1924.

——. "*Gojosōai no Taigi to Chōsen Mondai*." *Chōsen Shakaijigyō* 4, no. 1 (1926): 1–47.

——. *Hanzoku Zaiakushi*. Tokyo: Daitōkaku, 1919.

——. "*Kosho Kobun o Tsujite Mitaru Chōsenjin no Shinsei*." *Chōsen* (December 1921): 54–77.

——. "*Naisenjin Ketsugō no Kitan*." *Kantō no Shinsai to Chōsenjin*. Keijō: Zaigai Chōsenjin Jijokenkai, 1923

——. *Nihonjin no Ketsui*. Tokyo: Dai Nihon Yūbenkai Kōdansha, 1932.

——. *Seisō to Tōhei*. Tokyo: Yakushinkai, 1914.

——. *Senman no Keiei: Chōsen Mondai no Konpon Kaiketsu*. Tokyo: Jiyūtōkyūsha, 1921.

Horowitz, Asher, and Gad Horowitz. "An Ethical Orientation for Marxism: Geras and Levinas," *Rethinking Marxism* 5, no. 2 (2003): 181–95.

Hotei Toshihiro. *Ilche Malgi Ilbonŏ Sosŏl Yŏgu*. Master's thesis, Seoul National University, 1996.

Hwang Chongyŏn. "1930*nyŏndae Kojŏn Puhŭng Undong ŭi Munhakjŏk Ŭiŭi*." *Hanguk Munhak Yŏngu* 11 (1988): 217–60.

———. *"Chŏng Chiyong ŭi Sanmun gwa Chŏntong eŭi Chihyang." Hanguk Muhank Yŏnggu* 10 (1987): 237–56.

Hyŏn Yŏngsŏp. *Chōsenjin no Susumubeki Michi.* Seoul: Rokki Renmei, 1938.

Hyppolite, Jean. *Genesis and Structure of Hegel's Phenomenology of Spirit.* Evanston, Ill.: Northwestern University Press, 1974.

Im Chongguk. *Ch'inil Munhangnon.* Seoul: Pyŏngwha, 1966.

Im Hwa. *"Chosŏn Munhak Yŏngu ŭi Ilgwaje." Tong-a Ilbo,* January 13, 14, 16, 18, 19, and 20, 1940.

Im Insik. *"Chosŏn Munhak ŭi Sinjŏngse wa Hyŏndae Chesang 6–9." Chosŏn Chungang Ilbo,* February 2–5, 1936.

Imai Tōshiki. *"Minzoku to Toshi no Keitai." Shisō* (April 1937): 38–53.

Jakobson, Roman. "On Linguistic Aspects of Translation." In *Theories of Translation,* edited by Rainer Schulte and John Biguenet, 144–51. Chicago: University of Chicago Press, 1992.

Jameson, Fredric. *The Political Unconscious.* Ithaca, N.Y.: Cornell University Press, 1981.

———. "Third-World Literature in the Era of Multinational Capitalism." *Social Text,* no. 15 (Autumn 1986): 65–88.

Kajii Wataru. *"Chōsen Bungaku Honyaku no Ashiato." Kikan Sanzenri.* 12 parts. no. 22 (1980): 203–15; no. 23 (1980): 230–39; no. 24 (1980): 175–85; no. 25 (1981): 198–208; no. 26 (1981): 204–13; no. 27 (1981): 204–24; no. 28 (1981): 225–35; no. 29 (1982): 196–205; no. 30 (1982): 162–72; no. 31 (1982): 216–26; no. 32 (1982): 217–27; no. 33 (1983): 200–51.

———. *"Kim Soun Tōma Seita no Chōsenshi Ronsō." Chōsen Bungaku* (February 1971): 38–50.

Kamisaka Taizō. *"Honshi no Chōsengo Kenkyūran Setchi." Chōsen Keisatsu Shinbun,* June 15, 1929.

Kang Samhŭi. *"Sŏgu Kyoyangjŭi esŏ Tongyangjok Sekero." Oeguk Munhak* (Winter 1994): 304–20.

Kang Tŏksang. *Kantōdaishinsai.* Tokyo: Chūōkōronsha, 1975.

Kant, Immanuel. *The Philosophy of Law.* Edinburgh: T. & T. Clark, 1887.

Karatani, Kojin. *Origins of Modern Japanese Literature.* Durham, N.C.: Duke University Press, 1993.

———. *Transcritique.* Cambridge, Mass.: MIT Press, 2003.

Katō Norihiro. *"Haisengoron." Gunzō* 50, no. 1(1995): 252–94.

Kawamura Minato. *"Tōkyō de Shinda Otoko." Gendaishi Techō* (October and November, 1989): 122–30.

———. *"Yoidorebune" no Seishun.* Tokyo: Inpakuto Shuppankai, 2000.

Kim Chinyŏng, Kim Hyŏnju, and Kim Hŭich'an, eds. *Ch'unhyangjŏn Chŏnjip,* 17 vols. Seoul: Pakijŏng, 1997–2004.

Kim Hŭnggyu. *Munhak kwa Yŏksajŏk Ingan.* Seoul: Ch'angjak kwa Pip'yŏngsa, 1980.

Kim Hyejŏng. *"Kŭndae Ihu Kugŏgwa Kyojae Kaebal e Taehan Sajŏk Kŏmt'o." Kugŏ Kyoyuk Yŏngu* 13 (2004): 404–37.

Kim Namch'ŏn. *"Munhak ŭi Kyoyukjŏk Immu."* In *Haebang Konggan ŭi*

Pip'yŏng Munhak, edited by Song Kihan and Kim Oegon, 36–42. Seoul: T'aehaksa, 1991.

——. "*Tŭngpul.*" *Kokumin Bungaku* (March 1942): 106–25.

Kim Oegon. "*Chŏnhyang Munhak kwa Kŭndae ŭi Kŭkpok.*" *Oeguk Munhak* (Spring 1995): 330–50.

Kim Pyŏnggŏl. *Silp'aehan Insaeng, Silp'aehan Munhak*. Seoul: Ch'angjak kwa Pip'yŏngsa, 1994.

Kim Sarayng. "*Kusa Fukashi.*" In *Kim Saryang Zenshū*, edited by Kim Saryang Zenshū Henshū Iinkai, vol. 1, 147–70. Tokyo: Kawade Shobōshinsha, 1973–1974.

Kim Soun. *Chōsen Minyōshū*. Tokyo: Taibunkan, 1929.

——. *Chichi Iron no Kumo*. Tokyo: Kawade Shobō, 1940.

——. *Chosen Shishū*, 2 vols. Tokyo: Kōfūkan, 1943.

——. *Chōsen Shishū*. Tokyo: Sōgensha, 1953.

——. "*Okusoku to Dokudan no Meiro.*" *Bungaku* (June 1956): 86–101.

Kim Suyŏng. *Kim Suyŏng Chŏnjip*, edited by Kim Suhong., 2 vols. Seoul: Minumsa, 2005.

Kim Tonguk. *Jŭngbo Ch'unhyangjŏn Yŏngu*. Seoul: Yŏnsedaehakkyo Ch'ulpanbu, 1976.

Kim Yerim. "*1930nyŏndae Huban Mollak/Chaesaeng ŭi Sŏsa hwa Yŏksa Kihoek Yŏngu.*" *Hanguk Kŭndae Munhak Yŏngu* 6 (2003): 195–220.

Kim Yunsik. *Hanguk Kŭndae Munhak Sasang Yŏngu 1*. Seoul: Ilchisa, 1984.

——. "*Hanguk Kŭndaeshi Pŏnyŏk ŭi Munjechŏm.*" *Hyŏndae Munhak*, no.337 (1983): 132–47.

——. *Ilche Malgi Hanguk Chakka ŭi Ilbonŏ Kulssŭgi*. Seoul: Sŏul Taehak Ch'ulpanbu, 2003.

——. *Kim Yunsik Sŏnjip*, 2 vols. Seoul: Sol, 1996.

Kim Yunsik and Chŏng Houng. *Hangkuk Sosŏlsa*. Seoul: Munhak Tongne, 2000.

Kitahara Hakushū, "Jo" [Preface]. In *Chōsen Minyōshū*, edited and translated by Kim Soun. Tokyo: Taibunkan, 1929.

Ko Ŭn. *1950nyŏndae*. Seoul: Minŭnsa, 1973.

Kobayashi Hideo. "*Shisō to Jitsuseikatsu.*" Reprinted in *Gendai Nihon Bungaku Ronsōshi* 3: 126–30, edited by Hirano Ken, Odagiri Hideo, and Yamamoto Kenkichi, 3 vols. Tokyo: Miraisha, 1956.

Koike Kōshi. "*Chousen no Kotengei Ch'unhyangjŏn ni Tsuite.*" *Engei Gahō* 32, no. 5 (1938): 56–57.

Kongbosil. *Wŏllam Yi Sangjae Sŏnsaeng Yakchŏn*. Seoul: Kongbosil, 1956.

"*Kŏnsŏlgi ŭi Minjokmunhak.*" *Tong-a Ilbo*, January 3–6, March 6–23, 1935.

"*Kugŏ Pogŭp ŭn Chohŭna Chosŏnŏ Paech'ŏk ŭn Pulga.*" *Maeil Sinbo*, July 9, 1938.

Kwŏn Sŏngu. "*Yi T'aejun ŭi Sup'il Yŏngu.*" *Hanguk Munhak Iron gwa Pip'yŏng*, no. 22 (2004): 11–33.

Kwŏn T'aeŏk. "*Tonghwa Chŏngch'aeknon.*" *Yŏksa Hakpo*, no. 172 (2001): 335–65.

Kwŏn Yŏngmin. *Hanguk Minjok Munhangnon Yŏngu*. Seoul, Minŭmsa, 1988.
Kyōgoku Okikazu. *Kindai Nihongo no Kenkyū*. Tokyo: Tōensha, 1998.
Lee, Jin-Kyung. "Sovereign Aesthetics, Disciplining Emotion, and Racial Rehabilitation in Colonial Korea, 1910–1922." *Acta Koreana* 8, no. 1 (2005): 77–107.
Lefebvre, Henri. *Critique of Everyday Life*, 3 vols. London: Verso, 1992.
Lensen, George Alexander. *The Russian Push Toward Japan, 1697–1875*. Princeton, N.J.: Princeton University Press, 1959.
Levinas, Emmanuel. "Dialogue." In *Of God Who Comes to Mind*. Stanford, Calif.: Stanford University Press, 1986.
——. *Ethics and Infinity*. Pittsburgh: Duquesne University Press, 1985.
——. "Is Ontology Fundamental?" In *Basic Philosophical Writings*, edited by Adriaan T. Peperzak, Simon Critchley, and Robert Bernasconi. Bloomington: Indiana University Press, 1996.
——. *Otherwise than Being*. Pittsburgh: Duquesne University Press, 1998.
——. "Politics After." Reprinted in *Levinas Reader*, edited by Seán Hand. Oxford and Cambridge: Blackwell, 1989.
——. *Totality and Infinity*. Pittsburgh: Duquesne University Press, 1969.
Lippit, Seiji. *Topographies of Japanese Modernism*. New York: Columbia University Press, 2002.
Liu, Lydia H. "The Question of Meaning-Value in the Politics of Economy of the Sign." In *Token of Exchange*, edited by Lydia H. Liu. Durham, N.C.: Duke University Press, 1999.
Marx, Karl. "The British Rule in India." Reprinted in *Karl Marx on Colonialism and Modernization*, edited by Shlomo Avineri. Garden City, N.J.: Doubleday Anchor, 1969.
——. *A Contribution to the Critique of Political Economy*. New York: International, 1970.
——. *The Critique of the Gotha Programme*. New York: International, 1966.
——. *Grundrisse*. London: Penguin Books, 1993.
——. "On the Jewish Question." Reprinted in *The Portable Karl Marx*, edited by Eugene Kamenka. New York: Penguin Books, 1983.
Maseki Toshio. "*Taishōki ni Okeru Chōsenkan no Ittenkei*." *Nihon Kindashi Kenkyū* 8, no. 12: 28–38.
Mignolo, Walter D. "Dussel's Philosophy of Liberation." In *Thinking from the Underside of History*, edited by Linda Martin Alcoff and Eduardo Mendieta, 27–50. Lanham, Md.: Rowman & Littlefield, 2000.
Mikami Sanji and Takatsu Kuwasaburō. *Nihon Bungakushi*, 2 vols. Tokyo: Kinkōdō, 1890.
Miki Kiyoshi. "*Tōa Shisō no Konkyo*." *Kaizō* 12 (1938): 8–20.
Mitsui Takashi. "*Singminjiha Chosŏn esŏŭi Ŏnŏjibae*." *Han'il Minjok Munje Yŏn'gu* 4 (2003): 203–28.
Miyata Setsuko. *Chosŏn Minjung gwa 'Hwangminwha' Chŏngch'aek*. Translated by Yi Yŏng-rang. Seoul: Ilchogak, 1997.
Moore-Gilbert, Bart. *Postcolonial Theory*. London and New York: Verso, 1997.

Mortley, Raoul. *French Philosophers in Conversation*. London: Routledge, 1991.

"Munhakja ŭi Chagi Pip'an." In *Haebang Konggan ŭi Pip'yŏng Munhak*, edited by Song Kihan and Kim Oegon, 2: 164–72 . Seoul: T'aehaksa, 1991, 3 vols.

Murayama Tomoyoshi. *"Chōsen to no Kōryū."* *Asahi Shinbun*, September 15, 1938.

——. *"Ch'unhyangjŏn no Tsukiji Jōen ni Tsuite."* *Chōsen oyobi Manshū*. (March 1938): 59–60.

——. *"Ch'unhyangjŏn Yodan."* *Keijō Nippō*, May 31, 1938.

Najita, Tetsuo, and H. D. Harootunian. "Japan's Revolt Against the West." Reprinted in *Modern Japanese Thought*, edited by Bob Wakabayashi. Cambridge: Cambridge University Press, 1998.

Nakajima Atsushi. *"Junsa no Iru Fūkei: 1923nen no Hitotsu no Sukecchi."* Reprinted in *Nakajima Atsushi Zenshu*, edited by Hikami Hidehiro and Nakamura Mitsuo, 2: 50–64. Tokyo: Chikuma Shobō, 1976, 3 vols.

Nakanishi Inosuke. *"Futeisenjin."* Reprinted in *Chosen:"Gaichi" no Nihongo Bungakusen*, edited by Kurokawa Sō, 27–73. Tokyo: Shinjuku Shobō, 1996.

Nakarai Tōsui. *"Keirin Jōwa Ch'unhyangjŏn."* *Osaka Asahi Shinbun*, June 25–July 23, 1882.

Niranjana, Tejaswini. *Siting Translation* . Berkeley: University of California Press, 1992.

Nishio Kanji. *Kokumin no Rekishi*. Tokyo: Sankei Shinbun, 1999.

Nishizaki Kyōko. *"Aru Nōmin Bungakusha."* In *Kyōdō Kenkyū Tenkō*, edited by Shisōno Kagaku Kenkyūkai, 1: 218–37. Tokyo: Heibonsha, 1959, 3 vols.

No Yŏngt'aek. *"Ilchesigi ŭi Munmaengyul Ch'ui."* *Kuksagwan Nonch'ong* 51(1994): 109–59.

"Oesaek ŭi Chanjae nŭn Ajikto Namaitta." *Chosŏn Ilbo*, August 15, 1948.

Oguma Eiji. *Tan'ichi Minzoku no Shinwa no Kigen*. Tokyo: Shinyōsha, 1995.

——. *"Nihonjin" no Kyōkai*. Tokyo: Shinyōsha, 1998.

Ōzasa Yoshio. *Nihon Gendai Engekishi: Shōwa*, 3 vols. Tokyo: Hakusuisha, 1993–1995.

Paek Ch'ŏl. *Sinmunhak Sajosa*. Seoul: Singumunhwasa, 1982.

Pak Chonghwa. *"Minjok Munhak ŭi Wŏlli."* *Kyŏnghyangsinmun*, December 5, 1946.

Pak Hongmin. *"Pŏljaeng-i."* *Puin* 3 (1946): 44–46.

Pak Hŏnho. *Yi T'aejun gwa Hanguk Kŭndae Munhak ŭi Sŏngkyŏk*. Seoul: Somyŏng Ch'ulpan, 1999.

Pak Sŏngjin. *Sahoejinhwaron gwa Singminj Sahoesasang*. Seoul: Sŏin, 2003.

Pak Wonso. *"Nae an e Ŏnŏ Sadaejuŭi Yŏppogi."* Reprinted in *Tubu*, 172–98. Seoul: Ch'angjak kwa Pip'yŏngsa, 2002.

Rutt, Richard, and Kim Chong-un, trans. *Virtuous Women: Three Classic Korean Novels*. Seoul: Royal Asiatic Society Korea Branch, 1974.

Saegusa Toshikatsu. *"Kim Soun ŭn Muŏsŭl Haenŭga?"* In *Hanguk Kŭnade Munhank kwa Ilbon*. Seoul: Somyŏng Chulp'ansa, 2003, 288–347.

Said, Edward. *Orientalism*. New York: Vintage Books, 1979.

Sakai, Naoki. "Subject and Substratum: On Japanese Imperial Nationalism." *Cultural Studies* 14, no. 3 (2000): 462–530.

——. *Translation and Subjectivity*. Minneapolis: University of Minnesota, 1997.

"Sam Chŏnmunhakkyo Sa Kyosu Sam Sinmunsa Haggyebujang Munyejŏngch'aek Hoeŭi." Samch'olli 8, no. 6 (1936): 226–40.

Sand, Jordan. *House and Home in Modern Japan*. Cambridge, Mass.: Harvard University Asia Center, 2003.

Satō Haruo. *"Chōsen no Shijinra o Naichi no Shidan ni Mukahen to Suru no Ji."* In *Chichi Iron no Kumo*, translated and edited by Kim Soun. Tokyo: Kawade Shobō, 1940, 4–9.

Schmid, Andre. *Korea Between Empires 1895-1919*. (New York: Columbia University Press, 2002.

Shirakawa, Yutaka. *Shokuminchi Chōsen no Sakka to Nihon*. Okayama: Daigaku kyōiku shuppan, 1995.

Shisō no Kagaku Kenkyūkai, ed. *Kyōdō Kenkyū Tenkō*. 3 vols. Tokyo: Heibonsha, 1965.

Sin T'aehyŏn. *"Ch'unhyangjŏn* Jōen o Mite." *Chōsen*, no. 283 (1938): 47–61.

Sin Tonguk. *"Kim Namch'ŏn ŭi Sosŏl e Nat'anan Chisigin ŭi Chaa Hwangnip kwa Chŏnhyangja ŭi Chŏgungmunje." Tongyanghak* 21 (1991): 207–40.

Sŏl Sŏnggyŏng. *Ch'unhyangjŏn ŭi T'ongsijŏk Yŏngu*. Seoul: Yŏnsedaehakkyo Chulpanbu, 2000.

Son Chŏngsu. *Kaenyŏnsarosŏŭi Hanguk Kŭndae Pip'yŏngsa*. Seoul: Yŏkrak, 2002.

Sŏng Yunja. *"Ch'oe Chaesŏ ui Ch'inil Munhak Yŏngu."* Master thesis, Seoul National University, 2000.

Steiner, George. *After Babel*. Oxford: Oxford University Press, 1975.

Takagi Ichinosuke. *Kokubungaku Gojūnen*. Tokyo: Iwanami, 1967.

Takahama Kyoshi. *Chōsen*. Tōkyō: Jitsugyōnonihonsha, 1912.

Takahashi Tetsuya. *Kioku no Echika*. Tokyo: Iwanami Shoten, 1995.

Takasaki Sōji. *"Aru 'Chōsentsū' no Ikita Michi." Kikan Sanzenri*, no. 30 (1982): 104–15.

——. *Kenshō Nikkan Kaidan*. Tokyo: Iwanami Shoten, 1996.

Takata Yasuma. *Minzokuron*. Tokyo: Iwanami Shoten, 1942.

Tokuda Kyūichi. *"Atarashii Jōsei to Kore ni Taiōsuru Waga Tō no Seisaku."* In *Nihon Kyōsantō Gojūnen Mondai Shiryōshū* , edited by Mondai Bunken Henshū Iinkai, 1:11–17. Tokyo: Shin Nihon Shuppan, 1994, 3 vols.

Tōma, Seita. *"Aru Shijin no Shōgai, Ge—Chōsen no Shi ni Tsuite no Nōto II." Nihon Bungaku* 3, no. 7 (1954): 20–26.

——. *"Aru Shijin no Shōgai, Jō—Chōsen no Shi ni Tsuite no Nōto II." Nihon Bungaku* 3, no. 6 (1954): 25–34.

——. *"Furusato-Chōsen no Shi nit Tsuite no Nōto I." Nihon Bungaku* 3, no. 3 (1954): 39–51.

——. *"Gendai Chōsen Bungaku no Hitotsu no Mikata." Bungaku* (August 1956): 99–104.

——. "Shi to Minyō." *Bungaku* (July 1954): 61–77.

Tongyanghak Yŏnguso. *Hanhan Taesajŏng*. Seoul: Tanguk Taehakkyo, 2000.

Tsurumi Makoto. "Ch'unhyangjŏn—Kabukifū no Taishūka e no Tenkō to Shite." *Teikoku Daigaku Shinbun*, March 31, 1938.

UNESCO. "Broader and Easier Access to the World's Variety of Literary Works," http://portal.unesco.org/culture/en/ev.php-URL_ID=12312&URL_DO=DO_TOPIC&URL_SECTION=201.html (accessed March 1, 2013) .

Usui Jishō. "Minzoku Bunka Kyōdōtai." *Shisō* (April 1937): 13–36.

Williams, Raymond. *Keywords*. New York: Oxford University Press, 1985.

Yamada Hiroto. "Nihonjin Keisatsukan ni Taisuru Chōsengo Shōrei Seisaku." *Chōsenshi Kenkyūkai Ronbunshū* 38 (2004): 123–49.

Yanaihara Tadao. "Minzoku to Dentō." *Shisō* (April 1937): 1–12.

Yasuda Yojūrō. *Yasuda Yojūrō Zenshū*, 46 vols. Tokyo: Kōdansha, 1985–89.

Yi Chiwŏn. "1930 nyŏndae Chŏnban Minjokjuŭi Munhwaundongnon ŭi Sŏngkyŏk." *Kuksagwan Nonch'ong* 51 (1994): 161–84.

Yi Ch'ungu. *Kyŏngsŏng Chegukdaehak*. Seoul: Tarakwŏn, 1980.

Yi Chungyŏn. *Ch'aek, Sasŭl esŏ P'ullida*. Seoul: Hyean, 2005.

——. *Ch'aek ŭi Unmyŏng*. Seoul: Hyean, 2001.

Yi Hŭisŭng. "Ilsang Yongŏ e Issŏsŏ ŭi Ilbonjŏk Janjae." *Sinch'ŏnji* 2, no. 5 (1947): 60–67.

——. "Kuggŏran Muŏssinga?" *Sinch'ŏnji* 1, no. 3 (1946): 141–46.

——. "Kugŏ Kyoyuk ŭi Tangmyŏn Kwaje." *Chosŏn Kyoyuk* 1, no. 1 (1947): 33–42.

Yi Kŭngno. "Chosŏnŏ Sajŏn P'yŏnch'an e Taehaya." *Hangŭl* (May 1932): 12–14.

Yi Kwangsu. "Minjok Kaejoron." *Kaebyŏk* 23 (1922): 18–72.

——. "Muhak iran Hao." In *Hagun Hyŏndae Munhak Pip'yŏngsa* 1: 48–64. Seoul: Hanguk Haksul Chŏngbo, 2004.

——. "Sin Ch'eje wa Chosŏn Munhwa ŭi Chillo." *Maeil Sinbo*, September 10, 1940.

——. "Yakushishū ni Yosete." In *Chichi Iron no Kumo*, translated and edited by Kim Soun. Tokyo: Kawade Shobō, 1940, 10–11.

Yi Myŏnghŭi. "Munjang yi Poyŏjun 'Chŏnt'ong' ŭi Ŭimi wa Ŭiŭi." In *1930nyŏndae Huban ŭi Kŭndaesŏng gwa Chagi Sŏngch'al*, edited by Sanghŏ Munhakhoe, 383–406. Seoul: Kip'ŭnsaem, 1998.

Yi Myŏnghwa. "Chosŏn Ch'ongdokbu ŭi Ŏnŏ Tonghwa Chŏngch'aek." In *Hanguk Tongnip Undongsa Yŏngu,* edited by Tongnip Kinyŏmgwan Hanguk Tongnip Undongsa Yŏnguso, 9: 277–94. Ch'ŏnwŏngun: Tongnip Kinyŏmgwan Hanguk Tongnip Undongsa Yŏnguso, 1987–1995, 9 vols.

Yi Pyŏnghyŏk. "Ilcheha ŭi Ŏnŏ Saenghwal." *Ilcheha ŭi Singmin Chibae wa Saenghwalsang*. Seoul: Hanguk Chŏngsin Munhwawŏn, 1990.

Yi Sang. "Arŭmdaun Chosŏnmal." Reprinted in *Yi Sang Chŏnjip*. Seoul: Somyŏng Ch'ulpansa, 2009.

Yi Sanggyŏng. "Ilche Malgi Sosŏl e Nat'anan 'Naesŏn Kyŏrhon ŭi Ch'ŭngui." In *Ch'inil Munhak ŭi Naechok Nolli*, edited by Kim Chaeyong et al. Seoul: Yŏllak, 2003.

Yi T'aejun. "*Munjang Kanghwa.*" *Munjang.* 9 parts. (February through October 1939).
——. *Yi T'aejun Chŏnjip.* 18 vols. Seoul: Sŏŭm Ch'ulp'ansa, 1988.
——. "*Dai Ichigō Sen no Sōga.*" In *Kindai Chōsen bungaku Nihongo Sakuhinshū,* edited by Ōmura Masuo and Hotei Toshihiro, 5 vols. Tokyo: Rokuin Shobō, 2001, 5: 463–68.
Yi Ŭngho. *Mi Kunjŏnggi ŭi Hangŭl Ŭndongsa.* Seoul: Sŏngch'ŏngsa, 1974.
Yi Wŏndŏk. "*Hanil Hoedam gwa Ilbon ŭi Chŏnhu Ch'ŏri Oegyo.*" *Hanguk kwa Kukche Chŏngch'i* 1 (1996): 35–76.
Yi Wōnjo. "*Munhak kwa Ŏnŏ Ch'angjo.*" In *Haebang Konggan ŭi Pip'yŏng Munhak,* edited by Song Kihan and Kim Oegon, 1: 61–65. Seoul: T'aehaksa, 1991, 3 vols.
——. "*Sinhyŏp Kŭktan Kongyŏn ŭi Ch'unhyangjŏn Kwangukp'yŏng, ha.*" *Chosŏn Ilbo,* November 5, 1938.
Yi Yŏngjun. "Grand Affirmation: Kim Suyŏng's Poetic Vision." PhD diss., Harvard University, 2006.
Yonetani Masafumi. "*Miki Kiyoshi no 'Sekaishi no Testugaku.'*" *Hihyō Kūkan* 19 (1998): 40–67.
Yoshimoto Takaaki. "*Tenkōron.*" In Yoshimoto Takaaki, *Yoshimoto Takaaki Zenchosakushū,* 15 vols. Tokyo: Keisō Shobō, 1968, 13: 5–27.
Young, Robert. *Postcolonialism.* Malden and Oxford: Blackwell, 2001.
——. *White Mythologies.* London and New York: Routledge, 1990.
Yu Chino. *Yanghogi.* Seoul: Koryŏ Taehak Ch'ulpanbu, 1977.
Yu Chongho. "'*Chosŏn Sijip' Ilkki.*" In *Munhak ŭi Chŭlgŏum.* Seoul: Minŭmsa, 1993.
Yun Kŏnch'a. *Minzoku Gensō no Satetsu.* Tokyo: Iwanami Shoten, 1994.
Žižek, Salvoj. *Organs Without Bodies: Deleuze and Consequences.* London and New York: Routledge, 2004.

Index

Lightning Source UK Ltd.
Milton Keynes UK
UKHW011814250322
400626UK00001B/50